Collins

French

Phrase Book & Dictionary

Other languages in the *Collins Phrase Book & Dictionary* series:

GERMAN
GREEK
ITALIAN
JAPANESE
PORTUGUESE
SPANISH

These titles are also published in a Language pack containing
60-minute CD/cassette and phrase book

HarperCollins*Publishers*
Westerhill Road,
Bishopbriggs, Glasgow G64 2QT

www.collins.co.uk

First published 2004

Reprint 10 9 8 7 6 5 4 3 2

© HarperCollins*Publishers* 2004

ISBN 0 00-716529-3

Typeset by Davidson Pre-Press Graphics Ltd, Glasgow

Printed in Italy by Amadeus Srl

Introduction

Your *Collins Phrase Book & Dictionary* is a handy, quick-reference guide that will help you make the most of your stay abroad. Its clear layout will save you valuable time when you need that crucial word or phrase. There are four main sections in this book:

Everyday France – photoguide

Packed full of photos, this section allows you to see all the practical visual information that will help with using cash machines, driving on motorways, reading signs, etc.

Phrases

Practical topics are arranged thematically with an opening section Key talk containing vital phrases that should stand you in good stead in most situations.

Phrases are short, useful and each one has a pronunciation guide so that there is no problem saying them.

Eating out

This section contains phrases for ordering food and drink (and special requirements) plus a photoguide showing different eating places, menus and practical information to help choose the best options. The menu reader allows you to work out what to choose.

Dictionary

The practical 5000-word English-French and French-English Dictionary means that you won't be stuck for words.

And finally, there is a short Grammar section explaining how the language works.

So, just flick through the pages to find the information you need. Why not start with a look at Pronouncing French on page 6. From there on the going is easy with your *Collins Phrase Book & Dictionary*.

Useful websites

Currency Converters
www.x-rates.com

Foreign Office Advice
www.fco.gov.uk/travel/
countryadvice.asp

Passport Office
www.ukpa.gov.uk

Health advice
www.thetraveldoctor.com
www.doh.gov.uk/traveladvice

Pets
www.defra.gov.uk/animalh/
quarantine

Weather
www.bbc.co.uk/weather

Transport
www.aeroport.fr
(Info on France's 190 airports)
www.sncf.com
(French railways)
www.raileurope.com
*(Info on Train travel and
passes available)*
www.batobus.com
(Boat trips along Seine)

Driving
www.autoroutes.fr
(Traffic and road conditions)
www.saprr.fr *(Paris-Rhine-
Rhône motorway info)*

Sightseeing
www.franceguide.com
*(French Government Tourist
Office)*
www.cybevasion.com/france
(Info on France)
www.intermusées.com
(Info on museums and passes)
www.paris-tours-guides.com
www.paris.org *(Paris site)*
www.parisfree.com
www.handicap.gouv.fr
(Info for disabled)

Internet Cafés
www.cybercafes.com

Culture & Activities
www.louvre.fr/louvrea.htm
www.chateaux-france.com
www.opera-de-paris.fr
(Paris opera)
www.zingueurs.com
(Bars with music, theatre)
www.ski-nordic-france.com
(Cross-country skiing)

Hotels
www.francehotelreservation.com
www.hotels-france.com
www.hotel-restaurant-fr.com

Contents

Pronouncing French

We've tried to make the pronunciation under the phrases as clear as possible by breaking the words up with hyphens, but remember not to pause between syllables.

The consonants are not difficult, and are mostly pronounced as in English: **b**, **d**, **f**, **k**, **l**, **m**, **n**, **p**, **s**, **t**, **v**, **x** *and* **z**. *The letter* **h** *is always silent, and* **r** *should be pronounced at the back of the throat in the well-known French way, although an English 'r' will be understood. When* **c** *comes before the vowels* **e** *or* **i** *it is pronounced like 's'; otherwise it is a hard 'k'. Likewise,* **g** *before* **e** *or* **i** *is 'zh' like 's' in 'pleasure', not hard 'g'. The letter* **ç** *is pronounced the same as* **s**; **q** *is always like* **k** *in 'kick' (not the 'kw' sound in 'quick');* **ch** *is 'sh';* **gn** *is 'ny', something like the sound in 'onion'; and* **w** *is either 'v' or 'w'. Final consonants, especially* **s** *and* **n**, *are often silent, but sometimes not, for example when the following word begins with a vowel. Don't worry, just follow the pronunciation guide.*

The sound spelt **ou** *in French is something like 'oo' in English. To pronounce the sound written* **u**, *start by pronouncing 'ee' but pucker up and round your lips as if to say 'oo' – careful to keep your tongue in the 'ee' position! We use the symbol '<u>oo</u>' in the pronunciation guide. There are two* **o** *sounds in French; one is something like the 'o' in English 'hope' and one something like 'hop'. We've represented the first by 'oh' and the second by 'o' in the transcriptions. Meanwhile 'uh' represents both the rounded sounds of* **peu** *and* **peur**, *and also the sound (like 'a' in English 'ago' or 'sofa') found in* **je** *and* **se** *and the first syllables of* **retard** *and* **demain**. *Look out for the following letter combinations:* **au** *and* **eau** *are 'oh';* **oi** *is 'wa'; and* **ui** *is something like 'wee'.*

There are various 'nasalised' vowels in French. When you see a 'ñ' you should nasalise the vowel before it rather than pronouncing an **n**. *For example 'mañ' in the pronunciation guide represents 'm' plus the vowel in the well-known French words* **fin** *or* **rien**, *rather than the sounds in English 'man'. The others are 'uñ' (as in* **brun**) *and 'oñ', which we use to cover the similar vowel sounds in* **dans** *or* **en** *or* **blanc** *and* **mon** *or* **blond**.

OPEN 24 HOURS

Small shops tend to close between 12 and 2pm, but stay open later till about 7pm.

HERE
Ici, pronounced *ee-see*, means here.

PAY HERE

PAY HERE
The word *caisse* actually means till or cash box.

OUT OF ORDER

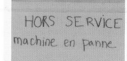

If something is working, you will see the words *en service*. The words *en panne* mean broken down.

ENTRANCE

Look out for the words *entrée libre* which means free entry (for museums, etc).

EXIT

sortie

Sortie is also used for exit on motorways.

CLOSED

FORBIDDEN

The word for forbidden is *interdit* or *défense de...*

PUSH   PULL

DANGER

OPENING HOURS

Horaires d'ouverture

Symbol for the euro. France is in the euro zone.

 Prices are generally written with a comma. This is 1 euro and 90 cents per kilo (*le kg*).

 PRICE Pronounced *pree*. The word stays the same in the plural *les prix*.

 Cash machines are known as *distributeurs de billets* and are widely available. You can carry out the transaction in English and it saves time queuing in banks to change money.

BANQUE (*boñk*) is the word for bank, but you will also see words such as *crédit* (*Crédit Agricole*) and *société* (*Société Générale*).

The euro is the currency of France. It breaks down into 100 euro cents. Notes: 5, 10, 20, 50, 100, 200, 500. Coins: 2 euro, 1 euro, 50 cent, 20 cent, 10 cent, 5 cent, 2 cent, 1 cent.

Although coins are officially *cents*, French people call them *centimes* (*soñ-teem*), a more familiar French term. Euro is pronounced *uh-roh*.

Euro notes are the same throughout Europe. The backs of coins carry different designs from each of the member European countries.

Cash machines operate as at home.

Annulation = cancel

Correction = error

Validation = proceed

Pièces acceptées = coins accepted

Ne rend pas la monnaie = no change given.

RECEIPT

BANKNOTES

carte de crédit

CREDIT CARD

carte bleue

DEBIT CARD

Tipping in France is not compulsory and should be simply an appreciation of good service. If you are dining in a restaurant, you might consider tipping the waiter 5-10% of the bill. In cafés it is customary to leave any loose change from the bill.

CANCEL

The red lozenge sign of the **tabac**. An extremely useful place, often it sells cigarettes, envelopes, stamps, transport tickets and lottery tickets. You can also have a flutter on the horses. If it is just a shop it is open till 7pm. If a bar is attached, it is open till late.

When friends or family meet up, they kiss each other on the cheeks (usually one on each cheek, but it depends on the region – 3 kisses in Paris, 4 in Normandy). It can be quite time consuming when 2 families meet up at the market in Normandy: 4 kisses to everyone, a quick chat, then 4 kisses again to say goodbye!

POLICE In small towns and villages you find *gendarmerie*, and in larger towns, *police*. You must report any crimes to them. The emergency no is 17.

À louer = to rent

FOR SALE
'Sold' in French is *Vendu* (voñ-doo).

LOCATION FOR HIRE

Don't be fooled into thinking it is the same word as in English! In French it is pronounced *loh-ka-syoñ*.

BEGINNERS

Initiation

Don't be fooled into thinking it is the same word as in English!

TOURIST INFORMATION

The tourist office is also known as the *Syndicat d'Initiative*. They have maps and brochures.

Most towns have a guide to the area. It is full of useful info such as emergency numbers for police, doctor, dentist, etc, as well as details of hotels, restaurants, shops, sporting activities, etc.

ROOMS AVAILABLE

A *chambre d'hôte* is bed and breakfast.

ON HOLIDAY

The main French holiday is the first half of August. Roads are particularly busy every Saturday when France is on the move.

UNPATROLLED BEACH

Beaches that have no lifeguards don't generally have showers or many facilities. The word for beach is *plage* (plazh).

Postboxes are yellow, as is the main colour for the French post office logo.

You will see name of village or town as you enter it, and as you leave.

BOTTLE BANK
Recycling banks for glass (*verre*), paper (*papiers*) and plastic (*plastique*) can be found everywhere.

 SWIMMING POOL
Most French towns have a municipal pool.

TOILETS
Many public toilets (especially in shopping centres) aren't free. Make sure you have about 35 euro cents on you.

Douche
SHOWER

Salle de bain
BATHROOM

 DAMES
LADIES
Ladies and men's toilets are generally shown with a pictogram.

MESSIEURS
GENTS
WC is pronounced *vay say*.

DRINKING WATER
The word for water is *eau* (*oh*).

chaud
HOT

froid
COLD

ENGAGED

LIBRE
VACANT

Timetables

LES JOURS	THE DAYS
lundi *luñ-dee*	**Monday**
mardi *mar-dee*	**Tuesday**
mercredi *mer-kruh-dee*	**Wednesday**
jeudi *zhuh-dee*	**Thursday**
vendredi *voñ-druh-dee*	**Friday**
samedi *sam-dee*	**Saturday**
dimanche *dee-moñsh*	**Sunday**

In French, neither months nor days start with a capital letter as they do in English.

LES MOIS	THE MONTHS
janvier *zhoñv-yay*	**January**
février *fev-ree-yay*	**February**
mars *mars*	**March**
avril *av-reel*	**April**
mai *may*	**May**
juin *zhwañ*	**June**
juillet *zhwee-yay*	**July**
août *oot*	**August**
septembre *sept-oñb-ruh*	**September**
octobre *ok-tob-ruh*	**October**
novembre *nov-oñb-ruh*	**November**
décembre *day-soñb-ruh*	**December**

BUS TIMETABLE

Service normal	normal service
Service du samedi et service réduit en vacances scolaires	Saturday (*samedi*) service and reduced service in school hols
Service des dimanches et fêtes	Sundays (*dimanches*) and holidays (*fêtes*) service
Pas de service	No service
Service été	Summer (*été*) service

TIMETABLE

Horaires = times

à partir du 2 mai = with effect from 2 May

demain	TOMORROW	aujourd'hui	TODAY

12

READING THE TRAIN TIMETABLE

JOURS DE CIRCULATION ET SERVICES DISPONIBLES

1. les sam.
2. jusqu'au 25 juin : les ven, sam, dim et fêtes sauf le 1er juin ; circule du 26 juin au 3 sept : tous les jours;du 8 sept au 3 nov : les ven, sam et dim;les 10, 17, 24 nov et 1er déc.

jours de circulation = days of service
services disponibles = services available
les sam = Saturdays ; *jusqu'au* = until
les ven, sam, dim et fêtes = Fri, Sat, Sun and hols
sauf = except for *le 1er juin* = 1st of June
circule du 26 juin au 3 sept = operates from 26 June til 3 Sep
tous les jours = every day/daily

TICKET À OBLITÉRER

Bus tickets need to be punched into the machine on bus, it slices off a corner and stamps it. It is for 2 trips. See the top left white band still to be stamped, and bottom left corner still to be sliced off.

Train tickets (and bus tickets) must be validated (*composté*) in the orange machines you find as you go on to the platforms. If you forget to do this, you will be liable to a fine.

CARNET

A book of 10 tickets or multiple-journey ticket is called *un carnet* (*uñ kar-nay*). A train ticket is called *un billet* (*uñ bee-yay*) and a bus ticket is *un ticket* (*uñ tee-kay*). A ticket to a museum or art gallery is *une entrée* (<u>*oon*</u> *oñ-tray*), i.e. entrance fee.

Carte (*kart*) is the word for card or pass. *Carte Musées* is a pass for museums in Paris. *Carte Orange* (*kart oh-roñzh*) is a travel pass (weekly, monthly or yearly) for Paris. Take spare passport photos in case you need them for various passes.

Getting around

PLACE

place (*plass*) = square

RUE

rue (*roo*) = road or street

BOULEVARD

boulevard (*bool-var*) = road (usually quite wide and tree-lined).

IMPASSE

impasse = cul de sac

1er étage
1ST FLOOR

rez-de-chaussée
GRND FLOOR **rdc**

sous-sol
BASEMENT **s-s**

Vieux Port
Les Plages
Vieille Ville
→

Vieux Port (*vee-uh por*) = old harbour
les Plages (*lay plazh*) = beaches
Vieille Ville (*vee-ay veel*) = old town

L.B.L
← Syndicat Initiative i
✉ ✕ Hôtel de LA PAIX

Syndicat d'Initiative is another word for tourist office. Hotels are signposted. The knife and fork means it has a restaurant (open to non-residents).

Hôtel de Ville

TOWN HALL don't be fooled by the word *hôtel*.

← P CENTRE VILLE

TOWN CENTRE

Musée

MUSEUM

GARE ROUTIERE
LA POSTE

French towns are well sign-posted.
gare routière = bus station
la poste = post office

← Librairie · Papeterie · Disques
← Régie Lamartine. Immobilier
Intermarché ←

As well as hotels, local amenities, shops and supermarkets (such as *Intermarché* here), are signposted.

Bus stops often have the time-table and service. Routes are generally numbered and colour-coded. Bus stop = *l'arrêt de bus* (la-ray duh *boos*).

Gare routière **BUS STATION**

Bus stop. Remember to punch your ticket into the machine near the driver. This validates the ticket.

Logo for French railway. The word for station is *la gare* (la gar).

You must validate your ticket before boarding the train.

Arrivée → **ARRIVALS**

↓ Départ **DEPARTURES**

↙ Métro
← Tram
← Bus
← ℹ

The symbol for the *Métro* is M. Lines are numbered. Connecting lines are *Correspondance*. Public transport is generally integrated and you can use tickets on bus, tram and underground.

DEPARTURE BOARD

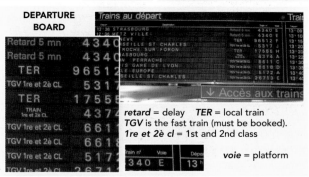

Trains au départ

Retard 5 mn	4340	
Retard 5 mn	4340	
TER	96512	
TGV 1re et 2è CL	531	
TER	17555	
TRAIN 1re et 2è CL	4372	
TGV 1re et 2è CL	661	
TGV 1re et 2è CL	6618	
TGV 1re et 2è CL	5172	
TGV 1re et 2è CL	2671	

↓ *Accès aux trains*

retard = delay   **TER** = local train
TGV is the fast train (must be booked).
1re et 2è cl = 1st and 2nd class

train n°	Voie	Dépa
340 E	13	

voie = platform

15

Driving

If you don't see your destination signposted, follow the *autres directions* (other routes) or

toutes directions (all routes). To get to the town centre, follow *centre ville*.

 HEAVY VEHICLES

 DETOUR

 RALENTIR
SLOW DOWN

 GIVE WAY
Indicates a roundabout and reminds drivers to give way.

 **FRENCH SPEED LIMITS**
In built-up areas on open roads on motorways. Remember speeds are in kilometres per hour. When it rains, the speed limit is reduced by 20 kph on the motorway and 10 kph on all other roads.

 PARKING PAY AT METER

 PRIORITY ROAD

RAPPEL **REMINDER**
restriction still in force

WEEKLY MARKET NO PARKING SAT FROM MIDNIGHT TO 3.30 PM

 NO PARKING
CAR EXIT

PARKING RESTRICTIONS

 no parking on pavement

3 minutes only

 no parking anywhere along road

Green roads are major French routes (E = European, N = National). Motorways are signposted blue with **A** for *Autoroute*. The yellow D-roads (*départementale*) are what we would term b- or secondary roads. However, these can be good roads with little traffic. Many French roads have a solid white central line. You should not overtake or cross this line.

You pay a toll on most French motorways. Don't use the orange 't' lane. These are for drivers with a special device in their car, i.e. pre-paid. They can just drive through.

 EXIT/ JUNCTION 14

 In towns, local destinations are signposted in white. Motorways are signposted in blue.

PETROL

← SANS PLOMB 95 →	unleaded 95 octane
← SANS PLOMB 98 →	unleaded 98 octane
← SUPER	leaded super
← GAZ OIL	diesel

95-octane petrol is usually fine for most cars, unless they have powerful engines or are towing a caravan.

 If main roads are busy, look out for the Bis signs – these indicate alternative (and less busy) routes to main towns.

 AIRE DE... Don't be fooled by the word *aire*, it means area not air.

 DIESEL is spelt in a number of ways, *gazole*, *gaz oil* and *gasoil*. It is usually the black pump.

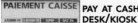 **PAY AT CASH DESK/KIOSK**

Shopping

SALES

PAY HERE

SPECIAL OFFER
Look out for these signs in the supermarkets.

Intermarché is one of the big chains. Supermarkets are generally out of town and sell cheaper petrol 24 hours a day. Pay-at-pump machines won't accept UK cards with the magnetic strip.

SUPERMARKET
Welcomes you Mon to Sat from 8.30am to 9pm. Late night shopping on Fri till 10pm. Sunday opening is not very common in France. Most small shops close between 12 and 2pm.

la pièce (*la pyess*) means per item, in this case per lettuce. Otherwise produce is generally sold by the weight (*le kg* = per kilo).

MARKET
Larger towns will have a daily market and smaller ones a weekly market.

PHARMACY
You can recognise the pharmacy by the green cross. If you are worried about a medical condition, ask the pharmacist for advice. They are medically trained and often able to supply suitable medication. If you need over-the-counter medicine (for headaches, etc), buy them here. They aren't sold in supermarkets.

DUTY PHARMACY

If the address of the duty pharmacy is not posted, ask at the local police station. Details will also be printed in the local paper.

BAKER'S

A *baguette* (*bag-et*) is a French stick.
A thinner version is *une ficelle* (*oon fee-sell*).
A fatter round country loaf is *un pain* (*uñ pañ*). Some bakers specialise in different types of bread: *seigle* (*say-gluh*) – rye; *complet* (*koñ-play*) – wholemeal. Bakers often sell sandwiches and bake at least twice a day. Some open Sun mornings, so look out for people clutching baguettes to find them.

ORGANIC EGGS Look out for the words *biologique* (*bee-o-loh-zheek*) or *bio* which means organic.

Look out for offers – 3 for the price of 2.

MILK
Look for the colour-coding for milk. Here, red is whole milk (*entier oñt-yay*), blue is semi-skimmed (*demi-écrémé duh-mee ay-kray-may*) and green is skimmed (*écrémé ay-kray-may*).

PLUS 1 FREE SLICE
tranche (*troñsh*) = slice
gratuite (*gra-tweet*)= free
jambon cuit (*zhoñ-boñ kwee*) = cooked ham
Ham is sold by the slice.

à emporter

TO TAKE AWAY

WATER Look out for the colour-coding used for sparkling (*pétillante pay-tee-yoñt*) and still (*plate plat*) water.
It can vary from brand to brand.

HERE
6 sausages
pure pork
no colouring
20€

Keeping in touch

EXPRESS POST For a slightly higher price you can get a quicker service.

Post offices and postboxes are easy to spot with the yellow and blue logo. You can also access the internet from larger post offices.

Most French pay phones take phonecards and credit cards, not coins. *Décrochez* = lift handset.

M. et Mme Bertillon
16, rue des Poissons
14290 Orbec
France

Addressing an envelope: house number, road, postcode, town and country

Some postboxes have 2 slots, one for local mail. *Autres destinations* = elsewhere. *Heures des levées* = collection times. *Jours ouvrables* = weekdays, *Samedi* = Sat. *Bureau le plus proche* = nearest post office.

French phonecards are sold in units: 50 (*cinquante unités* sañ-koñt <u>oo</u>-nee-tay) or 120 (*cent vingt unités* soñ vañ <u>oo</u>-nee-tay)

French phone numbers are given in 2 digits, sometimes written with full stops in between.

The word for 'at' is *arrobase* (ar-roh-baz).

01.	44.	79.	04.	57.
zéro un	quarante-quatre	soixante-dix-neuf	zéro quatre	cinquante-sept

www.
www dot is *trois double-vay point* (trwa doo-bluh-vay pwañ).

tél: .... (phone)
mél: .... (e-mail)

*on forms **mél** is used for e-mail address*

- The French are quite formal, especially the older generation. Only use the familiar 'you' **tu** with children or someone you know as a friend. Otherwise stick with the more formal **vous**.
- **Salut** is more informal than **bonjour**.
- The easiest way to ask for something is to name it & add please, **s'il vous plaît**.

yes	**no**	**that's fine**	**don't mention it**
oui	non	très bien	de rien
wee	*noñ*	*tray byañ*	*duh ryañ*

please		**thank you**	**thanks very much**
s'il vous plaît		merci	merci beaucoup
seel voo play		*mehr-see*	*mehr-see boh-koo*

hello/hi	**goodbye**	**good evening**	**goodnight**
bonjour/salut	au revoir	bonsoir	bonne nuit
boñ-zhoor/sa-loo	*oh ruh-vwar*	*boñ swar*	*bon nwee*

excuse me	**sorry!**	**what?**
excusez-moi	pardon!	comment?
eks-koo-zay mwa	*par-doñ*	*ko-moñ*

a...	**a coffee**	**2 coffees**
un... ('le' words)	un café	deux cafés
uñ...	*uñ ka-fay*	*duh ka-fay*

a...	**a bottle**	**2 bottles**
une... ('la' words)	une bouteille	deux bouteilles
oon...	*oon boo-tay*	*duh boo-tay*

a coffee and two beers, please
un café et deux bières, s'il vous plaît
uñ ka-fay ay duh byehr seel voo play

I'd like...	**we'd like...**
je voudrais...	nous voudrions...
zhuh voo-dray...	*noo voo-dree-oñ...*

Key Talk

- When someone offers you something, simply replying **merci** can be misleading. Depending on the tone of your voice, it can mean 'yes, please' or 'no, thank you'. Make sure you stress – **oui, merci** or **non, merci**. Otherwise you might not get that second helping you were offered!
- **Super** (<u>soo</u>-pehr) means 'great!'.

I'd like an ice cream
je voudrais une glace
zhuh voo-dray <u>oon</u> glass

we'd like to visit Paris
nous voudrions visiter Paris
noo voo-dree-oñ vee-zee-tay pa-ree

do you have...?
est-ce que vous avez...? *[or simply]*
ess kuh vooz av-ay...

vous avez...?
vooz av-ay...

do you have any milk?
vous avez du lait?
vooz av-ay <u>doo</u> lay

do you have stamps?
est-ce que vous avez des timbres?
ess kuh vooz av-ay day tañb-ruh

do you have a map?
vous avez une carte?
vooz av-ay <u>oon</u> kart

do you have cheese?
est-ce que vous avez du fromage?
ess kuh vooz av-ay <u>doo</u> fro-mazh

how much is it?
c'est combien?
say koñ-byañ

how much is...?
c'est combien...?
say koñ-byañ...

how much is the cheese?
c'est combien le fromage?
say koñ-byañ luh fro-mazh

how much is the ticket?
c'est combien le billet?
say koñ-byañ luh bee-yay

how much is a kilo?
c'est combien le kilo?
say koñ-byañ luh kee-loh

how much is it each?
c'est combien, pièce?
say koñ-byañ pyess

where is...?
où est...?
oo ay...

where are...?
où sont...?
oo soñ...

Key Talk

● In French you can turn a statement into a question, simply by changing your intonation and putting a question mark in your voice: **Vous avez une chambre?**
● You might find French spoken in rural areas more difficult to understand. The southern French accent is quite pronounced. People roll their 'r's and have a twang.

where is the station?
où est la gare?
oo ay la gar

where are the toilets?
où sont les toilettes?
oo soñ lay twa-let

is there/are there…?
est-ce qu'il y a…?
ess keel ee a…

is there a restaurant?
est-ce qu'il y a un restaurant?
ess keel ee a uñ res-toh-roñ

where is there a chemist?
où est-ce qu'il y a une pharmacie?
oo ess keel ee a <u>oo</u>n far-ma-see

are there children?
est-ce qu'il y a des enfants?
ess keel ee a dayz oñ-foñ

is there a swimming pool?
est-ce qu'il y a une piscine?
ess keel ee a <u>oo</u>n pee-seen

there is no…
il n'y a pas de…
eel nee a pa duh…

there is no hot water
il n'y a pas d'eau chaude
eel nee a pa doh shohd

there are no towels
il n'y a pas de serviettes
eel nee a pa de sehr-vyet

I need…
j'ai besoin de…
zhay buhz-wañ duh…

I need a receipt
j'ai besoin d'un reçu
zhay buhz-wañ duñ ruh-s<u>oo</u>

I need to phone
j'ai besoin de téléphoner
zhay buhz-wañ duh tay-lay-foh-nay

Key Talk

can I...?	**can we...?**
est-ce que je peux...?	est-ce que nous pouvons...?
ess kuh zhuh puh...	*ess kuh noo poo-voñ...*

can I pay?
est-ce que je peux payer?
ess kuh zhuh puh pay-ay

can we go in?
est-ce que nous pouvons entrer?
ess kuh noo poo-voñ oñ-tray

where can I...?
où est-ce que je peux...?
oo ess kuh zhuh puh...

where can I buy bread?
où est-ce que je peux acheter du pain?
oo ess kuh zhuh puh ash-tay doo pañ

when?
quand?
koñ

when (at what time)?
à quelle heure?
a kel uhr

when does the train leave?
quand part le train?
koñ par luh trañ

when does the film end?
à quelle heure finit le film?
a kel uhr fee-nee luh feelm

when does it open?
ça ouvre à quelle heure?
sa oovr a kel uhr

when does it close?
ça ferme à quelle heure?
sa fehrm a kel uhr

yesterday	**today**	**tomorrow**
hier	aujourd'hui	demain
yehr	*oh-zhoor-dwee*	*duh-mañ*

this morning	**this afternoon**	**tonight**
ce matin	cet après-midi	ce soir
suh ma-tañ	*set ap-ray mee-dee*	*suh swar*

is it open?
est-ce que c'est ouvert?
ess kuh say oo-vehr

is it closed?
est-ce que c'est fermé?
ess kuh say fehr-may

Key Talk

- The equivalent to Mr is **Monsieur**, abbreviated to **M.**
- The equivalent to Mrs or Ms is **Madame**, abbreviated to **Mme.**
- The equivalent to Miss is **Mademoiselle**, abbreviated to **Mlle.**
- Use **bonjour Madame** & **bonjour Monsieur**, not just **bonjour**.

hello
bonjour monsieur/madame
boñ-zhoor muh-syuh/ma-dam

how are you?
comment ça va?
ko-mañ sa va

my name is...
je m'appelle...
zhuh ma-pel...

I don't understand
je ne comprends pas
zhuh nuh koñ-proñ pa

this is my husband/my wife
voici mon mari/ma femme
vwa-see moñ ma-ree/ma fam

fine, thanks, and you?
très bien, merci, et vous?
tray byañ mehr-see ay voo

what is your name?
comment vous appelez-vous?
ko-moñ vooz ap-lay voo

do you speak English?
est-ce que vous parlez anglais?
ess kuh voo par-lay oñ-glay

thank you very much for your kindness
merci beaucoup pour votre gentillesse
mehr-see boh-koo poor vot-ruh zhoñ-tee-ess

the meal was delicious
le repas était délicieux
luh ruh-pa ay-tay day-lees-yuh

I have enjoyed myself very much
je me suis très bien amusé(e)
zhuh muh swee tray byañ a-moo-zay

we'd like to come back
nous voudrions revenir
noo voo-dree-oñ ruh-vuh-neer

here is my address
voici mon adresse
vwa-see mon ad-ress

Money – changing

● France is in the eurozone. Euro is pronounced uh-roh; cent, known as **centime**, is pronounced soñ-teem.
● Banks are generally open Mon to Fri till about 5pm, closed Sat pm and Sun.
● Cash machines are widespread and you will be able to use English instructions. It avoids wasting time in bank queues.

where can I change money?
où est-ce que je peux changer de l'argent?
oo ess kuh zhuh puh shoñ-zhay duh lar-zhoñ

where is the bank?
où est la banque?
oo ay la boñk

where is the bureau de change?
où est le bureau de change?
oo ay luh boo-roh duh shoñzh

when does the bank open?
la banque ouvre à quelle heure?
la boñk oovr a kel uhr

when does it close?
elle ferme à quelle heure?
el fehrm a kel uhr

I want to cash these traveller's cheques
je voudrais changer ces chèques de voyage
zhuh voo-dray shoñ-zhay say shek duh vwa-yazh

what is the rate...?
à combien est...?
a koñ-byañ ay...

for pounds
la livre sterling
la leev-ruh stehr-leeng

for dollars
le dollar
luh do-lar

I want to change £50
je voudrais changer cinquante livres
zhuh voo-dray shoñ-zhay sañ-koñt leev-ruh

where is there a cash dispenser?
où est-ce qu'il y a un distributeur de billets?
oo ess keel ee a uñ dees-tree-boo-tuhr duh bee-yay

I'd like small notes
je voudrais des petites coupures
zhuh voo-dray day puh-teet koo-poor

spending – Money

- *Credit cards are widely accepted, but French cards use a mirco chip rather than magnetic strip. It can be a problem with UK cards.*
- *Magnetic strip bank cards don't work in automated machines such as pay-at-pump or at train ticket machines.*
- *Take your bank's phone number in case of problems.*

how much is it?
c'est combien?
say koñ-byañ

where do I pay?
où est-ce qu'il faut payer?
oo ess keel foh pay-ay

I want to pay
je voudrais payer
zhuh voo-dray pay-ay

we want to pay separately
nous voulons payer séparément
noo voo-loñ pay-ay say-pa-ray-moñ

can I pay by credit card?
je peux payer avec ma carte de crédit?
zhuh puh pay-ay a-vek ma kart duh kray-dee

how many euros is it?
ça fait combien d'euros?
sa fay koñ-byañ duh-roh

how much is that in pounds?
ça fait combien en livres?
sa fay koñ-byañ oñ leev-ruh

do you accept traveller's cheques?
vous acceptez les chèques de voyage?
vooz ak-sep-tay lay shek duh vwa-yazh

how much is it...?
c'est combien...?
say koñ-byañ...

per person
par personne
par pehr-son

per night
par nuit
par nwee

per kilo
le kilo
luh kee-loh

are service and VAT included?
le service et la TVA sont compris?
luh sehr-veess ay la tay-vay-a soñ koñ-pree

I need a receipt
j'ai besoin d'un reçu
zhay buhz-wañ duñ ruh-soo

do you require a deposit?
est-ce qu'il faut verser des arrhes?
ess keel foh vehr-say dayz ahr

Airport

to the airport, please
à l'aéroport, s'il vous plaît
a la-ehr-oh-por seel voo play

how do I get into town?
pour aller en ville, s'il vous plaît?
poor al-ay oñ veel seel voo play

which bus goes to the town centre?
quel bus va au centre-ville?
kel boos va oh soñ-truh-veel

how much is it...?	**to the town centre**	**to the airport**
c'est combien...?	pour aller en ville	pour aller à l'aéroport
say koñ-byañ...	*poor al-ay oñ veel*	*poor al-ay a la-ehr-o-por*

where do I check in for...?
où est l'enregistrement pour...?
oo ay loñ-rezh-ees-truh-moñ poor...

which gate is it for the flight to...?
quelle est la porte d'embarquement pour le vol à destination de...?
kel ay la port doñ-bar-kuh-moñ poor luh vol a des-tee-nass-yoñ duh...

boarding will take place at gate number...
l'embarquement a lieu porte numéro...
loñ-bar-kuh-moñ a lyuh port noo-may-roh...

last call for passengers on flight...
dernier appel pour les passsagers du vol...
dehrn-yay a-pel poor lay pa-sa-zhay doo vol...

28

Customs & Passports

- *EU citizens with nothing to declare can use the blue customs channels.*
- *There's no restriction by quantity or value on goods purchased by travellers in another EU country, provided they are for their own personal use (this covers gifts). Check guidelines on* ***www.hmce.gov.uk***.

I have nothing to declare
je n'ai rien à déclarer
zhuh nay ryañ a day-kla-ray

here is...	**my passport**	**my green card**
voici...	mon passeport	ma carte verte
vwa-see...	*moñ pass-por*	*ma kart vehrt*

do I have to pay duty on this?
je dois payer des droits de douane sur ça?
zhuh dwa pay-ay day drwa duh dwan <u>soor</u> sa

it's for my own personal use
c'est pour mon usage personnel
say poor moñ <u>ooz</u>-azh pehr-son-el

we're going to...	**here is the receipt**
nous allons en...	voici le reçu
nooz a-loñ oñ...	*vwa-see luh ruh-<u>soo</u>*

the children are on this passport
les enfants sont sur ce passeport
layz oñ-foñ soñ <u>soor</u> suh pass-por

I'm...	**British**	**Australian**
je suis...	britannique	australien(ne) *m/f*
zhuh swee...	*bree-ta-neek*	*ohs-tral-yañ (-yen)*

I bought them in France
je les ai achetés en France
zhuh layz ay ash-tay oñ froñs

Asking the Way – questions

- You can also ask the way simply by asking **le musée, s'il vous plaît?** Nothing more complicated is required.
- **Tabacs** sell maps. Get free transport maps at metro and bus stations.
- You can also attract someone's attention with **pardon, Monsieur/Madame.**

excuse me, please
excusez-moi, s'il vous plaît
eks-k<u>oo</u>-zay-mwa seel voo play

where is...?
où est...?
oo ay...

where is the nearest...?
où est le/la ... le/la plus proche?
oo ay luh/la ... luh/la pl<u>oo</u> prosh

how do I get to...?
pour aller à...?
poor al-ay a...

is this the right way to...?
c'est la bonne direction pour...?
say la bon dee-reks-yoñ poor...

the...
le/la...
luh/la...

is it far?
c'est loin?
say lwañ

can I walk there?
on peut y aller à pied?
oñ puh ee al-ay a pyay

is there a bus that goes to...?
il y a un bus pour aller à/au...?
eel ee a uñ b<u>oo</u>s poor al-ay a/oh...

we're looking for...
nous cherchons...
noo shehr-shoñ...

we're lost
nous sommes perdus
noo som pehr-d<u>oo</u>

can you show me on the map?
pouvez-vous me montrer sur la carte?
poo-vay-voo muh moñ-tray s<u>oo</u>r la kart

answers – Asking the Way

ROUT
BARRÉ

- Key words are 'right' **droite** (drwat), 'left' **gauche** (gohsh), and 'straight on' **tout droit** (too drwa).
- Learn 'roundabout' **rond-point** (roñ-pwañ), 'crossroads' **carrefour** (kar-foor), 'square' **place** (plass), 'centre of town' **centre ville** (soñ-truh veel), 'exit' **sortie** (sor-tee) and 'follow' **suivre** (sweev-ruh).

keep going straight ahead
continuez tout droit
koñ-tee-noo-ay too drwa

you have to turn round
vous devez faire demi-tour
voo duh-vay fehr duh-mee-toor

turn...
tournez...
toor-nay...

right
à droite
a drwat

left
à gauche
a gohsh

keep going...
continuez...
koñ-tee-noo-ay...

as far as...
jusqu'à...
zhoos-ka...

as far as the church
jusqu'à l'église
zhoos-ka lay-gleez

cross...
traversez...
tra-ver-say...

the street
la rue
la roo

the square
la place
la plass

take...
prenez...
pruh-nay...

the first/second (road) on the right
la première/deuxième à droite
la pruhm-yehr/duhz-yem a drwat

it's...
c'est...
say...

after the traffic lights
après les feux
a-pray lay fuh

the road to...
la direction de...
la dee-rek-syon duh...

follow the signs for...
suivez les panneaux indicateurs en direction de...
swee-vay lay pan-oh añ-dee-ka-tuhr oñ dee-rek-syoñ duh...

Bus

- France has a national rail network so coach travel isn't so common as you might expect.
- Don't rely on a bus service in a small airport, the one bus scheduled may have left if there's a delay to your arrival.
- In cities, after the underground has stopped, you find night buses. In Paris the **Noctambus** runs from 1–5.30am at a flat rate.

where is the bus station?
où est la gare routière?
oo ay la gar root-yehr

I want to go...
je voudrais aller...
zhuh voo-dray al-ay...

to the station
à la gare
a la gar

to the museum
au musée
oh moo-zay

to the city centre
au centre-ville
oh soñ-truh-veel

to Paris
à Paris
a pa-ree

is there a bus that goes there?
est-ce qu'il y a un bus pour y aller?
ess keel ee a uñ boos poor ee al-ay

which bus do I take for...?
quel bus dois-je prendre pour aller à...?
kel boos dwa-zhuh proñdr poor al-ay a...

where do I get the bus to...?
où est-ce qu'on prend le bus pour aller à...?
oo ess koñ proñ luh boos poor al-ay a...

how often are the buses?
les bus passent tous les combien?
lay boos pass too lay koñ-byañ

can you tell me when to get off?
pourriez-vous me dire quand descendre?
poo-ree-ay voo muh deer koñ day-soñdr

Underground

- A book of 10 tickets (**carnet** kar-nay) is cheaper than buying single tickets. They can be used by a group of people.
- The **Carte Paris Visite** (for 1, 2, 3, or 5 days) is great value.
- Children between 4 and 11 get a reduced rate. Under 4s are free.
- The Paris metro runs until 12.30 at night.

where is the nearest metro station?
où est la station de métro la plus proche?
oo ay la stass-yoñ duh may-troh la ploo prosh

ten tickets, please
un carnet, s'il vous plaît
uñ kar-nay seel voo play

do you have an underground map?
est-ce que vous avez un plan du métro?
ess kuh vooz av-ay uñ ploñ doo may-troh

I want to go to...
je voudrais aller à...
zhuh voo-dray al-ay a...

can I go by underground?
est-ce que je peux y aller en métro?
ess kuh zhuh puh ee al-ay oñ may-troh

do I have to change?
est-ce qu'il faut changer?
ess keel foh shoñ-zhay

where?
où?
oo

which line is it for...?
c'est quelle ligne pour...?
say kel leen-yuh poor...

which station is it for the Louvre?
c'est quelle station pour le Louvre?
say kel stass-yoñ poor luh loovr

what is the next stop?
quel est le prochain arrêt?
kel ay luh pro-shañ ar-reh

Train

● *France has a highly efficient national rail network. Check offers and info on **www.sncf.com**.*
● *The highspeed TGV train must be booked in advance.*
● *Get reductions for 2 (or more) travelling on return trips.*
● *Tickets must be validated before boarding the train. Machines are orange and at the beginning of the platform.*

where is the station?
où est la gare?
oo ay la gar

to the station, please
à la gare, s'il vous plaît
a la gar seel voo play

a single to...
un aller simple pour...
uñ al-ay sañpl poor...

2 singles to...
deux allers simples pour...
duhz al-ay sañ-pluh poor...

a return to...
un aller retour pour...
uñ al-ay ruh-toor poor...

2 returns to...
deux allers retours pour...
duhz al-ay ruh-toor poor...

a child's return to...
un aller retour enfant pour...
uñ al-ay ruh-toor oñ-foñ poor...

1st class	**2nd class**	**smoking**	**non smoking**
première classe	seconde classe	fumeur	non fumeur
pruhm-yehr klass	*suh-goñd klass*	*foo-muhr*	*noñ foo-muhr*

do I have to pay a supplement?
je dois payer un supplément?
zhuh dwa pay-ay uñ soop-lay-moñ

is my pass valid on this train?
est-ce que ma carte est valable dans ce train?
ess kuh ma kart ay va-labl doñ suh trañ

I want to book...	**a seat**	**a couchette**
je voudrais réserver...	une place	une couchette
zhuh voo-dray ray-zehr-vay...	*oon plass*	*oon koo-shet*

- *Children under 4 travel free.*
- *A Swiss Pass (for cheap travel on Swiss trains) must be bought before arriving in Switzerland.*
- *Check **www.raileurope.com** before your trip for different options (including the Swiss Pass).*
- *Remember to validate tickets for both outward and return trips.*

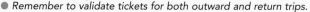

do you have a train timetable?
est-ce que vous avez un horaire des trains?
ess kuh vooz av-ay un o-rehr day trañ

do I need to change?
est-ce qu'il faut changer?
ess keel foh shoñ-zhay

where?
où?
oo

which platform does it leave from?
il part de quel quai?
eel par duh kel kay

does the train to ... leave from this platform?
le train pour ... part de ce quai?
luh trañ poor ... par duh suh kay

is this the train for...?
c'est le train pour...?
say luh trañ poor...

is this seat free?
cette place est libre?
set plass ay leebr

I think this is my seat
je crois que c'est ma place
zhuh krwah kuh say ma plass

where is the left-luggage?
où est la consigne?
oo ay la koñ-seen-yuh

Taxi

- Get a taxi from a taxi stand – generally located at stations. In smaller towns you may have to phone for one.
- The taxi is free if the roof sign is lit.
- In Paris there are 3 fare rates: A, B, and C. These correspond to inner and outer zones. Taxi zone maps can be found near to stands.

to the airport, please
à l'aéroport, s'il vous plaît
a la-ehr-o-por seel voo play

to the station, please
à la gare, s'il vous plaît
a la gar seel voo play

to this address, please
à cette adresse, s'il vous plaît
a set a-dress seel voo play

how much will it cost?
combien ça coûtera?
koñ-byañ sa koo-tra

it's too much
c'est trop
say troh

how much is it to the town centre?
combien ça coûte pour aller jusqu'au centre-ville?
koñ-byañ sa koot poor al-ay zh<u>oo</u>-skoh soñ-truh-veel

where can I get a taxi?
où est-ce que je peux prendre un taxi?
oo ess kuh zhuh puh proñdr uñ tak-see

please order me a taxi
pouvez-vous m'appeler un taxi?
poo-vay voo map-lay uñ tak-see

can I have a receipt?
est-ce que je peux avoir un reçu?
ess kuh zhuh puh av-war uñ ruh-s<u>oo</u>

I've nothing smaller
je n'ai pas de monnaie
zhuh nay pa duh mon-ay

keep the change
gardez la monnaie
gar-day la mon-ay

Boat

- In Paris take a **batobus** trip along the Seine with 8 sight-seeing stops. Visit their website **www.batobus.com**.
- Other French cities with rivers have adopted **bateaux-mouches**. Ask at the tourist offices about trips.
- In Switzerland the Swiss Pass includes travel on some lake steamers.

1 ticket	**2 tickets**	**single**	**round trip**
un billet	deux billets	un aller simple	un aller retour
uñ bee-yay	*duh bee-yay*	*uñ al-ay sañpl*	*uñ al-ay ruh-toor*

is there a tourist ticket?
est-ce qu'il y a un billet touristique?
ess keel ee a uñ bee-yay too-rees-teek

are there any boat trips?
est-ce qu'il y a des excursions en bateau?
ess keel ee a dayz ek-skoors-yoñ oñ ba-toh

how long is the trip?
le voyage dure combien de temps?
luh vwa-yazh door koñ-byañ duh toñ

when is the next boat?
à quelle heure part le prochain bateau?
a kel uhr par luh pro-shañ ba-toh

when does the boat leave?
à quelle heure part le bateau?
a kel uhr par luh ba-toh

have you a timetable?
vous avez un horaire?
vooz av-ay un o-rehr

can we eat on board?
on peut manger sur le bateau?
oñ puh moñ-zhay soor luh ba-toh

can we hire a boat?
on peut louer un bateau?
oñ puh loo-ay uñ ba-toh

Car – driving

- In wet weather the French motorway speed limit is reduced from 130 to 110kph and by 10kph on all other roads.
- Don't overtake or cross a solid white line.
- Flashing headlights don't mean 'you go', rather 'I'm coming through'. Take special care at pedestrian crossings.
- Flashing amber lights mean proceed with caution.

can I park here?
on peut se garer ici?
oñ puh suh gar-ay ee-see

where can I park?
où est-ce que je peux me garer?
oo ess kuh zhuh puh muh ga-ray

is there a car park?
est-ce qu'il y a un parking?
ess keel ee a uñ par-keeng

we're going to...
nous allons à...
nooz a-loñ a...

what's the best route?
quelle est le meilleur itinéraire?
kel ay luh me-yuhr ee-tee-nay-rehr

how do I get onto the motorway?
pour rejoindre l'autoroute, s'il vous plaît?
poor ruh-zhwañ-druh loh-toh-root seel voo play

which exit is it for...?
c'est quelle sortie pour...?
say kel sor-tee poor...

is the pass open?
est-ce que le col est ouvert?
ess kuh luh kol ayt oo-vehr

do I need snow chains?
est-ce qu'il faut des chaînes?
ess keel foh day shen

- *Petrol is more expensive at motorway service stations.*
- *Big supermarkets sell petrol (24/7), but you can't use pay-at-pump with magnetic-strip bank cards. To be safe get petrol when the kiosk is manned.*
- *95-octane petrol is usually adequate unless you have a powerful engine or are towing a caravan.*

is there a petrol station near here?
est-ce qu'il y a une station-service près d'ici?
ess keel ee a oon stass-yoñ-sehr-vees pray dee-see

fill it up, please
le plein, s'il vous plaît
luh plañ seel voo play

30 euros of unleaded
trente euros de sans plomb
troñt uh-roh duh soñ ploñ

of diesel
de gasoil
duh gaz-wal

pump number...
pompe numéro...
poñp noo-may-roh...

that's my car
voilà ma voiture
vwa-la ma vwa-toor

where is the air line?
où se trouve le compresseur?
oo suh troov luh koñ-pre-suhr

where is the water?
où se trouve l'eau?
oo suh troov loh

please check...
s'il vous plaît, vérifiez...
seel voo play vay-reef-yay...

the tyre pressure
la pression des pneus
la press-yoñ day pnuh

the oil
l'huile
lweel

the water
l'eau
loh

do you take credit cards?
vous acceptez les cartes de crédit?
vooz ak-sep-tay lay kart duh kray-dee

Car – problems/breakdown

- *Motorways have emergency phones every 2km. The police will automatically know your location if you use them.*
- *If you break down, put on hazard lights and place a warning triangle 30m behind the car.*
- *It is compulsory in France to carry a first aid kit.*
- *Dial 112 from mobiles for emergency services.*

my car has broken down
ma voiture est en panne
ma vwa-toor ayt oñ pan

what do I do?
qu'est-ce que je dois faire?
kes kuh zhuh dwa fehr

I'm on my own (female)
je suis seule
zhuh swee suhl

I have children in the car
j'ai des enfants dans la voiture
zhay dayz oñ-foñ doñ la vwa-toor

where is the nearest garage?
où est le garage le plus proche?
oo ay luh ga-razh luh ploo prosh

is it serious?
c'est grave?
say grav

can you repair it?
est-ce que vous pouvez le réparer?
ess kuh voo poo-vay luh re-pa-ray

when will it be ready?
ça sera prêt quand?
sa suh-ra pray koñ

how much will it cost?
combien ça va coûter?
koñ-byañ sa va koo-tay

the car won't start
la voiture ne démarre pas
la vwa-toor nuh day-mar pa

I have a flat tyre
j'ai un pneu crevé
zhay uñ pnuh kruh-vay

the engine is overheating
le moteur surchauffe
luh mo-tuhr soor-shohf

the battery is flat
la batterie est à plat
la ba-tree ay ta pla

can you replace the windscreen?
pouvez-vous changer le pare-brise?
poo-vay voo shoñzhay luh par-breez

hire – Car

- To avoid problems, book a car in advance. If you buy your air ticket on the internet, many airlines offer car hire.
- Drivers under 25 may have to pay a young driver's supplement.
- Take care driving: in some French towns cars coming from the right have right of way. It usually isn't indicated.

LOCATION
VEHICULES

I would like to hire a car
je voudrais louer une voiture
zhuh voo-dray loo-ay oon vwa-toor

for one day
pour un jour
poor uñ zhoor

for ... days
pour ... jours
poor ... zhoor

I would like...
je voudrais...
zhuh voo-dray...

a large car
une grosse voiture
oon grohss vwa-toor

a small car
une petite voiture
oon puh-teet vwa-toor

a cheaper car
une voiture moins chère
oon vwa-toor mwañ shehr

an automatic
une automatique
oon oh-toh-ma-teek

is fully comprehensive insurance included?
est-ce que l'assurance tous-risques est comprise?
ess kuh lass-oo-roñss too reesk ay koñ-preez

what do we do if we break down?
qu'est-ce qu'il faut faire si la voiture tombe en panne?
kess keel foh fehr see la vwa-toor toñb oñ pan

when must I return the car by?
quand dois-je rapporter la voiture?
koñ dwazh ra-por-tay la vwa-toor

can you show me the controls?
pouvez-vous me montrer les commandes?
poo-vay voo muh moñ-tray lay ko-moñd

where are the documents?
où sont les papiers?
oo soñ lay pap-yay

do you have a baby seat?
vous avez un siège-auto?
vooz av-ay uñ syezh oh-toh

Shopping – holiday

- The **tabac** sells a wide range of useful things: stamps, phonecards, transport and lottery tickets.
- Smaller shops close on Mondays.
- When buying presents, most shops will offer to giftwrap free of charge. There is also a gift-wrapping area in many supermarkets. Ask for **un paquet-cadeau** (uñ pa-kay ka-doh)

do you sell...?
est-ce que vous vendez...?
ess kuh voo voñ-day...

stamps
des timbres
day tañb-ruh

batteries for this camera
des piles pour cet appareil
day peel poor set a-pa-ray

where can you buy...?
où est-ce qu'on peut acheter...?
oo ess koñ puh ash-tay...

stamps
des timbres
day tañb-ruh

films
des pellicules
day pe-lee-kool

10 stamps
dix timbres
dee tañbr

for postcards
pour cartes postales
poor kart pos-tal

to Britain
pour la Grande-Bretagne
poor la groñd bruh-tan-yuh

a colour film
une pellicule couleur
oon pe-lee-kool koo-luhr

a tape for this video camera
une cassette vidéo pour ce caméscope
oon ka-set vee-day-oh poor suh ka-may-skop

I'm looking for a present
je cherche un cadeau
zhuh shehrsh uñ ka-doh

have you anything cheaper?
vous avez quelque chose de moins cher?
vooz av-ay kel-kuh shohz duh mwañ shehr

it's a gift
c'est un cadeau
sayt uñ ka-doh

could you wrap it up?
vous pouvez me l'envelopper?
voo poo-vay muh loñv-lop-ay

clothes – Shopping

- There are a number of good French department stores. Look out for **Printemps**, **Monoprix** and **Galeries Lafayette**.
- Taking things back to a shop after you've bought them is not as accepted as in the UK. You'll need a good reason for asking for a refund.
- Sunday is not a shopping day in France.

can I try this on?
est-ce que je peux l'essayer?
ess kuh zhuh puh lay-say-yay

where are the changing rooms?
où sont les cabines d'essayage?
oo soñ lay ka-been day-say-yazh

it's too big
c'est trop grand
say troh groñ

have you a smaller size?
vous l'avez en plus petit?
voo lav-ay oñ ploo puh-tee

it's too small
c'est trop petit
say troh puh-tee

have you a larger size?
vous l'avez en plus grand?
voo lav-ay oñ ploo groñ

it's too expensive
c'est trop cher
say troh shehr

I'm just looking
je regarde seulement
zhuh ruh-gard suhl-moñ

I'll take this one
je prends celui-ci
zhuh proñ suhl-wee-see

I take a size 6 shoe
je fais du trente-neuf
zhuh fay doo troñt-nuhf

what shoe size are you?
quelle pointure faites-vous?
kel pwañ-toor fet-voo

does it fit?
ça vous va?
sa voo va

Shopping – food

- Smaller shops generally close between 12 and 2pm.
- Supermarkets are generally open all day Mon–Sat. Sun opening is not as common as in the UK.
- Supermarkets include **Géant**, **Casino**, **Intermarché** and **Carrefour**.
- You will need euro coins to release the shopping trolley.

where can I buy...?
où est-ce que je peux acheter...?
oo ess kuh zhuh puh ash-tay...

fruit	bread	milk
des fruits	du pain	du lait
day frwee	*doo pañ*	*doo lay*

where is the supermarket?
où est le supermarché?
oo ay luh soo-pehr-mar-shay

where is the baker's?
où est la boulangerie?
oo ay la boo-loñzh-ree

where is the market?
où est le marché?
oo ay luh mar-shay

which day is the market?
c'est quel jour, le marché?
say kel zhoor luh mar-shay

it's my turn
c'est à moi
sayt a mwa

that's enough
ça suffit
sa soo-fee

a litre of...	milk	beer	water
un litre de...	lait	bière	eau
uñ leetr duh...	*lay*	*byehr*	*oh*

a bottle of...	wine	beer	water
une bouteille de...	vin	bière	eau
oon boo-tay duh...	*vañ*	*byehr*	*oh*

a can of...	coke	beer	tonic water
une boîte de...	coca	bière	tonic
oon bwat duh...	*ko-ka*	*byehr*	*to-neek*

a packet of...	biscuits	sugar
un paquet de...	biscuits	sucre
uñ pa-kay duh...	*bee-skwee*	*sookr*

food – Shopping

- Fruit and veg must be weighed and stickered before taking it to the check-out.
- Bread is generally bought daily from the local baker's, **boulangerie** (boo-loñzh-ree).
- Supermarkets don't sell medicine. For paracetamol, cough medicine, etc, you will need to go to a pharmacy.

100 grams of...
cent grammes de...
soñ gram duh...

cheese
fromage
fro-mazh

ham
jambon
zhoñ-boñ

250 grams of...
250 grammes de...
duh soñ sañ-koñt gram duh...

butter
beurre
buhr

mince
viande hachée
vyoñd ash-ay

a kilo of...
un kilo de...
uñ kee-loh duh...

potatoes
pommes de terre
pom duh ter

apples
pommes
pom

8 slices of...
huit tranches de...
wee troñsh duh...

ham
jambon
joñ-boñ

salami
saucisson
soh-see-soñ

a loaf of bread
un pain
uñ pañ

a baguette
une baguette
oon ba-get

six eggs
six œufs
seez uh

a tin of...
une boîte de...
oon bwat duh...

tomatoes
tomates
to-mat

peas
petits pois
puh-tee pwa

a jar of...
un pot de...
uñ poh duh...

jam
confiture
koñ-fee-toor

honey
miel
myel

can I help you?
vous désirez?
voo day-zee-ray

is that everything?
ce sera tout?
suh suh-ra too

would you like a bag?
vous voulez un sac?
voo voo-lay uñ sak

Sightseeing

- The French Tourist Office website is **www.franceguide.com**.
- Most French national museums close on Tues. Local museums generally close Mon.
- In Paris a **carte musée-monuments** (valid for 1, 3 or 5 days) lets you visit over 70 museums and monuments. See **www.intermusees.com**.

where is the tourist office?
où est le syndicat d'initiative?
oo ay luh sañ-dee-ka dee-nee-sya-teev

do you have a town guide?
vous avez un plan de la ville?
vooz av-ay uñ ploñ duh la veel

we want to visit...
nous voulons visiter...
noo voo-loñ vee-zee-tay...

have you any leaflets?
vous avez des brochures?
vooz av-ay day bro-shoor

is it open to the public?
est-ce que c'est ouvert au public?
ess kuh say too-vehr oh poob-leek

are there any sightseeing tours?
est-ce qu'il y a des visites guidées?
ess keel ee a day vee-zeet gee-day

when does it leave?
à quelle heure part-il?
a kel uhr part-eel

where does it leave from?
il part d'où?
eel par doo

how much is it to get in?
c'est combien l'entrée?
say koñ-byañ loñ-tray

are there reductions for...?
est-ce qu'il y a des réductions pour...?
ess keel ee a day ray-dooks-yoñ poor...

students
les étudiants
layz ay-tood-yoñ

children
les enfants
layz oñ-foñ

senior citizens
les seniors
lay sayñ-yor

Beach

- Many French beaches have lifeguards during the tourist season. These beaches will also generally have showers.
- Most French towns have a municipal pool. Males may be refused entry with swimming trunks that are like long baggy shorts (because they may have been worn as shorts rather than just for swimming).

can you recommend a quiet beach?
est-ce que vous connaissez une plage tranquille?
ess kuh voo ko-ness-ay <u>oo</u>n plazh troñ-keel

is there a swimming pool?
est-ce qu'il y a une piscine?
ess keel ee a <u>oo</u>n pee-seen

can we swim in the river?
on peut nager dans la rivière?
oñ puh na-zhay doñ la reev-yehr

is the water clean?
est-ce que l'eau est propre?
ess kuh loh ay propr

is the water deep?
est-ce que l'eau est profonde?
ess kuh loh ay pro-foñd

is the water cold?
est-ce que l'eau est froide?
ess kuh loh ay frwad

is it dangerous?
est-ce que c'est dangereux?
ess kuh say doñ-zhuh-ruh

are there currents?
est-ce qu'il y a des courants?
ess keel ee a day koo-roñ

where can we...?
où est-ce qu'on peut faire...?
oo ess koñ puh fehr...

surf
du surf
d<u>oo</u> suhrf

scuba dive
de la plongée
duh la ploñ-zhay

can we hire...?
est-ce qu'on peut louer...?
ess koñ puh loo-ay...

a sunshade
un parasol
uñ pa-ra-sol

a deck chair
un transat
uñ troñ-zat

a beach hut
une cabine
<u>oo</u>n ka-been

Sport

- *Local tourist offices have details of sporting facilities. There is also information in the local regional magazine.*
- **Location** *(loh-ka-syoñ)* means hire.
- **Initiation** *(ee-nee-see-a-syoñ)* means beginners.
- *French towns signpost their sporting facilities (**tennis, piscine, parc des sports**).*

where can we...?
où est-ce qu'on peut...?
oo ess koñ puh...

play tennis
jouer au tennis
zhway oh ten-ees

play golf
jouer au golf
zhway oh golf

go riding
faire du cheval
fehr <u>doo</u> shuh-val

go fishing
pêcher
pesh-ay

how much is it...?
c'est combien...?
say koñ-byañ...

per hour
l'heure
luhr

per day
la journée
la zhoor-nay

can I hire...?
je peux louer...?
zhuh puh loo-ay...

rackets
des raquettes
day ra-ket

golf clubs
des clubs de golf
day klub duh golf

how do I book a court?
comment dois-je faire pour réserver un court?
ko-moñ dwazh fehr poor ray-zehr-vay uñ koor

do I need a fishing permit?
est-ce qu'il faut avoir un permis de pêche?
ess keel foh av-war uñ per-mee duh pesh

is there a football match?
est-ce qu'il y a un match de football?
ess keel ee a uñ match duh foot-bol

where is there a sports shop?
où est-ce qu'il y a un magasin de sports?
oo ess keel ee a uñ ma-ga-zañ duh spor

- Take some passport-sized photos with you. It will save time when getting your ski pass organized.
- For cross-country skiing, visit **www.ski-nordic-france.com**.
- Check **www.snow-forecast.com** or **www.bbc.co.uk/weather/sports/skiing**.
- A map of the ski runs is **une carte des pistes** (<u>oo</u>n kart day peest).

Initiat

I'd like to hire skis
je voudrais louer des skis
zhuh voo-dray loo-ay day skee

how much is a pass?
c'est combien le forfait?
say koñ-byañ luh for-fay

I'm a beginner
je suis débutant
zhuh swee day-boo-toñ

is there a map of the ski runs?
il y a une carte des pistes?
eel ee a oon kart day peest

which is an easy run?
laquelle de ces pistes est facile?
la-kel duh say peest ay fa-seel

my skis are...	**too long**	**too short**
mes skis sont...	trop longs	trop courts
may skee soñ...	*troh loñ*	*troh koor*

my bindings...	**are too loose**	**are too tight**
mes fixations...	ne sont pas assez serrées	sont trop serrées
may feek-sass-yoñ...	*nuh soñ pa as-ay ser-ay*	*soñ troh ser-ay*

can you adjust my bindings?
pourriez-vous régler mes fixations?
poo-ree-ay voo ray-glay may feek-sass-yoñ

where can we go cross-country skiing?
où est-ce qu'on peut faire du ski de fond?
oo ess koñ puh fehr doo skee duh foñ

what is your shoe size?
quelle pointure faites-vous?
kel pwañ-toor fet voo

Nightlife – popular

- Check what's on from posters, the tourist office or if you are in Paris from **Pariscope** (similar to London's Time Out).
- French people don't generally follow a 'round' system. They might just have one or two drinks when out.
- Try night-time rollerblading in Paris. Ask at the tourist office about **randonnée en roller**.

what is there to do at night?
qu'est-ce qu'on peut faire le soir?
kess koñ puh fehr luh swar

which is a good bar?
vous connaissez un bon bar?
voo ko-ness-ay uñ boñ bar

which is a good disco?
vous connaissez une bonne discothèque?
voo ko-ness-ay <u>oon</u> bon dees-ko-tek

where do local people go at night?
où est-ce que les gens du coin vont le soir?
oo ess kuh lay zhoñ <u>doo</u> kwañ voñ luh swar

it isn't a dangerous area?
ce n'est pas un quartier dangereux?
suh nay paz uñ kart-yay doñ-zhuh-ruh

are there any good concerts?
est-ce qu'il y a de bons concerts?
ess keel ee a duh boñ koñ-sehr

do you want to dance?
tu veux danser?
<u>too</u> vuh doñ-say

my name is...
je m'appelle...
zhuh ma-pel...

what's your name?
comment t'appelles-tu?
ko-moñ ta-pel <u>too</u>

cultural – Nightlife

- *Blockbuster films are usually dubbed, arty ones subtitled. **VO** = original version (subtitled); **VF** = French version (dubbed).*
- *The first day of summer (21 June) is music night (**fête de la musique**). Anyone can go into the street & play music so you see lots of bands. Some towns organize big concerts. Everything is free.*

are there any local festivals?
est-ce qu'il y a des fêtes dans la région?
ess keel ee a day fet doñ la rezh-yon

we'd like to go...
nous voudrions aller...
noo voo-dree-oñ al-ay...

to the theatre
au théâtre
oh tay-atr

to the opera
à l'opéra
a lo-pay-ra

to the cinema
au cinéma
oh see-nay-ma

to a concert
à un concert
a uñ koñ-sehr

what's on?
quels sont les spectacles à l'affiche?
kel soñ lay spek-takl a la-feesh

do I need to book?
est-ce qu'il faut réserver?
ess keel foh ray-zehr-vay

how much are tickets?
c'est combien l'entrée?
say koñ-byañ loñ-tray

when does the performance end?
quand finit la représentation?
koñ fee-nee la ruh-pray-zoñ-tass-yoñ

is there an interval?
est-ce qu'il y a un entracte?
ess keel ee a uñ oñ-trakt

2 tickets...
deux billets...
duh bee-yay...

for tonight
pour ce soir
poor suh swar

for tomorrow night
pour demain soir
poor duh-mañ swar

for 5th August
pour le cinq août
poor luh sañk oot

Hotel

- **Chambres d'hôte** (shoñ-bruh doht) is like bed and breakfast. If they provide evening meals, it is table d'hôte.
- Local tourist offices can help with local accommodation.
- Most French towns signpost hotels.
- No frills hotels such as **Formule 1** and **Étap Hôtel** offer good rates.

have you a room for tonight?
vous avez une chambre pour ce soir?
vooz av-ay <u>oo</u>n shoñb-ruh poor suh swar

single
pour une personne
poor <u>oo</u>n pehr-son

double
pour deux personnes
poor duh pehr-son

for a family
pour une famille
poor <u>oo</u>n fa-mee-yuh

with a bath
avec bain
a-vek bañ

with a shower
avec douche
a-vek doosh

how much is it per night?
c'est combien par nuit?
say koñ-byañ par nwee

is breakfast included?
le petit déjeuner est compris?
luh puh-tee day-zhuh-nay ay koñ-pree

I booked a room
j'ai réservé une chambre
zhay ray-zehr-vay <u>oo</u>n shoñb-ruh

my name is…
je m'appelle…
zhuh ma-pel…

I'd like to see the room
je voudrais voir la chambre
zhuh voo-dray vwar la shoñb-ruh

are the rooms air-conditioned?
les chambres sont climatisées?
lay shoñb-ruh soñ klee-ma-tee-zay

have you anything less expensive?
vous avez quelque chose de moins cher?
vooz av-ay kel-kuh shohz duh mwañ shehr

can I leave this in the safe?
je peux laisser cela dans le coffre?
zhuh puh less-ay suh-la doñ luh kof-ruh

can I have my key, please
ma clé, s'il vous plaît
ma klay seel voo play

are there any messages for me?
il y a des messages pour moi?
eel ee a day mess-azh poor mwa

come in!
entrez!
oñ-tray

please come back later
s'il vous plaît, revenez plus tard
seel voo play ruh-vuh-nay ploo tar

I'd like breakfast in my room
je voudrais le petit déjeuner dans ma chambre
zhuh voo-dray luh puh-tee day-zhuh-nay doñ ma shoñb-ruh

please bring...
pouvez-vous m'apporter...
poo-vay voo ma-por-tay...

toilet paper
du papier hygiénique
doo pap-yay ee-zhyen-eek

soap
du savon
doo sa-voñ

clean towels
des serviettes propres
day sehr-vyet propr

a glass
un verre
uñ vehr

please clean...
pouvez-vous nettoyer...
poo-vay voo ne-twa-yay...

my room
ma chambre
ma shoñb-ruh

the bath
la baignoire
la ben-war

please call me...
pouvez-vous m'appeler...
poo-vay voo map-lay...

at 7 o'clock
à sept heures
a set uhr

is there a laundry service?
vous avez un service de blanchisserie?
vooz av-ay uñ sehr-veess duh bloñ-shees-ree

I'm leaving tomorrow
je pars demain
zhuh par duh-mañ

could you prepare the bill?
pouvez-vous préparer la note?
poo-vay-voo pray-pa-ray la not

Self-catering

- Voltage in France and Switzerland is 220 with 2-pronged plugs.
- Take an adaptor for any electrical appliances you pack.
- Rubbish is collected from collection bins in the street and not collected from houses. Bins are easy to spot and emptied daily in towns.
- The word for neighbours is **les voisins** (lay vwah-zañ).

which is the key for this door?
quelle est la clé de cette porte?
kel ay la klay duh set port

please show us how this works
montrez-nous comment ça marche, s'il vous plaît
moñ-tray-noo ko-moñ sa marsh seel voo play

how does ... work?	**the cooker**	**the heating**
comment fonctionne...?	**la cuisinière**	**le chauffage**
ko-moñ foñks-yon...	*la kwee-zeen-yehr*	*luh shoh-fazh*

	the washing machine	**the dryer**
	la machine à laver	**le séchoir**
	la ma-sheen a lav-ay	*luh saysh-war*

who do I contact if there are any problems?
qui faut-il contacter s'il y a un problème?
kee foht-eel koñ-tak-tay seel ee a uñ prob-lem

we need extra...	**cutlery**	**sheets**
il faut encore des...	**couverts**	**draps**
eel foh oñ-kor day...	*koo-vehr*	*dra*

the gas has run out	**what do I do?**
il n'y a plus de gaz	**qu'est-ce qu'il faut faire?**
eel nee a ploo duh gaz	*kes keel foh fehr*

where are the fuses?	**where do I put the rubbish?**
où sont les fusibles?	**où est-ce que je dois mettre la poubelle?**
oo soñ lay foo-zee-bluh	*oo ess kuh zhuh dwa metr la poo-bel*

Camping & Caravanning

- There is an additional charge for caravans on French motorways. Check details on **www.saprr.fr**.
- Speed limits for cars towing caravans are lower than normal speed limits.
- In Switzerland it is 50kph in built-up areas and 80kph on other roads.

we're looking for a campsite
nous cherchons un camping
noo shehr-shoñ uñ koñ-peeng

have you a list of campsites?
avez-vous un guide des campings?
av-ay-voo uñ geed day koñ-peeng

where is the campsite?
où est le camping?
oo ay luh koñ-peeng

have you any vacancies?
il vous reste des places?
eel voo rest day plass

how much is it per night?
c'est combien la nuit?
say koñ-byañ la nwee

we'd like to stay for ... nights
nous voudrions rester ... nuits
noo voo-dree-oñ res-tay ... nwee

is the campsite near the beach?
est-ce que le camping est près de la plage?
ess kuh luh koñ-peeng ay pray duh la plazh

can we have a more sheltered site?
est-ce que nous pouvons avoir un emplacement plus abrité?
ess kuh noo poo-voñ av-war un oñ-plass-moñ plooz ab-ree-tay

this site is very muddy
ce terrain est très boueux
suh tay-rañ ay tray boo-uh

is there another site?
il y a un autre emplacement?
eel ee a un ohtr oñ-plass-moñ

can we camp here?
est-ce qu'on peut camper ici?
ess koñ puh koñ-pay ee-see

can we park our caravan here?
est-ce que nous pouvons mettre notre caravane ici?
ess kuh noo poo-voñ metr notr ka-ra-van ee-see

Children

nfan

- The word for child is **enfant** (oñ-foñ).
- Generally children under 4 travel free on public transport. Between 4 and 12, they pay half price.
- In France children under 10 must travel in the back of the car and be strapped in using an appropriate restraint or child seat.

a child's ticket
un billet tarif enfant
uñ bee-yay ta-reef oñ-foñ

he/she is ... years old
il/elle a ... ans
eel/el a ... oñ

is there a reduction for children?
est-ce qu'il y a une réduction pour les enfants?
ess keel ee a oon ray-dooks-yoñ poor layz oñ-foñ

do you have a children's menu?
est-ce que vous avez un menu enfant?
ess kuh vooz av-ay uñ muh-noo oñ-foñ

do you have...?
est-ce que vous avez...?
ess kuh vooz av-ay...

a high chair
une chaise de bébé
oon shehz duh bay-bay

a cot
un lit d'enfant
uñ lee doñ-foñ

what is there for children to do?
quelles sont les activités prévues pour les enfants?
kel soñ layz ak-tee-vee-tay pray-voo poor layz oñ-foñ

is there a playpark near here?
il y a une aire de jeux près d'ici?
eel ee a oon ehr duh zhuh pray dee-see

is it safe for children?
c'est sans danger pour les enfants?
say soñ doñ-zhay poor layz oñ-foñ

he/she is 10 years old
il/elle a dix ans
eel/el a deez oñ

do you have children?
est-ce que vous avez des enfants?
ess kuh vooz av-ay dayz oñ-foñ

I have two children
j'ai deux enfants
zhay duhz oñ-foñ

Special Needs

- *Visit **www.handicap.gouv.fr** (French only) to check facilities for the disabled.*
- *The word for disabled is **handicapé** (oñ-dee-ka-pay). There are often discounts for entrance fees, etc.*
- *The French Tourist Office has a list of hotels which offer facilities for the disabled.*

is it possible to visit ... with a wheelchair?
est-ce qu'on peut visiter ... en fauteuil roulant?
ess koñ puh vee-zee-tay ... oñ foh-tuhy roo-loñ

do you have toilets for the disabled?
est-ce que vous avez des toilettes pour handicapés?
ess kuh vooz av-ay day twa-let poor oñ-dee-ka-pay

I need a bedroom on the ground floor
j'ai besoin d'une chambre au rez-de-chaussée
zhay buhz-wañ d<u>oo</u>n shoñbr oh ray duh shoh-say

is there a lift?
est-ce qu'il y a un ascenseur?
ess keel ee a uñ ass-oñ-suhr

where is the lift?
où est l'ascenseur?
oo ay lass-oñ-suhr

I can't walk far
je ne peux pas aller très loin à pied
zhuh nuh puh paz al-ay tray lwañ a pyay

are there many steps?
il y a beaucoup de marches?
eel ee a boh-koo duh marsh

is there an entrance for wheelchairs?
est-ce qu'il y a une entrée pour les fauteuils roulants?
ess keel ee a <u>oo</u>n oñ-tray poor lay foh-tuhy roo-loñ

can I travel on this train with a wheelchair?
est-ce que je peux prendre ce train avec un fauteuil roulant?
ess kuh zhuh puh proñdr suh trañ a-vek uñ foh-tuhy roo-loñ

is there a reduction for the disabled?
est-ce qu'il y a une réduction pour les handicapés?
ess keel ee a <u>oo</u>n ray-dooks-yoñ poor lay oñ-dee-kap-ay

Exchange Visitors

● These phrases are intended for families hosting French-speaking visitors. We've used the more familiar **tu** (rather than the more formal **vous**) form.
● French people generally eat dinner 7.30/8pm – visitors might not be used to eating early. Eating in front of the TV is unheard of in France!

what would you like for breakfast?
qu'est-ce que tu veux manger pour le petit déjeuner?
kess kuh <u>too</u> vuh moñ-zhay poor luh puh-tee day-zhuh-nay

what would you like to eat/drink?
qu'est-ce que tu veux manger/boire?
kess kuh <u>too</u> vuh moñ-zhay/bwar

did you sleep well?
tu as bien dormi?
<u>too</u> a byañ dor-mee

would you like to take a shower?
tu veux prendre une douche?
<u>too</u> vuh proñdr <u>oon</u> doosh

what would you like to do today?
qu'est-ce que tu veux faire aujourd'hui?
kess kuh <u>too</u> vuh fehr oh-zhoor-dwee

would you like to go shopping?
tu veux aller faire du shopping?
<u>too</u> vuh al-ay fehr <u>doo</u> shop-eeng

I will pick you up at...
je passerai te prendre à...
zhuh pass-ray tuh proñdr a...

did you enjoy yourself?
est-ce que tu t'es bien amusé?
ess kuh <u>too</u> tay byan a-m<u>oo</u>-zay

take care
fais attention à toi
fayz a-toñs-yon a twa

please be back by...
tâche de rentrer avant...
tash duh roñ-tray a-voñ...

we'll be in bed when you get back
nous serons au lit lorsque tu rentreras
noo suh-roñ oh lee lors-kuh <u>too</u> roñ-truh-ra

58

Exchange Visitors

- If invited to a French family for a meal, take chocolates or flowers, rather than wine. They will probably have chosen the wine to go with the food. Sparkling wine is a good option.
- Take care to use the more formal **vous** form until you are invited to **tutoyer** (use the informal **tu**), especially with older people.

I like...
j'aime bien...
zhem byañ...

I don't like...
je n'aime pas...
zhuh nem pa...

that was delicious
c'était délicieux
se-tay day-lee-syuh

thank you very much
merci beaucoup
mehr-see boh-koo

may I phone home?
est-ce que je peux téléphoner chez moi?
ess kuh zhuh puh tay-lay-foh-nay shay mwa

can you take me by car?
est-ce que vous pouvez m'emmener en voiture?
ess kuh voo poo-vay moñm-nay oñ vwa-toor

can I borrow...?
je peux emprunter...?
zhuh puh oñ-pruñ-tay...

an iron
un fer à repasser
uñ fehr a ruh-pass-ay

a hairdryer
un sèche-cheveux
uñ sesh-shuh-vuh

what time do I have to get up?
à quelle heure faut-il que je me lève?
a kel uhr foht-eel kuh zhuh muh lev

could you call me?
pouvez-vous m'appeler?
poo-vay voo map-lay

I'm leaving in a week
je m'en vais dans une semaine
zhuh moñ vay doñz oon suh-men

thanks for everything
merci pour tout
mehr-see poor too

I've had a great time
j'ai passé des moments formidables
zhay pass-ay day mo-moñ for-mee-dabl

Problems

- *Always try to speak in French – however bad! And then ask if there is someone who does speak some English.*
- *Try to stay calm. Not understanding each other can often aggravate the situation.*
- *Try to be as polite as possible, using* **monsieur** *or* **madame** *and the polite* **vous** *form.*

can you help me?
pouvez-vous m'aider?
poo-vay voo may-day

I don't speak French
je ne parle pas français
zhuh nuh parl pa froñ-say

do you speak English?
parlez-vous anglais?
par-lay voo oñ-glay

does anyone speak English?
il y a quelqu'un qui parle anglais?
eel ee a kel-kuñ kee parl oñ-glay

I'm lost
je me suis perdu
zhuh muh swee pehr-doo

how do I get to...?
pour aller à...?
poor al-ay a...

I'm late
je suis en retard
zhuh swee oñ ruh-tar

I need to get to...
je dois aller à...
zhuh dwa al-ay a...

I've missed...
j'ai manqué...
zhay moñ-kay...

my plane
mon avion
mon av-yoñ

my connection
ma correspondance
ma ko-res-poñ-doñs

I've lost...
j'ai perdu...
zhay pehr-doo...

my money
mon argent
mon ar-zhoñ

my passport
mon passeport
moñ pass-por

my luggage has not arrived
mes bagages ne sont pas arrivés
may ba-gazh nuh soñ paz a-ree-vay

I've left my bag in...
j'ai laissé mon sac dans...
zhay less-ay moñ sak doñ...

leave me alone!
laissez-moi tranquille!
less-ay-mwa troñ-keel

I have no money
je n'ai pas d'argent
zhuh nay pa dar-zhoñ

go away!
allez-vous-en!
al-ay vooz-oñ

Complaints

- *You can try complaining, but you may find that French shopkeepers and waiters aren't so worried about customers' opinions as they are in the UK.*
- *You'll need a good reason for getting a refund from a shop.*
- *You might be surprised at the way people queue in France – it's usually every man (or woman) for himself!*

Accue

the light
la lumière
la <u>loom</u>-yehr

the air conditioning
la climatisation
la klee-ma-tee-zas-yoñ

...doesn't work
...ne marche pas
...nuh marsh pa

the room is dirty
la chambre est sale
la shoñbr ay sal

the bath is dirty
la baignoire est sale
la ben-war ay sal

there is no...
il n'y a pas...
eel nee a pa...

hot water
d'eau chaude
doh shohd

toilet paper
de papier hygiénique
duh pap-yay ee-zhyen-eek

it is too noisy
il y a trop de bruit
eel ee a troh duh brwee

the room is too small
la chambre est trop petite
la shoñbr ay troh puh-teet

this isn't what I ordered
ce n'est pas ce que j'ai commandé
suh nay pa suh kuh zhay ko-moñ-day

there is a mistake
il y a une erreur
eel ee a <u>oon</u> e-ruhr

I want to complain
je veux faire une réclamation
zhuh vuh fehr <u>oon</u> ray-kla-mass-yoñ

I want a refund
je veux être remboursé
zhuh vuh etr roñ-boor-say

we've been waiting for a very long time
nous attendons depuis très longtemps
nooz a-toñ-doñ duh-pwee tray loñ-toñ

this is broken
c'est cassé
say kass-ay

can you repair it?
pouvez-vous le réparer?
poo-vay-voo luh ray-pa-ray

Emergencies

- *Emergency numbers in France: Police – 17, Ambulance – 15, Fire brigade – 18.*
- *Dial 112 from a mobile for all emergency numbers.*
- *You find **Gendarmerie** in villages, **Police** in towns.*
- *If you've been robbed or attacked, go to the police station to report it and fill in a form. A copy is needed for insurance.*

help!
au secours!
oh suh-koor

can you help me?
pouvez-vous m'aider?
poo-vay-voo may-day

there's been an accident
il y a eu un accident
eel ee a <u>oo</u> un ak-see-doñ

someone is injured
il y a un blessé
eel ee a uñ bless-ay

call...
appelez...
ap-lay...

the police
la police
la po-leess

an ambulance
une ambulance
<u>oo</u>n oñ-<u>boo</u>-loñs

the fire brigade
les pompiers
lay poñ-pyay

he was driving too fast
il allait trop vite
eel al-ay troh veet

I need a report for my insurance
il me faut un constat pour mon assurance
eel muh foh uñ koñ-sta poor mon ass-<u>oo</u>-roñss

I've been robbed
on m'a volé
oñ ma vol-ay

I have no money
je n'ai pas d'argent
zhuh nay pa dar-zhoñ

my car has been broken into
on a forcé ma voiture
on a for-say ma vwa-toor

my car has been stolen
on m'a volé ma voiture
oñ ma vol-ay ma vwa-toor

I've been attacked
on m'a attaqué
oñ ma a-tak-ay

I've been raped
on m'a violée
oñ ma vyol-ay

that man keeps following me
cet homme me suit
set om muh swee

how much is the fine?
c'est combien l'amende?
say koñ-byañ lam-oñd

can I pay at the police station?
est-ce que je peux payer au commissariat de police?
ess kuh zhuh puh pay-ay oh ko-mee-sar-ya duh po-leess

I would like to phone my embassy
je voudrais appeler mon ambassade
zhuh voo-dray ap-lay mon oñ-ba-sad

where is the British consulate?
où est le consulat britannique?
oo ay luh koñ-soo-la bree-ta-neek

I'm very sorry, officer
je suis vraiment désolé(e), monsieur l'agent
zhuh swee vray-moñ day-zoh-lay muh-syuh la-zhoñ

we're on our way
nous arrivons
nooz a-ree-voñ

Health

● *Take a stamped E111 form (from post offices). You can keep it for future trips (unless you change address).*
● *If you need a doctor, look for one who is* **conventionné** *(working within French national health). Get a signed statement of treatment to reclaim any expenses. This only applies for emergency treatment.*

have you something for...?
avez-vous quelque chose contre...?
av-ay-voo kel-kuh shohz koñtr...

flu	**diarrhoea**
la grippe	la diarrhée
la greep	*la dee-ar-ay*

is it safe to give to children?
c'est sans danger pour les enfants?
say soñ doñ-zhay poor layz oñ-foñ

I don't feel well
je me sens mal
zhuh muh soñ mal

I need a doctor
j'ai besoin d'un médecin
zhay buhz-wañ duñ mayd-sañ

my son/daughter is ill
mon fils/ma fille est malade
moñ feess/ma fee ay ma-lad

he/she has a temperature
il/elle a de la fièvre
eel/el a duh la fyehv-ruh

I'm taking these drugs
je prends ces médicaments
zhuh proñ say may-dee-ka-moñ

I have high blood pressure
j'ai de la tension
zhay duh la toñss-yoñ

I'm pregnant
je suis enceinte
zhuh sweez oñ-sañt

I'm on the pill
je prends la pilule
zhuh proñ la pee-lool

I'm allergic to penicillin
je suis allergique à la pénicilline
zhuh sweez a-lehr-zheek a la pe-nee-see-leen

my blood group is...
mon groupe sanguin est...
moñ groop soñ-gañ ay...

I'm breastfeeding
j'allaite mon enfant
zha-let mon oñ-foñ

can I take this medicine?
est-ce que je peux prendre ce médicament?
ess kuh zhuh puh proñd-ruh suh may-dee-ka-moñ

will he/she have to go to hospital?
est-ce qu'il/qu'elle devra aller à l'hôpital?
ess keel/kel duhv-ra al-ay a lop-ee-tal

I need to go to casualty
je dois aller aux urgences
zhuh dwa al-ay ohz <u>oor</u>-zhoñss

where is the hospital?
où est l'hôpital?
oo ay lop-ee-tal

when are visiting hours?
quelles sont les heures de visite?
kel soñ layz uhr duh vee-zeet

which ward?
quel service?
kel sehr-veess

I need to see a dentist
j'ai besoin de voir un dentiste
zhay buhz-wañ duh vwar uñ doñ-teest

I have toothache
j'ai mal aux dents
zhay mal oh doñ

the filling has come out
le plombage est parti
luh ploñ-bazh ay par-tee

it hurts
ça me fait mal
sa muh fay mal

my dentures are broken
mon dentier est cassé
moñ doñt-yay ay kass-ay

can you repair them?
vous pouvez le réparer?
voo poo-vay luh ray-par-ay

I have an abscess
j'ai un abcès
zhay un ab-seh

can you write me a prescription?
pouvez-vous me faire une ordonnance?
poo-vay voo muh fehr <u>oon</u> or-donn-oñs

Business

- *Office hours in France are generally 9 to 12pm and 1.30 to 5pm.*
- *Long lunches rather than formal meetings might be the best way of finding out about a French business.*
- *French company websites end .fr.*
- *If a French bank holiday falls on a Thursday, Friday also becomes a holiday, making it into a long weekend.*

I'm...
je suis...
zhuh swee...

here's my card
voici ma carte de visite
vwa-see ma kart duh vee-zeet

I'm from Jones Ltd
je suis de la compagnie Jones
zhuh swee duh la koñ-pan-yee Jones

I'd like to arrange a meeting with Mr/Ms...
j'aimerais arranger une entrevue avec Monsieur/Madame...
zhay-muh-ray a-roñ-zhay oon oñ-truh-voo a-vek muh-syuh/ma-dam...

on 4 May at 11 o'clock
pour le quatre mai à onze heures
poor luh katr may a oñz uhr

can we meet at a restaurant?
est-ce que nous pouvons nous rencontrer dans un restaurant?
ess kuh noo poo-voñ noo roñ-koñ-tray doñz uñ res-toh-roñ

I will confirm by fax
je confirmerai par fax
zhuh koñ-feer-muh-ray par faks

I'm staying at Hotel...
je suis à l'Hôtel...
zhuh swee a loh-tel...

how do I get to your office?
comment se rend-on à votre bureau?
ko-moñ suh roñ-toñ a votr boo-roh

here is some information about my company
voici de la documentation concernant ma compagnie
vwa-see duh la do-koo-moñ-tass-yoñ koñ-sehr-noñ ma koñ-pan-yee

I have an appointment with... at ... o'clock
j'ai rendez-vous avec...   à ... heures
zhay roñ-day-voo a-vek...   a ... uhr

I'm delighted to meet you
je suis enchanté de faire votre connaissance
zhuh sweez oñ-shoñ-tay duh fehr votr ko-nay-soñs

my French isn't very good
mon français n'est pas très bon
moñ froñ-say nay pa tray boñ

I need an interpreter
j'ai besoin d'un interprète
zhay buhz-wañ dun añ-tehr-pret

what is the name of the managing director?
comment s'appelle le directeur?
ko-moñ sa-pel luh dee-rek-tuhr

I would like some information about the company
je voudrais des renseignements sur l'entreprise
zhuh voo-dray day roñ-sen-yuh-moñ <u>soor</u> loñ-truh-preez

do you have a press office?
est-ce que vous avez un service de presse?
ess kuh vooz av-ay uñ sehr-veess duh press

can you photocopy this for me?
pouvez-vous me photocopier ça?
poo-vay voo muh fo-to-kop-yay sa

is there a business centre?
est-ce qu'il y a un service de secrétariat?
ess keel ee a uñ sehr-veess duh suh-kray-ta-ree-a

do you have an appointment?
est-ce que vous avez rendez-vous?
ess kuh vooz a-vay roñ-day-voo

Phoning

● *International dialling codes: UK 0044; USA/Canada 001;*
Australia 0061.
 ● *Cheap rates: from 7pm Mon-Fri, all day Sat/Sun and hols.*
 ● *Most phone boxes don't take coins, just cards.*
 ● *You can buy phonecards at 50 or 120 units.*
 ● *All French phone numbers include the area code.*

a phonecard
une télécarte
<u>oo</u>n tay-lay-kart

I want to make a phone call
je voudrais téléphoner
zhuh voo-dray tay-lay-foh-nay

I wish to make a reverse charge call
je voudrais téléphoner en PCV
zhuh voo-dray tay-lay-foh-nay oñ pay-say-vay

can I speak to...?
je peux parler à...?
zhuh puh par-lay a...

this is...
c'est...
say...

Monsieur Citron please
Monsieur Citron s'il vous plaît
muh-syuh see-troñ seel voo play

I'll call back later
je vais rappeler plus tard
zhuh vay rap-lay pl<u>oo</u> tar

can you give me an outside line, please?
est-ce que je peux avoir la ligne, s'il vous plaît?
ess kuh zhuh puh av-war la leen-yuh seel voo play

hello?
allô?
a-loh

who is calling?
c'est de la part de qui?
say duh la par duh kee

it's engaged
c'est occupé
say o-k<u>oo</u>-pay

do you have a mobile?
vous avez un portable?
vooz a-vay uñ por-tab-luh

my mobile number is...
le numéro de mon portable est le...
luh n<u>oo</u>-may-ro duh moñ por-tab-luh ay luh...

E-mail/Fax

- Internet cafés are on the increase. Visit **www.cybercafes.com**.
- *www.* is **trois w point** *(trwa doob-luh vay pwañ)*.
- The French for @ is **arrobase** *(a-ro-baz)*.
- The ending for French e-addresses is **.fr**
- **Mél** on a form is for e-mail address (like **Tél** for phone number).

I want to send an e-mail
je voudrais envoyer un e-mail
zhuh voo-dray oñ-vwa-yay uñ ee-mehl

what's your e-mail address?
quelle est votre addresse e-mail?
kel ay votr a-dress ee-mehl

my e-mail address is...
mon adresse e-mail est...
moñ a-dress ee-mehl ay...

caz.smith@anycompany.co.uk
caz point smith arrobase anycompany point co point uk
caz pwañ smith a-roh-baz anycompany pwañ say oh pwañ <u>oo</u> ka

did you get my e-mail?
est-ce que vous avez reçu mon e-mail?
ess kuh vooz av-ay ruh-s<u>oo</u> mon ee-mehl

I want to send a fax
je voudrais envoyer un fax
zhuh voo-dray oñ-vwa-yay uñ faks

do you have a fax?
vous avez un fax?
vooz av-ay uñ faks

what's your fax number?
quel est votre numéro de fax?
kel ay votr n<u>oo</u>-may-ro duh faks

did you get my fax?
vous avez reçu mon fax?
vooz av-ay ruh-s<u>oo</u> moñ faks

Numbers

0	**zéro**	*zay-ro*
1	**un**	*uñ*
2	**deux**	*duh*
3	**trois**	*trwa*
4	**quatre**	*kat-ruh*
5	**cinq**	*sañk*
6	**six**	*seess*
7	**sept**	*set*
8	**huit**	*weet*
9	**neuf**	*nuhf*
10	**dix**	*deess*
11	**onze**	*oñz*
12	**douze**	*dooz*
13	**treize**	*trez*
14	**quatorze**	*ka-torz*
15	**quinze**	*kañz*
16	**seize**	*sez*
17	**dix-sept**	*dees-set*
18	**dix-huit**	*dees-weet*
19	**dix-neuf**	*dees-nuhf*
20	**vingt**	*vañ*
21	**vingt et un**	*vañt-ay-uñ*
22	**vingt-deux**	*vañ-duh*
30	**trente**	*troñt*
40	**quarante**	*ka-roñt*
50	**cinquante**	*sañ-koñt*
60	**soixante**	*swa-soñt*
70	**soixante-dix**	*swa-soñt-deess*
80	**quatre-vingts**	*kat-ruh-vañ*
90	**quatre-vingt-dix**	*kat-ruh-vañ-deess*
100	**cent**	*soñ*
110	**cent dix**	*soñ deess*
200	**deux cents**	*duh soñ*
1,000	**mille**	*meel*
1,000,000	**un million**	*uñ meel-yoñ*

1st	**premier**	*pruhm-yay*
2nd	**deuxième**	*duhz-yem*
3rd	**troisième**	*trwaz-yem*
4th	**quatrième**	*katree-yem*
5th	**cinquième**	*sañk-yem*
6th	**sixième**	*seez-yem*
7th	**septième**	*set-yem*
8th	**huitième**	*weet-yem*
9th	**neuvième**	*nuhv-yem*
10th	**dixième**	*deez-yem*

Monday	**lundi** *luñ-dee*
Tuesday	**mardi** *mar-dee*
Wednesday	**mercredi** *mer-kruh-dee*
Thursday	**jeudi** *zhuh-dee*
Friday	**vendredi** *voñ-druh-dee*
Saturday	**samedi** *sam-dee*
Sunday	**dimanche** *dee-moñsh*

January	**janvier** *zhoñv-yay*
February	**février** *fayv-ree-ay*
March	**mars** *mars*
April	**avril** *av-reel*
May	**mai** *may*
June	**juin** *zhwañ*
July	**juillet** *zhwee-yay*
August	**août** *oot*
September	**septembre** *sep-toñ-bruh*
October	**octobre** *ok-toh-bruh*
November	**novembre** *noh-voñ-bruh*
December	**décembre** *day-soñ-bruh*

what's the date?
quelle est la date d'aujourd'hui?
kel ay la dat doh-zhoor-dwee

which day?
quel jour?
kel zhoor

which month?
quel mois?
kel mwa

March 5th
le cinq mars
luh sañk marss

July 6th
le six juillet
luh see jwee-yay

2004
deux mille quatre
duh meel kat-ruh

on Saturday
samedi
sam-dee

on Saturdays
le samedi
luh sam-dee

every Saturday
tous les samedis
too lay sam-dee

this Saturday
samedi qui vient
sam-dee kee vyañ

next Saturday
samedi prochain
sam-dee pro-shañ

last Saturday
samedi dernier
sam-dee dern-yay

please can you confirm the date?
vous pouvez me confirmer la date, s'il vous plaît?
voo poo-vay muh koñ-feer-may la dat seel voo play

Time

● am = **du matin** (d<u>oo</u> ma-tañ)
● pm = **de l'après-midi** (duh lap-ray-mee-dee)
● The 24-hour clock is used a lot more in Europe than in Britain.
● With the 24-hour clock the words **quart** (quarter) and **demie** (half) aren't used. 15 (**quinze**) and 30 (**trente**) are used.

what time is it, please?
quelle heure est-il, s'il vous plaît?
kel uhr ayt-eel seel voo play

it's 1 o'clock
il est une heure
eel ay <u>oo</u>n uhr

it's 3 o'clock
il est trois heures
eel ay trwaz uhr

it's half past 8
il est huit heures et demie
eel ay weet uhr ay duh-mee

in an hour
dans une heure
doñz <u>oo</u>n uhr

half an hour
une demi-heure
<u>oo</u>n duh-mee uhr

until 8 o'clock
jusqu'à huit heures
j<u>oo</u>s-ka weet uhr

it is half past 10
il est dix heures et demie
eel ay deez uhr ay duh-mee

at 10 am
à dix heures
a deez uhr

at 2200
à vingt-deux heures
a vañ-duhz uhr

at midday
à midi
a mee-dee

at midnight
à minuit
a meen-wee

soon
bientôt
byañ-toh

later
plus tard
pl<u>oo</u> tar

am
du matin
d<u>oo</u> ma-tañ

pm
du soir
d<u>oo</u> swar

72

La cuisine française

French cuisine is among the best in the world. The French take their food very seriously and what they eat largely depends on what is available locally and in season.

In Brittany with its craggy coastline, you find fish and superb seafood, along with sweet and savoury pancakes. Normandy boasts apples and rich dairy produce which you can sample in **tarte normande** (apple tart), cider and **calvados** (apple brandy).

Southern France enjoys the flavours of the sun and Mediterranean – tomatoes, olives, basil, garlic, anchovies and saffron. Try **pissaladière** (similar to pizza) and **tapenade** (rich anchovy and olive paste). Corsica mingles the flavours of France and Italy and makes use of wild boar.

Eastern France shares border and tastes with its German neighbours. You find sauerkraut and pork as well as **quiche lorraine**.

Western France boasts Bordeaux wine, truffles and goose liver. Stews are cooked in red wine with wild mushrooms.

Central France, a largely rural area, specialises in heavy, hearty dishes to see through the long winter months. Taste the earthy flavours in the Puy lentils, potatoes, cheese and pork.

The Pyrenees separate France and Spain but not influences. You find them in the bean and vegetable stews with spicy pork sausage similar to **chorizo**.

Paris, naturally, takes a pinch from here, a **soupçon** from there, and serves them up elegantly in rich smooth sauces.

Breakfast (**le petit déjeuner**) is a light meal, usually fresh bread or croissants with butter and jam and strong black coffee, with or without hot milk. The main meal of the day in France used to be lunch (**le déjeuner**), served between 12.30 and 2pm. Nowadays lunch may be lighter with the evening meal (**le dîner**) being the main meal, usually served between 7.30 and 8.30pm.

Ordering drinks

- You don't need to order at the bar. Take a seat and a waiter will take your order.
- Try a shandy, **un panaché** (uñ pan-a-shay), or cordial and lemonade, **un diabolo** (uñ dee-a-bo-lo): either mint, **menthe** (moñt) or strawberry, **fraise** (frehz).
- 'Cheers!' in French is **santé** (soñ-tay).

a black coffee
un café noir
uñ ka-fay nwar

a white coffee
un café crème/un café au lait
uñ ka-fay krem/uñ ka-fay oh lay

a tea
un thé
uñ tay

with milk
au lait
oh lay

with lemon
au citron
oh see-troñ

a bottle of mineral water
une bouteille d'eau minérale
oon boo-tay doh mee-nay-ral

sparkling
gazeuse
gaz-uhz

still
plate
plat

a beer
une bière
oon byehr

a shandy
un panaché
uñ pa-na-shay

a half pint
un demi
uñ duh-mee

what beers do you have?
qu'est-ce que vous avez comme bières?
kess kuh vooz a-vay kom byehr

the wine list, please
la carte des vins, s'il vous plaît
la kart day vañ seel voo play

a bottle of house wine
un pichet de vin
uñ pee-shay duh vañ

a glass of wine white/red
un verre de vin blanc/rouge
uñ vehr duh vañ bloñ/roozh

a bottle of red wine
une bouteille de vin rouge
oon boo-tay duh vañ roozh

a bottle of white wine
une bouteille de vin blanc
oon boo-tay duh vañ bloñ

would you like a drink?
voulez-vous boire quelque chose?
voo-lay voo bwar kel-kuh shoz

what will you have?
qu'est-ce que vous prenez?
kess kuh voo pruh-nay

Ordering food

- By law, French restaurants must offer one set-price menu, many offer 2 or 3.
- *Au choix* (oh shwah) means 'choice of'.
- A children's menu is **un menu enfant** (uñ muh-<u>noo</u> oñ-foñ).
- It is polite to wish **bon appétit** (boñ a-pay-tee). The reply is 'you, too', either **vous** or **toi aussi** (vooz/twah oh-see).

can you recommend a good restaurant?
pouvez-vous nous recommander un bon restaurant?
poo-vay voo noo ruh-ko-moñ-day uñ boñ res-toh-roñ

I'd like to book a table
je voudrais réserver une table
zhuh voo-dray ray-zehr-vay <u>oo</u>n tabl

for … people
pour … personnes
poor … pehr-son

for tonight
pour ce soir
poor suh swar

at 8 pm
à huit heures
a weet uhr

the menu, please
le menu, s'il vous plaît
luh muh-<u>noo</u> seel voo play

is there a dish of the day?
est-ce qu'il y a un plat du jour?
ess keel ee a uñ pla <u>doo</u> zhoor

the 26-euro menu
le menu à vingt-six euros
luh muh-<u>noo</u> a vañ-seess uh-roh

I'll have this
je vais prendre ça
zhuh vay proñdr sa

what do you recommend?
qu'est-ce que vous me conseillez?
kess kuh voo muh koñ-say-ay

do you have any vegetarian dishes?
avez-vous des plats végétariens?
av-ay voo day pla vay-zhay-tar-yañ

excuse me!
excusez-moi!
eks-<u>koo</u>-zay mwa

some bread please
du pain s'il vous plaît
<u>doo</u> pañ seel voo play

some water please
de l'eau s'il vous plaît
duh loh seel voo play

the bill, please
l'addition, s'il vous plaît
la-dees-yoñ seel voo play

Special requirements

- *The words for gluten free are* **sans gluten** *(soñ* gloo*-ten).*
- **Fait avec du lait cru** *means made with unpasteurised milk.*
- **Biologique** *(bee-o-loh-zheek) or* **bio** *means organic.*
- *On labels,* **glucides** *(*gloo*-seed) are carbohydrates.*
  Lipides *(lee-peed) are fats.*
- *Decaffeinated is* **décaféiné** *(day-ka-fay-ee-nay).*

what's in this?
quels sont les ingrédients?
kel soñ lay añ-gray-dyoñ

I'm vegetarian
je suis végétarien(ne)
zhuh swee vay-zhay-tar-yañ(-ryeñ)

I don't eat pork
je ne mange pas de porc
zhuh nuh moñzh pa duh por

I'm allergic to shellfish
je suis allergique aux crustacés
zhuh swee a-lehr-zheek oh kroos-ta-say

I am allergic to peanuts
je suis allergique aux cacahuètes
zhuh swee a-lehr-zheek oh ka-ka-wet

I can't eat raw eggs
je ne peux pas manger d'œufs crus
zhuh nuh puh pa moñ-zhay duh kroo

I don't eat fish
je ne mange pas de poisson
zhuh nuh moñzh pa duh pwa-soñ

I can't eat liver
je ne peux pas manger de foie
zhuh nuh puh pa moñ-zhay duh fwah

is it raw?
c'est cru?
say kroo

I am on a diet
je suis au régime
zhuh swee oh ray-zheem

I don't drink alcohol
je ne bois pas d'alcool
zhuh nuh bwa pa dal-kol

BAKER'S
Boulangeries open very early and sell sandwiches and snacks. You can get both breakfast and lunch there.

LA CREPERIE

PANCAKES Make a delicious meal of 2 or 3 *crêpes* as different courses. A savoury pancake is a *galette* and fillings include cheese, ham, eggs, sausage and tomato. Sweet fillings include chocolate, honey, banana, chestnut purée, almonds and jam.

BOUCHERIE CHARCUTERIE VOLAILLES

BUTCHER, PORK & POULTRY
The word *traiteur* means that they are also a deli and have dishes to take away.

ÉPICERIE FROMAGERIE

GROCER & CHEESEMONGER
There are over 350 varieties of French cheese. Ask for *un morceau* (uñ mor-soh), a bit.

BRASSERIE LE FRANÇAIS

Brasseries and Bistros serve a *plat du jour* (dish of the day) at almost any time of the day. Restaurants tend to only be open at meal times. *Bistro*

Y. Cadol PATISSIER CHOCOLATIER

CAKE SHOPS
Often have a tearoom (*Salon de thé*), serving mouth-watering cakes and generally weak tea with lemon. Try *chocolat chaud* (hot chocolate). Can be on the expensive side.

MARKET
Daily or weekly, you will find cheese and local specialities as well as tomatoes and fruit for the perfect picnic.

TABACS often have a bar or restaurant attached. They are usually good value and frequented by locals.

You don't have to go to the bar to order your drinks in a café. Find a table, sit down and the waiter will take your order. In small towns and villages you won't be asked to pay straightaway, but when you've finished. It's usual to leave any loose change on the table.

Hotels often have a restaurant attached. You don't have to be staying there to use it. They tend to be shut on Sunday.

A more rustic-style hotel, usually in the country. They often have a restaurant which non-residents can use.

Table d'hôte

B & B (*chambres d'hôtes*) might offer meals – generally home-cooked dishes using local farm produce.

LOGIS DE FRANCE
A chain of smallish hotels (around 18 rooms), usually family-run and with restaurants that make the most of regional produce and specialities.

TAKE-AWAY
pain = bread
viennoiserie = Danish pastries
tartes = tarts, pies
sucrées = sweet
salées = savoury
poulets rôtis = spit-roasted chickens
à emporter = take-away

Glacier

ICE-CREAM PARLOUR

Frites 500m

CHIPS Signals road-side café 500 metres away. Mediocre food, mostly chips.

à la cafétéria

Spécial enfants

menu

1 steak haché ou
3 bâtonnets de colin pané,
des frites, 1 dessert,
1 boisson,
1 gadget,
1 surprise !

Botakado

3 € 80

GRATUIT LE MARDI SOIR

Supermarket cafés offer standard kids' food – hamburger (*steak haché*) or fish fingers (*bâtonnets de colin pané*), with chips, dessert and toy.

PLATS DU JOUR

A café serving food will have one or more daily dishes. If they are in popular areas, it is worth going early before they run out.

MENU DU JOUR

A set-price daily menu. This is good value and often includes drink. Bread is always provided.

PIZZAS & OTHER TAKE-AWAY DISHES

Food is very expensive at service stations compared to other eating places in France. If you can get off the motorway, go to a village bakery, or take food with you.

RESTAURANT

As well as displaying the menu, restaurants and hotels display awards. Restaurants are generally open 12–2pm and 7-9.30pm.

IN A HURRY?

Meals don't always have to be slow affairs. Here you can have a salad (made up of your own choice) and drink. A drink (*boisson*) is included in the price.

Sandwiches are widely available. Either a *baguette* or half a *baguette*. Words to look out for are *rillettes* (pâté) and *cornichons* (gherkins).

Choosing dishes from the à la carte menu tends to be more expensive than opting for a set price menu. Restaurants generally offer several set price menus. There may be two menus of differing prices, a regional (*du terroir*) menu which lets you sample local dishes, and for the foodies, a **menu gourmand**.

Many set-price menus will include drink (**boisson**). Here the choice is between 1/4 litre of wine (**vin**), draught lager (**bière pression**), mineral water (**eau minérale**) or a soft fizzy drink (**soda**).

La Carte *Menu*

POTAGES *soups*

ENTRÉES *starter*

POISSONS *fish*

FRUITS DE MER
seafood

VIANDES *meat*

GIBIER et VOLAILLE
game and poultry

LÉGUMES *vegetables*

FROMAGES *cheeses*

DESSERTS *sweet*

BOISSONS *drinks*

By law French restaurants must display their menus outside the restaurant. You will be able to judge the type of food and cost before you go in.

Restaurants usually have different menus, varying in prices. Some are only available at lunchtime (*du midi*). The one below is lunchtimes only Mon to Fri. *Entrée* = starter, *plat* = main dish, *café* = coffee (usually of strong dark, variety).

Du lundi au vendredi
Menu du midi
7□50
ENTREE + PLAT + CAFE

Reading the menu

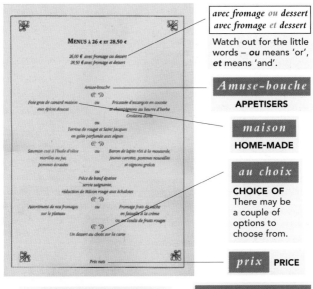

MENUS À 26 € ET 28,50 €

26,00 € avec fromage ou dessert
28,50 € avec fromage et dessert

Amuse-bouche

Foie gras de canard maison
aux épices douces

ou

Fricassée d'escargots en cocotte
et champignons au beurre d'herbe
Croûtons dorés

ou

Terrine de rouget et Saint Jacques
en gelée parfumée aux algues

Saumon cuit à l'huile d'olive
morilles au jus,
pommes écrasées

ou

Baron de lapin rôti à la moutarde,
jeunes carottes, pommes nouvelles
et oignons grelots

ou

Pièce de bœuf épaisse
servie saignante,
réduction de Mâcon rouge aux échalotes

Assortiment de nos fromages
sur le plateau

ou

Fromage frais de vache
en faisselle à la crème
ou au coulis de fruits rouges

Un dessert au choix sur la carte

Prix nets

---

avec fromage *ou* dessert
avec fromage *et* dessert

Watch out for the little words – *ou* means 'or', *et* means 'and'.

Amuse-bouche
APPETISERS

maison
HOME-MADE

au choix
CHOICE OF
There may be a couple of options to choose from.

prix PRICE

Menu du Terroir

If you want to try the regional dishes, this is the menu to choose.

avec sa garniture

Usually means with chips or rice and veg. *Garnis* means the same thing.

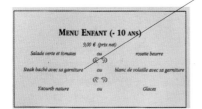

MENU ENFANT (- 10 ANS)

9,00 € (prix net)

Salade verte et tomates   ou   *rosette beurre*

Steak haché avec sa garniture   ou   *blanc de volaille avec sa garniture*

Yaourth nature   ou   *Glaces*

Menu Enfant

This menu is for children under 10 years (*-10 ans*). The choice is between green and tomato salad followed by hamburger and chips.

COFFEE If you ask for *un café* you'll get it small, strong and black. For a white coffee, ask for *un café au lait* (*uñ ka-fay oh lay*) or *un cappuccino*. You might get the cappuccino with a swirl of whipped cream.

It is cheaper to have a drink standing at the bar. If you are looking for a toilet and can only see a café or bar, you should buy something cheap at the bar, like a coffee, or a small glass of wine

COLD WATER AND HOT DRINKS Mineral water will be either sparkling or still.

In France, beer is generally lager. Draught beer is *bière pression* (*byehr pray-syoñ*). Half a pint is *un demi* (*uñ duh-mee*). If you want bitter, ask for *bière brune* (*byehr broon*).

To ask for the bill, attract the waiter's attention with *pardon* and ask for *l'addition, s'il vous plaît* (*lad-ees-yoñ seel voo play*).

service non compris

SERVICE NOT INCLUDED If you wish to tip, about 10% of the bill is fairly standard.

BOISSONS

DRINKS

DRINK NOT INCLUDED

boisson non comprise

CHAUD

HOT

FROID

COLD

READING THE WINE LABEL
Appellation contrôlée guarantees that the wine is from a demarcated area (not its quality). In this case, Côtes de Bourg.

mis en bouteille au means bottled at

Alcohol content. 11.5% is average, 14% would be pretty hefty.

Apéritifs et Digestifs

Carte des vins

WINE LIST

APERITIFS AND DIGESTIVES
French people love aperitifs. They can be a simple glass of Pernod with water or can involve Champagne, canapés and long chats.

You can buy a wide selection of French champagne at most super-markets. It makes a good gift to take if you have been invited by French friends for a meal. *Brut* = very dry, *sec* = dry, *demi-sec* = sweet, *doux* = very sweet.

Vin de pays simply means the wine has come from one area and not been blended. *Vin de table*, or *vin ordinaire* indicates that the wine has been blended and is usually sold in plastic bottles.

A

...à la/à l'/au/aux... 'in the style of...', or 'with...'
   au feu de bois *cooked over a wood fire*
   au four *baked*
   au porto *in port*
abats *offal, giblets*
abricot *apricot*
Abricotine *liqueur brandy with apricot flavouring*
agneau *lamb*
agrumes *citrus fruit*
aïado *roast shoulder of lamb stuffed with garlic and other ingredients*
aiglefin *haddock*
aïgo bouïdo *garlic soup*
ail *garlic*
aile *wing*
aïoli *rich garlic mayonnaise originated in the south and gives its name to the dish it is served with: cold steamed fish and vegetables. The mayonnaise is served on the side*
airelles *bilberries, cranberries*
algues *seaweed*
alicot *puréed potato with cheese*
allumettes *very thin chips*
amande *almond*
amuse-bouche *nibbles*
arlésienne, ...à l' *with tomatoes, onions, auber-gines, potatoes and rice*
armagnac *fine grape brandy from the Landes area*
armoricaine, ...à l' *cooked with brandy, wine, tomatoes and onions*
ananas *pineapple*
anchoïade *anchovy paste usually served on grilled French bread*
anchois *anchovies*

andouille, andouillette *spicy tripe sausage*
anglaise, ...à l' *poached or boiled*
anguille *eel*
anis *aniseed*
arachide *peanut (uncooked)*
araignée de mer *spider crab*
artichaut *artichoke*
   artichauts à la barigoule *artichokes in wine, with carrots, garlic, onions*
   artichauts châtelaine *artichokes stuffed with mushrooms*
asperge *asparagus*
aspic de volaille *chicken in aspic*
assiette *dish, platter*
   assiette anglaise *plate of assorted cold meats*
   assiette de charcuterie *plate of assorted pâtés and salami*
   assiette de crudités *selection of raw vegetables served with dip*
   assiette de pêcheur *assorted fish*
assortiment *selection*
aubergine *aubergine*
   aubergines farcies *stuffed aubergines*
aurin *grey mullet*
auvergnat, ...à l' *with cabbage, sausage and bacon*
avocat *avocado*

B

babas au rhum *rum baba*
baccala frittu *dried salt cod fried Corsica style*
Badoit *mineral water, very slightly sparkling*
baeckoffe *hotpot of pork, mutton and beef baked with potato layers from Alsace*

baguette *stick of French bread*

banane *banana*
  bananes flambées *bananas flambéed in brandy*

bar *sea-bass*

barbue *brill*

bardatte *cabbage stuffed with rabbit or hare*

barquette *small boat-shaped flan*

basilic *basil*

baudroie *fish soup with vegetables, garlic and herbs, monkfish*

bavarois *moulded cream and custard pudding, usually served with fruit*

Béarnaise, ...à la *sauce similar to mayonnaise but flavoured with tarragon. Traditionally served with steak*

bécasse *woodcock*

béchamel *classic white sauce made with milk, butter and flour*

beignets *fritters, doughnuts*

Bénédictine *herb liqueur on a brandy base*

betterave *beetroot*

beurre *butter*
  beurre blanc, ...à la *sauce of white wine and shallots with butter*

bien cuit *well done*

bière *beer*
  bière pression *draught beer*
  bière blonde *lager*
  bière brune *bitter*

bifteck *steak*

bigorneau *periwinkle*

biologique *organic*

bis *wholemeal (of bread or flour)*

biscuit de Savoie *sponge cake*

bisque *smooth rich seafood soup*
  bisque de homard *lobster soup*

blanc de volaille *chicken breast (white meat)*

blanquette *white meat stew served with a creamy white sauce*
  blanquette de veau *veal stew in white sauce*
  blanquette de volaille *chicken stew in white sauce*

blé *wheat*

blette *Swiss chard*

bleu *very rare*

bœuf *beef*
  bœuf bourguignon *beef in burgundy, onions and mushrooms*
  bœuf en daube *rich beef stew with wine, vegetables and herbs*

bombe *moulded ice cream dessert*

bonite *bonito, small tuna fish*

bonne femme, ...à la *cooked in white wine with mushrooms*

bordelaise, ...à la *cooked in a sauce of red wine, shallots and herbs*

bouchée *vol-au-vent*
  bouchée à la reine *vol-au-vent filled with chicken or veal in a white sauce*

boudin *pudding*
  boudin blanc *white pudding*
  boudin noir *black pudding*

bouillabaisse *rich seafood soup flavoured with saffron, originally from Marseilles*

bouilleture d'anguilles *eels cooked with prunes and red wine*

bouilli *boiled*

bouillon *stock*
  bouillon de légumes *vegetable stock*
  bouillon de poule *chicken stock*

boulangère, ...à la *baked with potatoes and onions*

boulettes meatballs
bouquet bunch, mixture
bourgeoise, ...à la with carrots, onions, bacon, celery and braised lettuce
bourguignonne, ...à la cooked in red wine, with onions, bacon and mushrooms
bourride fish stew traditionally served with garlic mayonnaise (aïoli)
brandade de morue dried salt cod puréed with cream and olive oil
brème bream
brioche sweet bun
   brioche aux fruits sweet bun with glacé fruit
brochet pike
brochette kebab
brocoli broccoli
brugnon nectarine
bulot whelk

C

cabillaud fresh cod
cacahuète peanut
café coffee
   café au lait coffee with hot milk
   café crème white coffee
   café décaféiné decaffeinated coffee
   café expresso espresso coffee
   café glacé iced coffee
   café irlandais Irish coffee
   café noir black coffee
caille quail
   caille sur canapé quail served on toast
caillettes rolled liver stuffed with spinach
cajou, noix de cashew nut
calisson almond sweet
calmar (or calamar) squid

calvados apple brandy made from cider (Normandy)
canard duck
   canard à l'orange roast duck with orange sauce
   canard périgourdin roast duck with prunes, **pâté de foie gras** and truffles
   canard Rouennais stuffed roast duck covered in red wine sauce
caneton duckling
cannelle cinnamon
câpres capers
carbonnade de bœuf braised beef
cardon cardoon
cari curry
carotte carrot
   carottes Vichy carrots cooked in butter and sugar
carpe carp
   carpe farcie carp stuffed with mushrooms or **foie gras**
carré persillé roast lamb Normandy style (with parsley)
carrelet plaice
carte des vins wine list
cassis blackcurrant, blackcurrant liqueur
cassoulet bean stew with pork or mutton or sausages. There are many regional variations
caviar caviar
   caviar blanc mullet roe
   caviar niçois a paste made with anchovies and olive oil
cédrat large citrus fruit, similar to a lemon
céleri celery; celeriac
   céleri rémoulade celeriac in a mustard and herb dressing
céleri-rave celeriac
cèpes boletus mushrooms, wild mushrooms

cèpes marinés *wild mushrooms marinated in oil, garlic and herbs*
cerfeuil *chervil*
cerise *cherry*
cervelas *smoked pork sausages, saveloy*
cervelle *brains (usually lamb or calf)*
champignon *mushroom*
champignons à la grecque *mushrooms cooked in wine, olive oil and herbs*
champignons de Paris *button mushrooms*
champignons périgourdine *mushrooms with truffles and **foie gras***
chanterelle *chanterelle (wild golden-coloured mushroom)*
chantilly *whipped cream*
charlotte *custard and fruit in lining of almond fingers*
Chartreuse *aromatic herb liqueur made by Carthusian monks*
chasseur *literally hunter-style, cooked with white wine, shallots, mushrooms and herbs*
châtaigne *chestnut*
châteaubriand *thick fillet steak*
châtelaine, ...à la *with artichoke hearts and chestnut purée*
chaud(e) *hot*
chaudrée rochelaise *a selection of fish stewed in red wine*
chauffé *heated*
chausson *a pasty filled with meat or seafood*
chausson aux pommes *apple turnover*
cheval, à *topped with a fried egg*
chèvre *goat*
chevreuil *venison*
chichi *doughnut shaped in a stick*

chicorée *chicory, endive*
chocolat *chocolate*
chocolat chaud *hot chocolate*
chou *cabbage*
choucroute *sauerkraut*
choucroute garnie *sauerkraut with various types of sausages*
chou-fleur *cauliflower*
choux brocolis *broccoli*
choux de Bruxelles *Brussels sprouts*
ciboule (or cive) *spring onion*
ciboulette *chives*
cidre *cider, sparkling (bouché) or still, quite strong*
cidre brut *dry cider*
cidre doux *sweet cider*
citron *lemon*
citron pressé *freshly squeezed lemon juice with water and sugar*
citron vert *lime*
citrouille *pumpkin*
civet *thick stew*
civet de langouste *crayfish in wine sauce*
civet de lièvre *hare stewed in wine, onions and mushrooms*
clafoutis *cherry pudding*
claire *type of oyster*
clou de girofle *clove*
cochon *pig*
coco *coconut*
cocotte, en *cooked in a small earthenware casserole*
cœur *heart*
cœurs d'artichauts *artichoke hearts*
cœurs de palmier *palm hearts*
cognac *high quality white grape brandy*
coing *quince*
Cointreau *orange-flavoured liqueur*

colbert, ...à la fried, with a coating of egg and breadcrumbs

colin hake

compote de fruits mixed stewed fruit

concombre cucumber

condé rich rice pudding with fruits

confit pieces of meat preserved in fat

confit d'oie goose meat preserved in its own fat

confit de canard duck meat preserved in its own fat

confiture jam

confiture d'oranges marmalade

congre conger eel

consommé clear soup, generally made from meat or fish stock

contre-filet sirloin fillet (beef)

coq au vin chicken cooked in red wine

coquelet cockerel

coques cockles

coquillages shellfish

coquilles Saint-Jacques scallops

coquilles Saint-Jacques à la provençale scallops with garlic sauce

coquilles Saint-Jacques scallops cooked in shell with a breadcrumb and white sauce topping

coquillettes pasta shells

cornichon gherkin

côtelette cutlet

côtelettes de veau veal cutlets

côte rib, chop

côtes de porc pork chops

cotriade fish stew (Brittany)

cou neck

coulibiac salmon cooked in puff pastry

coulis puréed fruit sauce

coupe goblet with ice cream

courge marrow

cousinat chestnut and cream soup

crabe crab

craquelots smoked herring

crème cream

crème anglaise fresh custard

crème au beurre butter cream with egg yolks and sugar

crème brûlée rich custard with caramelised sugar on top

crème caramel baked custard with caramelised sugar sauce

crème chantilly slightly sweetened whipped cream

crème fraîche sour cream

crème pâtissière thick fresh custard used in tarts and desserts

crème renversée (or crème caramel) custard with a caramelised top

crème de cream of... (soup)

crème d'Argenteuil white asparagus soup

crème de cresson watercress soup

crème de marrons chestnut purée

crème de menthe peppermint-flavoured liqueur

crêpes sweet and savoury pancakes

crêpes fourrées filled pancakes

crêpes Suzette pancakes with a Cointreau or Grand Marnier sauce, usually flambéed

crépinette type of sausage

crevette prawn

crevette grise shrimp

crevette rose large prawn

crevettes en terrine potted prawns

croûte, en in pastry
croûtes, croûtons, ...aux served with cubes of toasted or fried bread
cru raw
crudités assortment of raw vegetables (grated carrots, sliced tomatoes, etc) served as a starter
crustacés shellfish
cuisses de grenouille frogs' legs
cuit cooked
culotte rump steak
Curaçao orange-flavoured liqueur

D

darne fillet or steak
datte date
daube casserole with wine, herbs and garlic
dauphinoise, ...à la cooked in milk
daurade sea bream
désossé boned
diable, ...à la strong mustard seasoning
diabolo menthe mint cordial and lemonade
dinde turkey
diots au vin blanc pork sausages in white wine
dos back
duxelles fried mushrooms and shallots with cream

E

eau water
  eau de Seltz soda water
  eau-de-vie brandy (often made from plum, pear, etc)
  eau minérale mineral water
  eau minérale gazeuse sparkling mineral water
  eau du robinet tap water

échalote shallot
échine loin of pork
écrevisse freshwater crayfish
églefin haddock
emballé wrapped
émincé thinly sliced
en brochette cooked like a kebab (on a skewer)
encornet squid
endive chicory
entrecôte rib steak
entrées starters
entremets sweets (desserts)
épaule shoulder
éperlan whitebait
épice spice
épinards spinach
escalope escalope
escargots snails (generally cooked with strong seasonings)
  escargots à la bourguignonne snails with garlic butter
espadon swordfish
estouffade de bœuf beef stew cooked in red wine, herbs, onions, mushrooms and diced bacon
estragon tarragon
esturgeon sturgeon

F

faisan pheasant
farci(e) stuffed
faux-filet sirloin
faverolles haricot beans
favou(ille) tiny crab
fenouil fennel
férigoule thyme (in provençal dialect)
fermier free-range
feuille leaf
feuilleté in puff pastry
fèves broad beans
figue fig

filet *fillet steak*
  filet de bœuf en croûte *steak in pastry*
  filet de bœuf *tenderloin*
  filet mignon *small fillet steak*
financière, ...à la *in a rich sauce made with Madeira wine and truffles*
fine de claire *type of oyster*
fines herbes *mixed, chopped herbs*
flageolet *type of small green haricot bean*
flamande, ...à la *served with potatoes, cabbage, carrots and pork*
flambé(e) *doused with brandy or another spirit and set alight, usually cooked at your table*
flétan *halibut*
flocons d'avoine *oat flakes*
florentine *with spinach, usually served with mornay sauce*
foie *liver (usually calf's)*
  foie de volailles *chicken livers*
  foie gras *goose liver pâté*
fond d'artichaut *artichoke heart*
fondant au chocolat *rich chocolate flan*
fondue *a shared dish which is served in the middle of the table. Each person uses a long fork to dip their bread or meat into the pot*
  fondue (au fromage) *melted cheeses into which chunks of bread are dipped*
  fondue bourguignonne *small chunks of meat dipped into boiling oil and eaten with different sauces. The meat equivalent to cheese fondue*
forestière, ...à la *with bacon and mushroom*
fougasse *type of bread with various fillings*

fourré(e) *stuffed*
frais (fraîche) *fresh*
fraise *strawberry*
  fraises des bois *wild strawberries*
framboise *raspberry*
frappé *iced*
fricassée *a stew, usually chicken or veal, and vegetables*
frisée *curly endive*
frit(e) *fried*
friture *fried food, usually small fish*
froid(e) *cold*
fromage *cheese*
  fromage blanc *soft white cheese*
  fromage frais *creamy fresh cheese*
froment *wheat*
fruit *fruit*
  fruit de la passion *passion fruit*
  fruits de mer *shellfish, seafood*
fumé(e) *smoked*
fumet *fish stock*

G

galantine *meat in aspic*
galette *savoury buckwheat pancake*
gambas *large prawns*
garbure *thick vegetable and meat soup*
gargouillau *pear tart*
garni(e) *garnished i.e. served with something*
garnitures *side dishes*
gâteau *cake, gateau*
  gâteau Saint-Honoré *choux pastry cake filled with custard*
gaufres *waffles (often cream-filled)*
gazeuse *sparkling*
gelée *jelly, aspic*
genièvre *juniper berry*
génoise *sponge cake*

germes de soja *bean sprouts*
gésier *gizzard*
gibier *game*
gigot d'agneau *leg of lamb*
gigot de mer *large fish baked whole*
gingembre *ginger*
glace *ice cream*
goyave *guava*
grabure *bean, meat and vegetable stew*
Grand Marnier *tawny-coloured, orange-flavoured liqueur*
gratin, au *topped with cheese and breadcrumb and grilled*
gratin dauphinois *potatoes cooked in cream, garlic and Swiss cheese*
gratinée Lyonnaise *clear soup with eggs flavoured with Port wine and served with toasted french bread and grated cheese*
grenade *pomegranate*
grecque, ...à la *cooked in olive oil, garlic and herbs, can be served hot or cold*
grenouilles *frogs' legs*
grenouilles meunière *frogs' legs cooked in butter*
grillade *grilled meat*
grillé(e) *grilled*
gros mollet *lump fish*
groseille *redcurrant*
groseille à maquereau *gooseberry*

H

hachis *mince*
hareng *herring*
haricots *beans*
haricots beurre *butter beans*
haricots blancs *haricot beans*
haricots rouges *red kidney beans*
haricots verts *green beans, French beans*
herbes (fines herbes) *herbs*
hollandaise, sauce *sauce made of butter, egg yolks and lemon juice, served warm*
homard *lobster*
homard à l'armoricaine *lobster cooked with onions, tomatoes and wine*
homard thermidor *lobster served in cream sauce, topped with parmesan*
hors d'œuvre variés *selection of appetizers*
huile *oil*
huile d'arachide *groundnut oil*
huile de tournesol *sunflower oil*
huître *oyster*

I

îles flottantes *soft meringues floating on fresh custard*
Izarra vert *green-coloured herb liqueur*

J

jambon *ham*
jambon de Bayonne *cured raw ham from the Basque country*
jambon de Paris *boiled ham*
jardinière, ...à la *with peas and carrots, or other fresh vegetables*
julienne *vegetables cut into fine strips*
jus *juice, meat-based glaze or sauce*
au jus *in sauce*
jus de pomme *apple juice*
jus d'orange *orange juice*

K

kir white wine and **cassis** aperitif
kirsch a kind of **eau-de-vie** made from cherries (Alsace)
kugelhopf hat-shaped sugar-covered cake from Alsace

L

lait milk
  lait demi-écrémé semi-skimmed milk
  lait écrémé skimmed milk
  lait entier full-cream milk
laitue lettuce
lamproie à la bordelaise lamprey in red wine
langouste crayfish (saltwater)
  langouste froide crayfish served cold with mayonnaise and salad
langoustines large scampi
langue tongue
lapereau young rabbit
lapin rabbit
lard fat, streaky bacon
  lard fumé smoked bacon
lardon strip of fat, diced bacon
laurier bayleaf
légumes vegetables
lentilles lentils
levure yeast
lie de vin wine sediment, dregs of wine
lièvre hare
limande lemon sole
limousine, ...à la cooked with chestnuts and red cabbage
lotte de mer monkfish
loup de mer sea-bass
Lyonnaise, ...à la with onions

M

macaron macaroon
macédoine (de fruits) fresh fruit salad
macédoine de légumes mixed cooked vegetables
madeleine small sponge cake
magret de canard duck breast
maison home-made
maïs, maïs doux maize, sweetcorn
mange-tout sugar peas
mangue mango
maquereau mackerel
marcassin young wild boar
marinière, ...à la a sauce of white wine, onions and herbs (mussels or clams)
marmite casserole
marjolaine marjoram
marron chestnut
  marrons glacés candied chestnuts
  marrons Mont Blanc chestnut purée and cream on a rum-soaked sponge cake
matelote fresh-fish stew
  matelote à la normande sea-fish stew with cider, calvados and cream
médaillon thick, medal-sized slices of meat
melon melon
menthe mint, mint tea
merguez spicy, red sausage
meringues à la chantilly meringues filled with whipped cream
merlan whiting
merluche hake
mérou grouper
merveilles fritters flavoured with brandy
mignonnette small fillet of lamb
mijoté stewed
mille-feuille thin layers of pastry filled with cream
mirabelle small yellow plum, plum brandy from Alsace

mont-blanc *pudding made with chestnuts and cream*
morilles *mushrooms (morels)*
Mornay, sauce *cream and cheese sauce*
morue *dried salt cod*
moules *mussels*
  moules marinière *mussels cooked in white wine*
  moules poulette *mussels in wine, cream and mushroom sauce*
mourtairol *beef, chicken, ham and vegetable soup*
mousse au chocolat *chocolate mousse*
mousseline *mashed potatoes with cream and eggs*
moutarde *mustard*
mouton *mutton, sheep or lamb*
mûre *blackberry*
muscade *nutmeg*
myrtille *bilberry*

N

navet *turnip*
nectarine *nectarine*
niçoise, ...à la *with garlic and tomatoes*
noisette *hazelnut*
noisettes d'agneau *small round pieces of lamb*
noix *walnut, general term for a nut ; fillet cut of meat*
  noix de beurre *knob of butter*
  noix de Saint-Jacques *scallops*
  noix de veau *fillet of veal*
nouilles *noodles*

O

œuf *egg*
  œufs à la causalade *fried eggs with bacon*
  œufs à la coque *soft-boiled eggs*
  œufs au plat *fried eggs*
  œufs à la tourangelle *eggs served with red wine sauce*
  œufs Bénédicte *poached eggs on toast, with ham and hollandaise sauce*
  œufs brouillés *scrambled eggs*
  œufs durs *hard-boiled eggs*
  œufs en cocotte *eggs baked in individual containers*
  œufs frits *fried eggs*
oie *goose*
  oie farcie aux pruneaux *goose stuffed with prunes*
oignon *onion*
  oignons grelots *shallots, small onions*
olive *olive*
omelette *omelette*
  omelette brayaude *cheese and potato omelette*
  omelette nature *plain omelette*
  omelette norvégienne *baked Alaska*
onglet *cut of beef*
orange *orange*
orangeade *orangeade*
orge *barley*
os *bone*
oseille *sorrel*
oursin *sea urchin*

P

pain *bread, loaf of bread*
  pain au chocolat *croissant with chocolate filling*
  pain bagnat *bread roll with egg, olives, salad, tuna, anchovies and olive oil*
  pain bis *brown bread*
  pain complet *wholemeal bread*
  pain d'épice *ginger cake*
  pain de mie *white sliced loaf*
  pain de seigle *rye bread*

pain grillé *toast*
palmier *caramelized puff pastry*
palombe *wood pigeon*
palourde *clam*
pamplemousse *grapefruit*
panais *parsnip*
pané(e) *with breadcrumbs*
panini *toasted Italian sandwich*
panisse *thick chickpea flour pancake*
papillote, en *in filo pastry*
parfait *rich home-made ice cream*
Paris Brest *ring-shaped cake filled with praline-flavoured cream*
parisienne, ...à la *sautéed in butter with white wine, sauce and shallots*
parmentier *with potatoes*
pastèque *watermelon*
pastis *aniseed-based aperitif*
patate douce *sweet potato*
pâté *pâté*
   pâté de foie de volailles *chicken liver pâté*
   pâté en croûte *pâté encased in pastry*
pâtes *pasta*
   pâtes fraîches *fresh pasta*
paupiettes *meat slices stuffed and rolled, like beef olives*
pavé *thickly-cut steak*
pays d'auge, ...à la *cream and cider*
paysanne, ...à la *cooked with diced bacon and vegetables*
pêche *peach*
   pêches melba *poached peaches served with a raspberry sauce and vanilla ice cream or whipped cream*
pélandron *type of string bean*
perche *perch (fish)*
   perche du Menon *perch cooked in champagne*

perdreau (perdrix) *partridge*
Périgueux, sauce *with truffles*
Pernod *aperitif with aniseed flavour (pastis)*
persil *parsley*
persillé(e) *with parsley*
petit-beurre *butter biscuit*
petit farcis *stuffed tomatoes, aubergines, courgettes and peppers*
petit pain *roll*
petits fours *bite-sized cakes and pastries*
petits pois *small peas*
petit-suisse *a smooth mixture of cream and curds*
pieds et paquets *mutton or pork tripe and trotters*
pigeon *pigeon*
pignons *pine nuts*
pilon *drumstick (chicken)*
piment *chilli*
   piment doux *sweet pepper*
   piment fort *chilli*
pimenté *peppery hot*
pintade/pintadeau *guinea fowl*
pipérade *tomato, pepper and onion omelette*
piquant *spicy*
piquante, ...à la *gherkins, vinegar and shallots*
pissaladière *a kind of pizza made mainly in the Nice region, filled with onions, anchovies and black olives*
pistache *pistachio*
pistou *garlic, basil and olive oil sauce – similar to **pesto***
plat *dish*
   plat principal *main course*
plate *still*
plateau *tray*
   plateau de fromages *cheese-board*

plie *plaice*
poché(e) *poached*
poêlé *pan-fried*
pimenté *peppery hot*
point, …à *medium rare*
poire *pear*
  poires belle Hélène *poached pears with vanilla ice cream and chocolate sauce*
poireau *leek*
pois *peas*
  pois cassés *split peas*
  pois-chiches *chickpeas*
poisson *fish*
poitevin *pork-stuffed cabbage*
poitrine *breast*
poivre *pepper*
poivron *sweet pepper*
  poivron rouge *red pepper*
  poivron vert *green pepper*
pomme *apple*
pomme (de terre) *potato*
  pommes à l'anglaise *boiled potatoes*
  pommes à la vapeur *steamed potatoes*
  pommes allumettes *match-stick chips*
  pommes dauphine *potato croquettes*
  pommes duchesse *potato mashed then baked in the oven*
  pommes écrassées *mashed potatoes*
  pommes frites *fried potatoes*
  pommes Lyonnaise *potatoes fried with onions*
  pommes mousseline *potatoes mashed with cream*
  pommes rissolées *small potatoes deep-fried*
pompe aux grattons *pork flan*
porc *pork*
pot au feu *beef and vegetable stew*

potage *soup, generally creamed or thickened*
potée auvergnate *cabbage and meat soup*
potiron *type of pumpkin*
poulet *chicken*
  poulet basquaise *chicken stew with wine, tomatoes, mushrooms and peppers*
  poulet célestine *chicken cooked in white wine with mushrooms and onion*
  poulet demi-deuil *chicken breasts in a wine sauce*
  poulet Vallée d'Auge *chicken cooked with cider, calvados, apples and cream*
poulpe à la niçoise *octopus in tomato sauce*
pousses de soja *bean sprouts*
poussin *baby chicken*
poutargue *mullet roe paste*
praire *clam*
praliné *hazelnut flavoured*
primeurs *spring vegetables*
provençale, …à la *cooked with tomatoes, peppers, garlic and white wine*
prune *plum, plum brandy*
purée *mashed potatoes*

Q

quatre-quarts *cake made with equal parts of butter, flour, sugar, eggs*
quenelles *poached fish or meat mousse balls served in a sauce*
  quenelles de brochet *pike mousse in cream sauce*
quetsch *type of plum*
queue *tail*
  queue de bœuf *oxtail*
quiche Lorraine *flan with egg, fresh cream and diced back bacon*

R

râble saddle
radis radishes
ragoût stew, casserole
raie skate
raifort horseradish
raisin grape
raisin sec sultana, raisin
raïto red wine, olive, caper, garlic and shallot sauce
ramier wood pigeon
râpé(e) grated
rascasse scorpion fish
ratatouille tomatoes, aubergines, courgettes and garlic cooked in olive oil
rave turnip
raviolis pasta parcels of meat (in provençal dialect)
reine-claude greengage
rillettes coarse pâté (usually pork or goose)
  rillettes de canard coarse duck pâté
ris de veau calf sweetbread (generally thymus gland)
riz rice
rognon kidney
  rognons blancs testicles
  rognons sautés sauce madère sautéed kidneys served in Madeira sauce
romaine cos lettuce
romarin rosemary
romsteak rump steak
rond de gigot large slice of leg of lamb
rosbif roast beef
rôti roast
rouget red mullet
rouille spicy version of garlic mayonnaise (**aïoli**) served with fish stew or soup
roulade meat or fish, stuffed and rolled
roulé sweet or savoury roll
rouleau roll
rutabaga swede

S

sabayon dessert made with egg yolks, sugar and Marsala wine
sablé shortbread
safran saffron
saignant rare
Saint-Hubert game consommé flavoured with wine
salade lettuce, salad
  salade aveyronnaise cheese salad (made with Roquefort)
  salade de fruits fruit salad
  salade de saison mixed salad and/or greens in season
  salade lyonnaise salad dressed with croutons and bacon
  salade niçoise many variations on a famous theme: the basic ingredients are green beans, anchovies, black olives, green peppers
  salade russe mixed cooked vegetables in mayonnaise
  salade verte green salad
salé salted/spicy
salsifis salsify
sandwich sandwich
  sandwich croque-monsieur grilled gruyère cheese and ham sandwich
  sandwich croque-madame grilled cheese and bacon, sausage, chicken or egg sandwich
sanglier wild boar
sarrasin buckwheat
sarriette savory (herb)
sauce sauce
saucisse/saucisson sausage
saumon salmon

saumon fumé smoked salmon
saumon poché poached salmon
sauté(e) sautéed
sauté d'agneau lamb stew
savarin a filled ring-shaped cake
savoyarde, ...à la with gruyère cheese
scarole endive, escarole
sec dry or dried
seiche cuttlefish
sel salt
selle d'agneau saddle of lamb
semoule semolina
socca thin chickpea flour pancake
sole sole
 sole Albert sole in cream sauce with mustard
 sole cardinal sole cooked in wine, served with lobster sauce
 sole Normande sole cooked in a cream, cider and shrimp sauce
 sole Saint Germain grilled sole with butter and tarragon sauce
sole-limande lemon sole
soufflé light fluffy dish made with egg yolks and stiffly beaten egg whites combined with cheese, ham, fish, etc
soupe hearty thick soup
 soupe à l'oignon onion soup usually served with a crisp chunk of French bread in the dish with grated cheese on top
 soupe à la bière beer soup
 soupe au pistou vegetable soup with garlic and basil
 soupe aux choux cabbage soup with pork
 soupe de poisson fish soup
soupe anglaise trifle
steak steak
 steak au poivre steak with peppercorns

steak haché beefburger
steak tartare minced raw steak mixed with raw egg, chopped onion, tartare or worcester sauce, parsley and capers
St Raphaël aperitif (with quinine)
sucre sugar
sucré sweet
suprême de volaille breast of chicken in cream sauce

T

tagine North African casserole
tapendade rich olive spread made with black olives, capers and anchovies
tarte open tart, generally sweet
 tarte aux fraises strawberry tart
 tarte aux pommes apple tart
 tarte flambée thin pizza-like pastry topped with onion, cream and bacon
 tarte Normande apple tart
 tarte tatin upside down tart with caramelized apples or pears
 tarte tropézienne sponge cake filled with custard cream topped with nuts
tartine open sandwich
terrine terrine (refers to pot that pâté has been cooked in), pâté
 terrine de campagne pork and liver terrine
 terrine de porc et gibier pork and game terrine
terroir region, area
tête de veau calf's head
tétras grouse
thé tea
 thé au citron tea with lemon
 thé au lait tea with milk
 thé sans sucre tea without sugar
thermidor lobster grilled in its shell with cream sauce

thon *tuna fish*

tilleul *lime tea*

timbale *round dish in which a mixture of usually meat or fish is cooked. Often lined with pastry and served with a rich sauce*
  timbale d'écrevisses *crayfish in a cream, wine and brandy sauce*
  timbale de fruits *pastry base covered with fruits*

tisane *herbal tea*

tomate *tomato*
  tomates à la provençale *grilled tomatoes steeped in garlic*
  tomates farcies *stuffed tomatoes*

tomme *type of cheese*

tournedos *thick fillet steak*
  tournedos Rossini *thick fillet steak on fried bread with goose liver and truffles on top*

tourte à la viande *meat pie usually made with veal and pork*

tripe *tripe*
  tripes à la mode de Caen *tripe cooked with vegetables, herbs, cider and calvados*

truffade *potato pie with garlic and cheese originating in Auvergne*

truffe *truffle*

truffiat *potato cake*

truite *trout*
  truite aux amandes *trout covered with almonds*

turbot *turbot*

V

vacherin *large meringue filled with cream, ice cream and fruit*

vapeur, ...à la *steamed*

veau *calf, veal*

veau sauté Marengo *veal cooked in a casserole with white wine and garlic*

velouté *thick creamy white sauce made with fish, veal or chicken stock. Also used in soups*

venaison *venison*

verdure, en *garnished with green vegetables*

verjus *juice of unripe grapes*

vermicelle *vermicelli*

véronique, ...à la *with grapes, wine and cheese*

verveine *herbal tea made with verbena*

viande *meat*
  viande séchée *thin slices of cured beef*

vichyssoise *leek and potato soup, served cold*

viennoise *fried in egg and breadcrumbs*

vin *wine*
  vin blanc *white wine*
  vin de pays *local wine*
  vin de table *table wine*
  vin rosé *rosé wine*
  vin rouge *red wine*

vinaigrette *dressing of oil and vinegar*

vinaigre *vinegar*

violet *sea squirt*

volaille *poultry*

Y

yaourt *yoghurt*

Z

zewelwai *onion flan*

DICTIONARY
English-French
French-English

A

a(n) un (m)/une (f)
abbey l'abbaye (f)
able: to be able to pouvoir
abortion l'avortement (m)
about (approximately) vers ; environ
(concerning) au sujet de
   about 100 euros environ cent euros
   about 10 o'clock vers dix heures
above au-dessus (de)
   above the bed au-dessus du lit
   above the farm au-dessus de
   la ferme
abroad à l'étranger
abscess l'abcès (m)
accelerator l'accélérateur (m)
accent l'accent (m)
to accept accepter
   do you accept this card? vous
   acceptez cette carte?
access l'accès (m)
accident l'accident (m)
accident & emergency department
les urgences (fpl)
accommodation le logement
to accompany accompagner
account le compte
account number le numéro de
compte
to ache faire mal
   it aches ça fait mal
acid l'acide (m)
actor l'acteur (m)/l'actrice (f)
adaptor (electrical) l'adaptateur (m)
address l'adresse (f)
   here's my address voici mon adresse
   what is the address? quelle est
   l'adresse?
address book le carnet d'adresse
admission charge l'entrée (f)
to admit (to hospital) hospitaliser
adult l'adulte (m/f)
   for adults pour adultes
advance: in advance à l'avance
advertisement (in paper) l'annonce (f)
(on TV) la publicité
to advise conseiller

A&E les urgences (fpl)
aeroplane l'avion (m)
aerosol l'aérosol (m)
afraid: to be afraid of avoir peur de
after après
afternoon l'après-midi (m)
   in the afternoon l'après-midi
   this afternoon cet après-midi
   tomorrow afternoon demain après-
   midi
aftershave l'après-rasage (m)
again encore
against contre
age l'âge (m)
agency l'agence (f)
ago: a week ago il y a une semaine
to agree être d'accord
agreement l'accord (m)
AIDS le SIDA
airbag (in car) l'airbag (m)
airbed le matelas pneumatique
air-conditioning la climatisation
air freshener le désodorisant
airline la ligne aérienne
air mail: by airmail par avion
airplane l'avion (m)
airport l'aéroport (m)
airport bus la navette pour
   l'aéroport
air ticket le billet d'avion
aisle le couloir
alarm l'alarme (f)
alarm clock le réveil
alcohol l'alcool (m)
alcohol-free sans alcool
alcoholic drink la boisson alcoolisée
all tout(e)/tous/toutes
allergic allergique
   I'm allergic to... je suis allergique à...
allergy l'allergie (f)
to allow permettre
   it's not allowed c'est interdit
all right (agreed) d'accord
   are you all right? ça va?
almost presque
alone tout(e) seul(e)

Alps les Alpes *(fpl)*

already déjà

also aussi

altar l'autel *(m)*

always toujours

a.m. du matin

am: *I am* je suis

amber *(traffic light)* orange

ambulance l'ambulance *(f)*

America l'Amérique *(f)*

American américain(e)

amount *(total)* le montant

anaesthetic l'anesthésique *(m)*
  a local anaesthetic
  une anesthésie locale
  a general anaesthetic
  une anesthésie générale

anchor l'ancre *(f)*

and et

angina l'angine de poitrine *(f)*

angry fâché(e)

animal l'animal *(m)*

aniseed l'anis *(m)*

ankle la cheville

anniversary l'anniversaire *(m)*

to announce annoncer

announcement l'annonce *(f)*

annual annuel(-elle)

another un(e) autre
  another beer une autre bière

answer la réponse

to answer répondre à

answerphone le répondeur

antacid le comprimé contre les
brûlures d'estomac

antibiotic l'antibiotique *(m)*

antifreeze l'antigel *(m)*

antihistamine l'antihistaminique *(m)*

antiques les antiquités *(fpl)*

antique shop le magasin d'antiquités

antiseptic l'antiseptique *(m)*

any de (du/de la/des)
  have you any apples? vous avez des
  pommes?

anyone quelqu'un/personne

anything quelque chose/rien

anywhere quelque part

apartment l'appartement *(m)*

appendicitis l'appendicite *(f)*

apple la pomme

application form le formulaire

appointment le rendez-vous
  I have an appointment j'ai rendez-
  vous

approximately environ

apricot l'abricot *(m)*

April avril

architect l'architecte *(m/f)*

architecture l'architecture *(f)*

are: *you are* vous êtes
  we are nous sommes
  they are ils/elles sont

arm le bras

armbands *(for swimming)* les bracelets
  (mpl) gonflables

armchair le fauteuil

to arrange arranger

to arrest arrêter

arrival l'arrivée *(f)*

to arrive arriver

art l'art *(m)*

art gallery le musée

arthritis l'arthrite *(f)*

artichoke l'artichaut *(m)*

artificial artificiel

artist l'artiste *(m/f)*

ashtray le cendrier

to ask demander
  to ask a question poser une question

asparagus l'asperge *(f)*

aspirin l'aspirine *(f)*

asthma l'asthme *(m)*
  I have asthma je suis asthmatique

at à
  at my/your home chez moi/vous
  at 8 o'clock à huit heures
  at once tout de suite
  at night le soir

Atlantic Ocean l'Océan atlantique *(m)*

attachment *(to e-mail)* la pièce jointe

attack *(mugging)* l'agression *(f)*
  (medical) la crise

to attack agresser

attic le grenier

attractive séduisant(e)
aubergine l'aubergine (f)
auction la vente aux enchères
audience le public
August août
aunt la tante
au pair la jeune fille au pair
Australia l'Australie (f)
Australian australien(ne)
author l'écrivain (m) ;
l'auteur (m)
automatic automatique
automatic car la voiture à boîte
automatique
auto-teller le distributeur
automatique (de billets)
autumn l'automne (m)
available disponible
avalanche l'avalanche (f)
avenue l'avenue (f)
average moyen(ne)
to avoid éviter
awake: I was awake all night
je n'ai pas dormi de toute la nuit
awful affreux(-euse)
axle (car) l'essieu (m)

B

baby le bébé
baby food les petits pots (mpl)
baby milk (formula) le lait maternisé
baby's bottle le biberon
baby seat (car) le siège pour bébés
babysitter le/la babysitter
baby wipes les lingettes (fpl)
back (of body) le dos
backpack le sac à dos
bacon le bacon ; le lard
bad (food, weather) mauvais(e)
badminton le badminton
bag le sac (suitcase) la valise
baggage les bagages (mpl)
baggage allowance le poids
(de bagages) autorisé
baggage reclaim la livraison
des bagages

bait (for fishing) l'appât (m)
baked au four
baker's la boulangerie
balcony le balcon
bald (person) chauve
(tyre) lisse
ball (large: football, etc) le ballon
(small: golf, tennis, etc) la balle
ballet le ballet
balloon le ballon
banana la banane
band (music) le groupe
bandage le pansement
bank (money) la banque
(river) la rive ; le bord
bank account le compte en banque
banknote le billet de banque
bar le bar
bar of chocolate la tablette
de chocolat
barbecue le barbecue
to have a barbecue faire
un barbecue
barber's le coiffeur
to bark aboyer
barn la grange
barrel (wine, beer) le tonneau
basement le sous-sol
basil le basilic
basket le panier
basketball le basket-ball
bat (baseball, cricket) la batte
(animal) la chauve-souris
bath le bain
to have a bath prendre un bain
bathing cap le bonnet de bain
bathroom la salle de bains
with bathroom avec salle de bains
battery (for car) la batterie
(for radio, camera) la pile
bay (along coast) la baie
B&B la chambre d'hôte
to be être
beach la plage
private beach la plage privée
sandy beach la plage de sable
nudist beach la plage de nudistes

beach hut la cabine
bean le haricot
beard la barbe
beautiful beau (belle)
because parce que
to become devenir
bed le lit
  double bed le grand lit ;
  le lit de deux personnes
  single bed le lit d'une personne
  sofa bed le canapé-lit
  twin beds les lits jumeaux (mpl)
bed clothes les draps
  et couvertures (mpl)
bedroom la chambre à coucher
bee l'abeille (f)
beef le bœuf
beer la bière
before avant
to begin commencer
behind derrière
beige beige
Belgian belge
Belgium la Belgique
to believe croire
bell (church, school) la cloche
  (doorbell) la sonnette
to belong to appartenir à
below sous
belt la ceinture
bend (in road) le virage
berth (train, ship, etc) la couchette
beside (next to) à côté de
  beside the bank à côté de la
  banque
best le/la meilleur(e)
bet le pari
to bet on faire un pari sur
better meilleur(e)
  better than meilleur que
between entre
bib (baby's) le bavoir
bicycle la bicyclette ; le vélo
bicycle repair kit la boîte de rustines
bidet le bidet
big grand(e), gros(se)
bike (pushbike) le vélo
  (motorbike) la moto

bike lock l'antivol (m)
bikini le bikini
bill (restaurant) l'addition (f)
  (hotel) la note
  (for work done) la facture
bin (dustbin) la poubelle
bin liner le sac poubelle
binoculars les jumelles (fpl)
bird l'oiseau (m)
biro le stylo
birth la naissance
birth certificate l'acte de naissance
birthday l'anniversaire (m)
  happy birthday! bon anniversaire!
  my birthday is on… mon
  anniversaire c'est le…
birthday card la carte d'anniversaire
birthday present le cadeau
  d'anniversaire
biscuits les biscuits (mpl)
bit: *a bit (of)* un peu (de)
bite (animal) la morsure
  (insect) la piqûre
to bite (animal) mordre
  (insect) piquer
bitten (by animal) mordu(e)
  (by insect) piqué(e)
bitter amer(-ère)
black noir(e)
black ice le verglas
blanket la couverture
bleach l'eau de Javel (f)
to bleed saigner
blender (for food) le mixeur
blind (person) aveugle
blind (for window) le store
blister l'ampoule (f)
block of flats l'immeuble (m)
blocked bouché(e)
  the sink is blocked l'évier est bouché
blond (person) blond(e)
blood le sang
blood group le groupe sanguin
blood pressure la tension (artérielle)
blood test l'analyse de sang (f)
blouse le chemisier
blow-dry le brushing

blue bleu(e)
dark blue bleu foncé
light blue bleu clair
boar (wild) le sanglier
to board embarquer
boarding card la carte
d'embarquement
boat le bateau
(rowing) la barque
boat trip l'excursion en bateau (f)
body le corps
to boil faire bouillir
boiled bouilli(e)
boiler la chaudière
bomb la bombe
bone l'os (m) (fish) l'arête (f)
bonfire le feu
book le livre
to book (reserve) réserver
booking la réservation
booking office le bureau de location
bookshop la librairie
boots les bottes (fpl)
border (of country) la frontière
boring ennuyeux(-euse)
born: *to be born* naître
to borrow emprunter
boss le chef
both les deux
bottle la bouteille
a bottle of wine une bouteille de vin
a bottle of water une bouteille d'eau
a half-bottle une demi-bouteille
bottle opener l'ouvre-bouteilles (m)
bottom (of pool, etc) le fond
bowl (for soup, etc) le bol
bow tie le nœud papillon
box la boîte
box office le bureau de location
boxer shorts le caleçon
boy le garçon
boyfriend le copain
bra le soutien-gorge
bracelet le bracelet
brain le cerveau
brake(s) le(s) frein(s)

to brake freiner
brake fluid le liquide de freins
brake lights les feux de stop (mpl)
brake pads les plaquettes de
frein (fpl)
branch (of tree) la branche
(of company, etc) la succursale
brand (make) la marque
brass le cuivre
brave courageux(-euse)
bread le pain
(French stick) la baguette
(thin French stick) la ficelle
sliced bread le pain de mie
en tranches
bread roll le petit pain
to break casser
breakable fragile
breakdown (car) la panne
(nervous) la dépression
breakdown van la dépanneuse
breakfast le petit déjeuner
breast le sein
to breast-feed allaiter
to breathe respirer
brick la brique
bride la mariée
bridegroom le marié
bridge le pont
briefcase la serviette
Brillo® pad le tampon Jex®
to bring apporter
Britain la Grande-Bretagne
British britannique
brochure la brochure ; le dépliant
broken cassé(e)
my leg is broken je me suis cassé la
jambe
broken down en panne
bronchitis la bronchite
bronze le bronze
brooch la broche
broom (brush) le balai
brother le frère
brother-in-law le beau-frère
brown marron

bruise le bleu
brush la brosse
bubble bath le bain moussant
bucket le seau
buffet car *(train)* la voiture-buffet
to build construire
building l'immeuble *(m)*
bulb *(light)* l'ampoule *(f)*
bumbag la banane
bumper *(on car)* le pare-chocs
bunch *(of flowers)* le bouquet
  (of grapes) la grappe
bungee jumping le saut à l'élastique
bureau de change le bureau
  de change
burger le hamburger
burglar le/la cambrioleur(-euse)
burglar alarm le système d'alarme
to burn brûler
  to burn a CD graver
bus le bus
  (coach) le car
bus pass la carte de bus
bus station la gare routière
bus stop l'arrêt de bus *(m)*
bus ticket le ticket de bus
business les affaires *(fpl)*
  on business pour affaires
business card la carte de visite
business class la classe affaires
businessman/woman l'homme/
  la femme d'affaires
business trip le voyage d'affaires
busy occupé(e)
but mais
butcher's la boucherie
butter le beurre
button le bouton
to buy acheter
by *(via)* par
  (beside) à côté de
  by bus en bus
  by car en voiture
  by ship en bateau
  by train en train
bypass *(road)* la rocade

C

cab *(taxi)* le taxi
cabaret le cabaret
cabin *(on boat)* la cabine
cabin crew l'équipage *(m)*
cablecar le téléphérique ;
  le funiculaire
café le café
  internet café le cybercafé
cafetière la cafetière
cake *(large)* le gâteau
  (small) la pâtisserie ; le petit gâteau
cake shop la pâtisserie
calculator la calculatrice
calendar le calendrier
call *(telephone)* l'appel *(m)*
to call *(speak, phone)* appeler
calm calme
camcorder le caméscope
camera l'appareil photo *(m)*
  digital camera appareil photo
  numérique
camera case l'étui *(m)*
camera shop le magasin de photo
to camp camper
camping gas le butane
camping stove le camping-gaz®
campsite le camping
can *(to be able to)* pouvoir
  (to know how to) savoir
  I can je peux/sais
  we can nous pouvons/savons
can la boîte
can opener l'ouvre-boîtes *(m)*
Canada le Canada
Canadian canadien(ne)
canal le canal
to cancel annuler
cancellation l'annulation *(f)*
cancer le cancer
candle la bougie
canoe le kayak
canoeing: to go canoeing faire
  du canoë-kayak
cap *(hat)* la casquette
  (contraceptive) le diaphragme

capital (*city*) la capitale
car la voiture
car alarm l'alarme de voiture (*f*)
car ferry le ferry
car hire la location de voitures
car insurance l'assurance automobile (*f*)
car keys les clés de voiture (*fpl*)
car phone le téléphone de voiture
car park le parking
car parts les pièces pour voiture (*fpl*)
car radio l'autoradio (*m*)
car seat (*for child*) le siège pour enfant
carwash le lavage automatique
carafe le pichet
caravan la caravane
carburettor le carburateur
card la carte
  birthday card la carte d'anniversaire
  business card la carte de visite
  playing cards les cartes à jouer
cardboard le carton
cardigan le gilet
careful: *to be careful* faire attention
  careful! attention!
carpet (*rug*) le tapis
  (*fitted*) la moquette
carriage (*railway*) la voiture
carrot la carotte
to carry porter
carton (*cigarettes*) la cartouche
  (*milk, juice*) le brick
case (*suitcase*) la valise
cash l'argent liquide (*m*)
to cash (*cheque*) encaisser
cash desk la caisse
cash dispenser (*ATM*) le distributeur automatique (de billets)
cashier le/la caissier(-ière)
cashpoint le distributeur automatique (de billets)
casino le casino
casserole dish la cocotte
cassette la cassette
cassette player le magnétophone
castle le château

casualty dept les urgences (*fpl*)
cat le chat
cat food la nourriture pour chats
catalogue le catalogue
to catch (*bus, train*) prendre
cathedral la cathédrale
Catholic catholique
cauliflower le chou-fleur
cave la grotte
cavity (*in tooth*) la carie
CD le CD
  blank CD le CD vierge
CD player le lecteur de CD
ceiling le plafond
celery le céleri
cellar la cave
cellphone le téléphone cellulaire
cemetery le cimetière
centimetre le centimètre
central central(e)
central heating le chauffage central
central locking le verrouillage central
centre le centre
century le siècle
ceramic la céramique
cereal (*breakfast*) les céréales (*fpl*)
certain (*sure*) certain(e)
certificate le certificat
chain la chaîne
chair la chaise
chairlift le télésiège
chalet le chalet
chambermaid la femme de chambre
champagne le champagne
change (*coins*) la monnaie
to change changer
  to change money changer de l'argent
  to change clothes se changer
  to change bus changer d'autobus
  to change train changer de train
changing room la cabine d'essayage
Channel (*English*) la Manche
chapel la chapelle

charcoal le charbon de bois
charge *(fee)* le prix
to charge faire payer
charger *(battery)* le chargeur
charter flight le vol charter
cheap bon marché
cheaper moins cher
cheap rate le tarif réduit
to check vérifier
to check in enregistrer
check-in (desk) l'enregistrement
  des bagages *(m)*
  (at hotel) la réception
cheek la joue
cheers! santé!
cheese le fromage
chef le chef de cuisine
chemist's la pharmacie
cheque le chèque
cheque book le carnet de chèques
cheque card la carte d'identité
  bancaire
cherry la cerise
chest *(body)* la poitrine
chewing gum le chewing-gum
chicken le poulet
chickenpox la varicelle
child l'enfant *(m)*
child safety seat *(car)* le siège pour
  enfant
children les enfants
  for children pour enfants
chimney la cheminée
chin le menton
china la porcelaine
chips les frites
chocolate le chocolat
  drinking-chocolate le chocolat
  en poudre
  hot chocolate le chocolat chaud
chocolates les chocolats *(mpl)*
choir la chorale
to choose choisir
chop *(meat)* la côtelette
chopping board la planche à
  découper

christening le baptême
Christian name le prénom
Christmas Noël *(m)*
  merry Christmas! joyeux Noël!
Christmas card la carte de Noël
Christmas Eve la veille de Noël
church l'église *(f)*
cigar le cigare
cigarette la cigarette
cigarette lighter le briquet
cigarette paper le papier à cigarette
cinema le cinéma
circle *(theatre)* le balcon
circuit breaker le disjoncteur
circus le cirque
cistern *(toilet)* le réservoir de
  chasse d'eau
city la ville
city centre le centre-ville
class la classe
  first-class de première classe
  second-class de seconde classe
clean propre
to clean nettoyer
cleaner la femme de ménage
cleanser *(for face)* le démaquillant
clear clair(e)
client le client/la cliente
cliff *(along coast)* la falaise
  (in mountains) l'escarpement *(m)*
to climb *(mountain)* faire de la
  montagne
climbing boots les chaussures
  de montagne
Clingfilm® le film alimentaire
clinic la clinique
cloakroom le vestiaire
clock l'horloge *(f)*
close by proche
to close fermer
closed *(shop, etc)* fermé(e)
cloth *(rag)* le chiffon
  (fabric) le tissu
clothes les vêtements *(mpl)*
clothes line la corde à linge
clothes pegs les pinces à linge *(fpl)*

clothes shop le magasin de vêtements
cloudy nuageux(-euse)
club le club
clutch (in car) l'embrayage (m)
coach (bus) le car ; l'autocar (m)
coach station la gare routière
coach trip l'excursion en car (f)
coal le charbon
coast la côte
coastguard le garde-côte
coat le manteau
coat hanger le cintre
cockroach le cafard
cocktail le cocktail
cocoa le cacao
code le code
coffee le café
  white coffee le café au lait
  black coffee le café noir
  cappuccino le cappuccino
  decaffeinated coffee le café décaféiné
coil (IUD) le stérilet
coin la pièce de monnaie
Coke® le Coca®
colander la passoire
cold froid
  I'm cold j'ai froid
  it's cold il fait froid
cold water l'eau froide (f)
cold (illness) le rhume
  I have a cold j'ai un rhume
cold sore le bouton de fièvre
collar le col
collar bone la clavicule
colleague le/la collègue
to collect (someone) aller chercher
collection la collection
colour la couleur
colour-blind daltonien(ne)
colour film (for camera) la pellicule couleur
comb le peigne
to come venir
  (to arrive) arriver
  to come back revenir

to come in entrer
  come in! entrez!
comedy la comédie
comfortable confortable
company (firm) la compagnie ; la société
compartment le compartiment
compass la boussole
to complain faire une réclamation
complaint la plainte
to complete remplir
compulsory obligatoire
computer l'ordinateur (m)
computer disk (floppy) la disquette
computer game le jeu électronique
computer program le programme informatique
concert le concert
concert hall la salle de concert
concession la réduction
concussion la commotion (cérébrale)
conditioner l'après-shampooing (m)
condom le préservatif
conductor (in orchestra) le chef d'orchestre
conference la conférence
to confirm confirmer
confirmation la confirmation
confused: I am confused je m'y perds
congratulations! félicitations!
connection (train, bus, etc) la correspondance
constipated constipé(e)
consulate le consulat
to consult consulter
to contact contacter
contact lenses les verres de contact
contact lens cleaner le produit pour nettoyer les verres de contact
to continue continuer
contraceptive le contraceptif
contract le contrat
convenient: it's not convenient ça ne m'arrange pas
convulsions les convulsions (fpl)
to cook (be cooking) cuisiner

to cook a meal préparer un repas
cooked cuisiné
cooker la cuisinière
cool frais (fraîche)
cool-bag (for picnic) le sac isotherme
cool-box (for picnic) la glacière
copper le cuivre
copy (duplicate) la copie
to copy copier
cork le bouchon
corkscrew le tire-bouchon
corner le coin
cornflakes les corn-flakes (mpl)
corridor le couloir
cortisone la cortisone
cosmetics les produits de beauté
  (mpl)
cost le coût
to cost coûter
  how much does it cost? ça coûte
  combien?
costume (swimming) le maillot
  (de bain)
cot le lit d'enfant
cottage la maison de campagne
cotton le coton
cotton bud le coton-tige®
cotton wool le coton hydrophile
couchette la couchette
cough la toux
to cough tousser
cough mixture le sirop pour la toux
cough sweets les pastilles pour
  la gorge (fpl)
counter (shop, bar, etc) le comptoir
country (not town) la campagne
  (nation) le pays
countryside le paysage
couple (two people) le couple
  a couple of... deux ...
courgette la courgette
courier service le service de
  messageries
course (syllabus) le cours
  (of meal) le plat
cousin le/la cousin(e)

cover charge (restaurant) le couvert
cow la vache
crafts les objets artisanaux (mpl)
craftsperson l'artisan(e)
cramps (period pain) les règles
  douloureuses (fpl)
crash (car) l'accident (m) ; la collision
crash helmet le casque
cream (food, lotion) la crème
  soured cream la crème fermentée
  whipped cream la crème fouettée
credit card la carte de crédit
crime le crime
crisps les chips (fpl)
croissant le croissant
cross la croix
to cross (road, etc) traverser
cross-country skiing le ski de fond
cross-channel ferry le ferry qui
  traverse la Manche
crossing (by sea) la traversée
crossroads le carrefour ;
  le croisement
crossword puzzle les mots croisés
  (mpl)
crowd la foule
crowded bondé(e)
crown la couronne
cruise la croisière
crutches les béquilles (fpl)
to cry (weep) pleurer
crystal le cristal
cucumber le concombre
cufflinks les boutons de manchette
  (mpl)
cul-de-sac le cul-de-sac
cup la tasse
cupboard le placard
currant le raisin sec
currency la devise ; la monnaie
current (air, water) le courant
curtain le rideau
cushion le coussin
custom (tradition) la tradition
customer le/la client(e)
customs la douane
  (duty) les droits de douane (mpl)

customs declaration la déclaration de douane

to cut couper

cut la coupure

cutlery les couverts *(mpl)*

to cycle faire du vélo

cycle track la piste cyclable

cycling le cyclisme

cyst le kyste

cystitis la cystite

D

daily *(each day)* tous les jours

dairy produce les produits laitiers *(mpl)*

dam le barrage

damage les dégâts *(mpl)*

damp humide

dance le bal

to dance danser

danger le danger

dangerous dangereux(-euse)

dark l'obscurité *(f)*
  after dark à la nuit tombée

date la date

date of birth la date de naissance

daughter la fille

daughter-in-law la belle-fille ; la bru

dawn l'aube *(f)*

day le jour
  per day par jour
  every day tous les jours

dead mort(e)

deaf sourd(e)

dear *(expensive, in letter)* cher (chère) *(m(f))*

debts les créances

decaffeinated décaféiné(e)
  decaffeinated coffee le café décaféiné

December décembre

deckchair la chaise longue

to declare déclarer
  nothing to declare rien à déclarer

deep profond(e)

deep freeze le congélateur

deer le cerf

to defrost décongeler

to de-ice *(windscreen)* dégivrer

delay le retard
  how long is the delay? il y a combien de retard ?

delayed retardé(e)

delicatessen le traiteur *(f)*

delicious délicieux(-euse)

demonstration la manifestation

dental floss le fil dentaire

dentist le/la dentiste

dentures le dentier

deodorant le déodorant

to depart partir

department le rayon

department store le grand magasin

departure le départ

departure lounge la salle d'embarquement

deposit les arrhes *(fpl)*

to describe décrire

description la description

desk *(furniture)* le bureau *(information)* l'accueil *(m)*

dessert le dessert

details les détails *(mpl)*

detergent le détergent

detour la déviation

to develop *(photos)* faire développer

diabetes le diabète

diabetic diabétique
  I'm diabetic je suis diabétique

to dial *(a number)* composer

dialling code l'indicatif *(m)*

dialling tone la tonalité

diamond le diamant

diapers les couches (pour bébé) *(fpl)*

diaphragm le diaphragme

diarrhoea la diarrhée

diary l'agenda *(m)*

dice le dé

dictionary le dictionnaire

to die mourir

diesel le gazole

diet le régime

I'm on a diet je suis au régime
special diet le régime spécial
different différent(e)
difficult difficile
digital camera l'appareil photo numérique *(m)*
digital radio la radio numérique
to dilute diluer ; ajouter de l'eau à
dinghy le canot
dining room la salle à manger
dinner *(evening meal)* le dîner
to have dinner dîner
diplomat le diplomate
direct *(train, etc)* direct(e)
directions les indications *(fpl)*
to ask for directions demander le chemin
directory *(telephone)* l'annuaire *(m)*
directory enquiries (le service des) renseignements
dirty sale
disability: to have a disability être handicapé(e)
disabled *(person)* handicapé(e)
to disagree ne pas être d'accord
to disappear disparaître
disaster la catastrophe
disco la discothèque
discount le rabais
to discover découvrir
disease la maladie
dish le plat
dishtowel le torchon à vaisselle
dishwasher le lave-vaisselle
disinfectant le désinfectant
disk *(floppy)* la disquette
to dislocate *(joint)* disloquer
disposable jetable
distant lointain(e)
distilled water l'eau distillée *(f)*
district *(of town)* le quartier
to disturb déranger
to dive plonger
diversion la déviation
divorced divorcé(e)
DIY shop le magasin de bricolage

dizzy pris(e) de vertige
to do faire
doctor le médecin
documents les papiers
dog le chien
dog food la nourriture pour chiens
dog lead la laisse
doll la poupée
dollar le dollar
domestic flight le vol intérieur
donor card la carte de donneur d'organes
door la porte
doorbell la sonnette
double double
double bed le grand lit
double room la chambre pour deux personnes
doughnut le beignet
down: to go down descendre
to download télécharger
downstairs en bas
drain *(house)* le tuyau d'écoulement
draught le courant d'air
there's a draught il y a un courant d'air
draught lager la bière pression
drawer le tiroir
drawing le dessin
dress la robe
to dress s'habiller
dressing *(for food)* la vinaigrette
(for wound) le pansement
dressing gown le peignoir
drill *(tool)* la perceuse électrique
drink la boisson
to drink boire
drinking water l'eau potable *(f)*
to drive conduire
driver *(of car)* le conducteur/ la conductrice
driving licence le permis de conduire
drought la sécheresse
to drown se noyer
drug *(medicine)* le médicament
(narcotics) la drogue

drunk ivre ; soûl(e)
dry sec (sèche)
to dry sécher
dry-cleaner's le pressing
dummy (for baby) la tétine
during pendant
dust la poussière
duster le chiffon
dustpan and brush la pelle et la balayette
duty-free hors taxe
duvet la couette
duvet cover la housse de couette
dye la teinture
dynamo la dynamo

E

each chacun/chacune
ear l'oreille (f)
earlier plus tôt
early tôt
to earn gagner
earphones le casque
earplugs les boules Quiès® (fpl)
earrings les boucles d'oreille (fpl)
earth la terre
earthquake le tremblement de terre
east l'est (m)
Easter Pâques
  happy Easter! joyeuses Pâques!
easy facile
to eat manger
egg l'œuf (m)
  fried eggs les œufs sur le plat
  hard-boiled egg l'œuf dur
  scrambled eggs les œufs brouillés
  soft-boiled egg l'œuf à la coque
eggplant l'aubergine (f)
either ... or soit ... soit
elastic band l'élastique (m)
elastoplast® le sparadrap
elbow le coude
electric électrique
electric blanket la couverture chauffante
electric razor le rasoir électrique

electrician l'électricien (m)
electricity l'électricité (f)
electricity meter le compteur électrique
elevator l'ascenseur (m)
e-mail le e-mail
  to e-mail sb envoyer un e-mail à qn
e-mail address l'adresse électronique
  (on forms) le mél
embassy l'ambassade (f)
emergency l'urgence (f)
emergency exit la sortie de secours
empty vide
end la fin
engaged (to marry) fiancé(e)
  (phone, toilet, etc) occupé(e)
engine le moteur
England l'Angleterre (f)
English anglais(e)
  (language) l'anglais (m)
Englishman/-woman l'Anglais(e) (m/f)
to enjoy aimer
  I enjoy swimming j'aime nager
  I enjoy dancing j'aime danser
  enjoy your meal! bon appétit!
enough assez
  that's enough ça suffit
enquiry desk les renseignements (mpl)
to enter entrer
entertainment les divertissements (mpl)
entrance l'entrée (f)
entrance fee le prix d'entrée
envelope l'enveloppe (f)
epileptic épileptique
epileptic fit la crise d'épilepsie
equipment l'équipement (m)
equal égal
eraser la gomme
error l'erreur (f)
escalator l'escalator (m)
to escape s'échapper
essential indispensable
estate agent l'agence immobilière (f)
euro l'euro (m)
eurocheque l'eurochèque (m)

Europe l'Europe (f)
European européen(ne)
European Union l'Union européenne (f)
evening le soir
  this evening ce soir
  tomorrow evening demain soir
  in the evening le soir
  7 o'clock in the evening sept heures du soir
evening dress (man) la tenue de soirée
  (woman) la robe du soir
evening meal le dîner
every chaque
everyone tout le monde
everything tout
everywhere partout
examination l'examen (m)
example: *for example* par exemple
excellent excellent(e)
except sauf
excess baggage l'excédent de bagages (m)
exchange l'échange (m)
to exchange échanger
exchange rate le taux de change
exciting passionnant(e)
excursion l'excursion (f)
excuse: *excuse me!* excusez-moi!
  (to get by) pardon!
exercise l'exercice (m)
exhaust pipe le pot d'échappement
exhibition l'exposition (f)
exit la sortie
expenses les frais
expensive cher (chère)
expert l'expert(e) (m/f)
to expire (ticket, etc) expirer
to explain expliquer
explosion l'explosion (f)
to export exporter
express (train) le rapide
express (parcel, etc) en exprès
extension (electrical) la rallonge
extra (additional) supplémentaire
  (more) de plus
eye l'œil (m)
  eyes les yeux

eyebrows les sourcils (mpl)
eye drops les gouttes pour les yeux (fpl)
eyelashes les cils (mpl)
eyeliner l'eye-liner (m)
eye shadow le fard à paupières

F

fabric le tissu
face le visage
face cloth/glove le gant de toilette
facial les soins du visage (mpl)
facilities les installations (fpl)
factory l'usine (f)
to faint s'évanouir
fainted évanoui(e)
fair (hair) blond(e)
  (just) juste
fair (funfair) la fête foraine
fake faux (fausse)
fall (autumn) l'automne (m)
to fall tomber
  he has fallen il est tombé
false teeth le dentier
family la famille
famous célèbre
fan (handheld) l'éventail (m)
  (electric) le ventilateur
  (sports) le supporter
fan belt la courroie de ventilateur
fancy dress le déguisement
far loin
  is it far? c'est loin?
fare (bus, metro, etc) le prix du billet
farm la ferme
farmer le fermier
fashionable à la mode
fast rapide
  too fast trop vite
to fasten (seatbelt) attacher
fat gros (grosse)
  (noun) la graisse
father le père
father-in-law le beau-père
fault (defect) le défaut
  it's not my fault ce n'est pas de ma faute

favour le service
favourite préféré(e)
fax le fax
  by fax par fax
fax number le numéro de fax
to fax *(document)* faxer
  (person) envoyer un fax à
February février
to feed nourrir
to feel sentir
  I feel sick j'ai la nausée
  I don't feel well je ne me sens
  pas bien
feet les pieds *(mpl)*
felt-tip pen le feutre
female *(person)* féminin
ferry le ferry
festival le festival
to fetch aller chercher
fever la fièvre
few peu
  a few quelques-un(e)s
fiancé(e) le fiancé/la fiancée
field le champ
fig la figue
to fight se battre
file *(computer)* le fichier
  (for papers) le dossier
to fill remplir
to fill in *(form)* remplir
to fill up *(with petrol)* faire le plein
  fill it up! *(car)* le plein!
fillet le filet
filling *(in tooth)* le plombage
film le film *(for camera)* la pellicule
to find trouver
fine *(penalty)* la contravention
finger le doigt
to finish finir
finished fini(e)
fire le feu ; l'incendie *(m)*
fire alarm l'alarme d'incendie *(f)*
fire brigade les pompiers *(mpl)*
fire engine la voiture de pompiers
fire escape *(staircase)* l'échelle de
  secours *(f)*
fire exit la sortie de secours

fire extinguisher l'extincteur *(m)*
fireplace la cheminée
fireworks les feux d'artifice *(mpl)*
firm la compagnie
first premier(-ière)
first aid les premiers secours *(mpl)*
first aid kit la trousse de secours
first-class de première classe
first name le prénom
fish le poisson
to fish pêcher
fisherman le pêcheur
fishing la pêche
  to go fishing aller à la pêche
fishing permit le permis de pêche
fishing rod la canne à pêche
fishmonger's le/la marchand(e)
  de poisson
fit *(medical)* l'attaque *(f)*
to fit: *it doesn't fit me* ça ne me
  va pas
to fix *(repair)* réparer
  can you fix it? vous pouvez
  le réparer?
fizzy gazeux(-euse)
flag le drapeau
flames les flammes *(fpl)*
flash *(for camera)* le flash
flashlight la lampe de poche
flask le Thermos®
flat l'appartement *(m)*
flat *(level)* plat
  beer) éventé
flat tyre le pneu dégonflé
flavour le goût
  (of ice cream) le parfum
flaw le défaut
fleas les puces *(fpl)*
  flea market le marché aux puces
flesh la chair
flex *(electrical)* le fil
flight le vol
flip flops les tongs *(fpl)*
flippers les palmes *(fpl)*
flood l'inondation *(f)*
  flash flood la crue subite
floor *(of room)* le sol
  (storey) l'étage *(m)*

(on the) ground floor
(au) rez-de-chaussée
(on the) first floor
(au) premier étage
(on the) second floor
(au) deuxième étage
which floor? quel étage?

floorcloth la serpillère
florist's shop le magasin de fleurs
flour la farine
flower la fleur
flu la grippe
fly la mouche
to fly *(person)* aller en avion
(bird) voler
fly sheet le double toit
fog le brouillard
foggy: *it was foggy* il y avait du brouillard
foil le papier alu(minium)
to fold plier
to follow suivre
food la nourriture
food poisoning l'intoxication alimentaire *(f)*
foot le pied
to go on foot aller à pied
football le football
football match le match de football
football pitch le terrain de football
football player le/la joueur(-euse) de football
footpath le sentier
for pour
for me/you/us pour moi/vous/nous
for him/her pour lui/elle
forbidden interdit(e)
forehead le front
foreign étranger(-ère)
foreign currency les devises étrangères *(fpl)*
foreigner l'étranger(ère) *(m(f))*
forest la forêt
forever toujours
to forget oublier
fork *(for eating)* la fourchette
(in road) l'embranchement *(m)*

form *(document)* le formulaire
(shape, style) la forme
fortnight la quinzaine
forward en avant
foul *(football)* la faute
fountain la fontaine
four-wheel drive vehicle le quatre-quatre ; le 4 x 4
fox le renard
fracture la fracture
fragile fragile
fragrance le parfum
frame *(picture)* le cadre
France la France
in/to France en France
free *(not occupied)* libre
(costing nothing) gratuit(e)
freezer le congélateur
French français(e)
(language) le français
French beans les haricots verts *(mpl)*
French fries les frites *(fpl)*
French people les Français *(mpl)*
frequent fréquent(e)
fresh frais (fraîche)
fresh water l'eau douce *(f)*
Friday vendredi
fridge le frigo
fried frit(e)
friend l'ami(e) *(m/f)*
frog la grenouille
frogs' legs les cuisses de grenouille *(fpl)*
from de
I'm from England je suis anglais(e)
I'm from Scotland je suis écossais(e)
front le devant
in front of... devant...
front door la porte d'entrée
frost le gel
frozen gelé(e)
(food) surgelé(e)
fruit le fruit
dried fruit les fruits secs
fruit juice le jus de fruit
fruit salad la salade de fruits
to fry frire

frying-pan la poêle
fuel le combustible
fuel gauge l'indicateur de niveau d'essence (m)
fuel pump la pompe d'alimentation
fuel tank le réservoir d'essence
full plein(e)
  (occupied) complet(ète)
full board la pension complète
fumes (exhaust) les gaz d'échappement (mpl)
fun: to have fun s'amuser
funeral les obsèques (fpl)
funfair la fête foraine
funny (amusing) amusant(e)
furnished meublé(e)
furniture les meubles (mpl)
fuse le fusible
fuse box la boîte à fusibles
future l'avenir (m)

G

gallery la galerie
game le jeu
  (meat) le gibier
garage (for petrol) la station-service
  (for parking, repair) le garage
garden le jardin
garlic l'ail (m)
gas le gaz
gas cooker la gazinière
gas cylinder la bouteille de gaz
gastritis la gastrite
gate la porte
gay (person) homo
gear la vitesse
  in first gear en première
  in second gear en seconde
gearbox la boîte de vitesses
generous généreux(-euse)
gents (toilet) les toilettes pour hommes (fpl)
genuine authentique
German allemand(e)
  (language) l'allemand (m)
German measles la rubéole

Germany l'Allemagne (f)
to get (obtain) obtenir
  (to fetch) aller chercher
to get in (vehicle) monter
to get off (bus, etc) descendre
gift le cadeau
gift shop la boutique de souvenirs
girl la fille
girlfriend la copine
to give donner
to give back rendre
glacier le glacier
glass le verre
  a glass of water un verre d'eau
glasses les lunettes (fpl)
glasses case l'étui à lunettes (m)
gloves les gants (mpl)
glue la colle
to go aller
  I'm going to... je vais ...
  we're going to hire a car nous allons louer une voiture
to go back retourner
to go in entrer
to go out (leave) sortir
goat la chèvre
God Dieu (m)
goggles (for swimming) les lunettes de natation (fpl)
gold l'or (m)
  is it gold? c'est en or?
golf le golf
golf ball la balle de golf
golf clubs les clubs de golf (mpl)
golf course le terrain de golf
good bon (bonne)
  (that's) good! (c'est) bien!
  (for food) c'est bon!
good afternoon bonjour
goodbye au revoir
good day bonjour
good evening bonsoir
good morning bonjour
goodnight bonne nuit
goose l'oie (f)
gram le gramme

grandchildren les petits-enfants (mpl)
granddaughter la petite-fille
grandfather le grand-père
grandmother la grand-mère
grandparents les grands-parents (mpl)
grandson le petit-fils
grapefruit le pamplemousse
grapes le raisin
grass l'herbe (f)
grated (cheese) râpé(e)
grater la râpe
greasy gras (grasse)
great (big) grand(e)
    (wonderful) formidable
Great Britain la Grande-Bretagne
green vert(e)
green card (insurance) la carte verte
greengrocer's le magasin de fruits
    et légumes
greetings card la carte de vœux
grey gris(e)
grill (part of cooker) le gril
grilled grillé(e)
grocer's l'épicerie (f)
ground la terre ; le sol
ground floor le rez-de-chaussée
    on the ground floor au rez-de-
    chaussée
groundsheet le tapis de sol
group le groupe
guarantee la garantie
guard (on train) le chef de train
guest (house guest) l'invité(e)
    (in hotel) le/la client(e)
guesthouse la pension
guide (tourist guide) le/la guide
guidebook le guide
guided tour la visite guidée
guitar la guitare
gun (rifle) le fusil
    (pistol) le pistolet
gym (gymnasium) le gymnase
gym shoes les chaussons de gym

H

haemorrhoids les hémorroïdes (fpl)

hail la grêle
hair les cheveux (mpl)
hairbrush la brosse à cheveux
haircut la coupe (de cheveux)
hairdresser le/la coiffeur(-euse)
hairdryer le sèche-cheveux
hair dye la teinture pour les
    cheveux
hair gel le gel pour les cheveux
hairgrip la pince à cheveux
hair mousse la mousse coiffante
hair spray la laque
half la moitié
    half an hour une demi-heure
half board la demi-pension
half fare le demi-tarif
half-price à moitié prix
ham (cooked) le jambon
    (cured) le jambon cru
hamburger le hamburger
hammer le marteau
hand la main
handbag le sac à main
hand luggage les bagages
    à main (mpl)
hand-made fait main
handicapped handicapé(e)
handkerchief le mouchoir
handle la poignée
handlebars le guidon
handsome beau (belle)
hanger (coathanger) le cintre
hangover la gueule de bois
to hang up (telephone) raccrocher
hang-gliding le deltaplane
    to go hang-gliding faire du
    deltaplane
to happen arriver ; se passer
    what happened? qu'est-ce qui s'est
    passé?
happy heureux(-euse)
    happy birthday! bon anniversaire!
harbour le port
hard (not soft) dur(e)
    (not easy) difficile
hard disk le disque dur

hardware shop la quincaillerie
to harm someone faire du mal à
  quelqu'un
harvest *(grape)* les vendanges
hat le chapeau
to have avoir
to have to devoir
hay fever le rhume des foins
he il
head la tête
headache le mal de tête
  I have a headache j'ai mal à la tête
headlights les phares *(mpl)*
headphones les écouteurs *(mpl)*
head waiter le maître d'hôtel
health la santé
health food shop la boutique
  de produits diététiques
healthy sain(e)
to hear entendre
hearing aid la prothèse auditive
heart le cœur
heart attack la crise cardiaque
heartburn les brûlures d'estomac *(fpl)*
heater l'appareil de chauffage *(m)*
heating le chauffage
to heat up faire chauffer
heavy lourd(e)
heel le talon
heel bar le talon-minute
height la hauteur
helicopter l'hélicoptère *(m)*
hello bonjour!
  (on telephone) allô?
helmet le casque
help! au secours!
to help aider
  can you help me? vous pouvez
  m'aider?
hem l'ourlet *(m)*
hepatitis l'hépatite *(f)*
her son/sa/ses
  her passport son passeport
  her room sa chambre
  her suitcases ses valises
herb l'herbe *(f)*

herbal tea la tisane
here ici
  here is... voici...
hernia la hernie
hi! salut!
to hide *(something)* cacher
  (oneself) se cacher
high haut(e)
high blood pressure la tension
high chair la chaise de bébé
high tide la marée haute
hill la colline
hill walking la randonnée (de basse
  montagne)
him il ; lui
hip la hanche
hip replacement la pose d'une
  prothèse de la hanche
hire la location
  car hire la location de voitures
  bike hire la location de bicyclettes
  boat hire la location de bateaux
  ski hire la location de skis
to hire louer
hired car la voiture de location
his son/sa/ses
  his passport son passeport
  his room sa chambre
  his suitcases ses valises
historic historique
history l'histoire *(f)*
to hit frapper
to hitchhike faire du stop
HIV le VIH
hobby le passe-temps
to hold tenir *(contain)* contenir
hold-up *(in traffic)* l'embouteillage *(m)*
hole le trou
holiday les vacances
  on holiday en vacances *(fpl)*
home la maison
  at my/your/our home chez
  moi/vous/nous
homesick: to be homesick avoir le
  mal du pays
  I'm homesick j'ai le mal du pays
homosexual homosexuel(le)

honest honnête
honey le miel
honeymoon la lune de miel
hood (of car) le capot
hook (fishing) l'hameçon (m)
to hope espérer
  I hope so/not j'espère que oui/non
horn (of car) le klaxon
hors d'œuvre le hors-d'œuvre
horse le cheval
horse racing les courses de
  chevaux (fpl)
horse-riding: *to go horse-riding* faire
  du cheval
hosepipe le tuyau d'arrosage
hospital l'hôpital (m)
hostel (youth hostel) l'auberge
  de jeunesse (f)
hot chaud(e)
  I'm hot j'ai chaud
  it's hot (weather) il fait chaud
hot-water bottle la bouillotte
hotel l'hôtel (m)
hour l'heure (f)
  half an hour une demi-heure
  1 hour une heure
  2 hours deux heures
house la maison
househusband l'homme au foyer
housewife la femme au foyer
house wine le vin en pichet
housework: *to do the housework* faire
  le ménage
hovercraft l'aéroglisseur (m)
how? (in what way) comment?
  how much/many? combien?
  how are you? comment allez-vous?
hungry: *to be hungry* avoir faim
  I'm hungry j'ai faim
to hunt chasser
hunting permit le permis de chasse
hurry: *I'm in a hurry* je suis pressé
to hurt: *to hurt somebody* faire du
  mal à quelqu'un
  that hurts ça fait mal
husband le mari
hut (bathing/beach) la cabine
  (mountain) le refuge

hydrofoil l'hydrofoil (m)
hypodermic needle l'aiguille
  hypodermique (f)

I

I je
ice la glace
  (cube) le glaçon
  with/without ice avec/sans glaçons
ice cream la glace
ice lolly l'esquimau (m)
ice rink la patinoire
to ice skate faire du patin (à glace)
ice skates les patins (à glace) (mpl)
idea l'idée (f)
identity card la carte d'identité
if si
ignition l'allumage (m)
ignition key la clé de contact
ill malade
illness la maladie
immediately immédiatement
immersion heater le chauffe-eau
  électrique
immigration l'immigration (f)
immunisation l'immunisation (f)
to import importer
important important(e)
impossible impossible
to improve améliorer
in dans ; en ; à
  in 2 hours' time dans deux heures
  in France en France
  in Canada au Canada
  in London à Londres
in front of devant
included compris(e)
inconvenient gênant
to increase augmenter
indicator (car) le clignotant
indigestion l'indigestion (f)
indigestion tablets les comprimés
  pour les troubles digestifs (mpl)
indoors à l'intérieur
infection l'infection (f)
infectious infectieux(-euse)

information les renseignements (mpl)
information desk les renseignements (mpl)
information office le bureau de renseignements
ingredients les ingrédients (mpl)
inhaler l'inhalateur (m)
injection la piqûre
to injure blesser
injured blessé(e)
injury la blessure
inn l'auberge (f)
inner tube la chambre à air
inquiries les renseignements (mpl)
inquiry desk le bureau de renseignements
insect l'insecte (m)
insect bite la piqûre (d'insecte)
insect repellent le produit antimoustiques
inside à l'intérieur
instant coffee le café instantané
instead of au lieu de
instructor le moniteur/la monitrice
insulin l'insuline (f)
insurance l'assurance (f)
insurance certificate l'attestation d'assurance (f)
to insure assurer
insured assuré(e)
to intend to avoir l'intention de
interesting intéressant(e)
international international(e)
internet l'internet (m)
   internet café le cybercafé
interpreter l'interprète (m/f)
interval (theatre) l'entracte (m)
interview l'entrevue (f)
   (TV, etc) l'interview (f)
into dans ; en
   into town en ville
to introduce présenter
invitation l'invitation (f)
to invite inviter
invoice la facture
Ireland l'Irlande (f)

Irish irlandais(e)
iron (for clothes) le fer à repasser
   (metal) le fer
to iron repasser
ironing board la planche à repasser
ironmonger's la quincaillerie
is est
island l'île (f)
it il ; elle
Italian italien(ne)
Italy l'Italie (f)
to itch démanger
   it itches ça me démange
item l'article (m)
itemized bill la facture détaillée

J

jack (for car) le cric
jacket la veste
   waterproof jacket l'anorak (m)
jam (food) la confiture
jammed (stuck) coincé(e)
January janvier
jar (honey, jam, etc) le pot
jaundice la jaunisse
jaw la mâchoire
jealous jaloux(-ouse)
jeans le jean
jellyfish la méduse
jet ski le jet-ski
jetty (landing pier) l'embarcadère (m)
Jew le Juif/la Juive
jeweller's la bijouterie
jewellery les bijoux (mpl)
Jewish juif (juive)
job le travail ; l'emploi (m)
to jog faire du jogging
to join (become member) s'inscrire
to join in participer
joint (body) l'articulation (f)
to joke plaisanter
joke la plaisanterie
journalist le/la journaliste
journey le voyage
judge le juge
jug le pichet

juice le jus
  fruit juice le jus de fruit
  orange juice le jus d'orange
  a carton of juice un brick de jus de fruits
July juillet
to jump sauter
jumper le pull
jump leads les câbles de raccordement pour batterie *(mpl)*
junction *(road)* le croisement ; le carrefour
June juin
just: *just two* deux seulement
  I've just arrived je viens d'arriver

K

to keep *(retain)* garder
kennel la niche
kettle la bouilloire
key la clé
  the car key la clé de la voiture
keyboard le clavier
keyring le porte-clés
to kick donner un coup de pied à
kid *(child)* le gosse
kidneys *(in body)* les reins *(mpl)*
kill tuer
kilo(gram) le kilo
kilometre le kilomètre
kind *(person)* gentil(-ille)
kind *(sort)* la sorte
kiosk *(newsstand)* le kiosque
  (phone box) la cabine
kiss le baiser
to kiss embrasser
kitchen la cuisine
kitchen paper l'essuie-tout *(m)*
kite *(toy)* le cerf-volant
knee le genou
knickers la culotte
knife le couteau
to knit tricoter
to knock *(on door)* frapper
to knock down *(in car)* renverser
to knock over *(vase, glass, etc)* faire tomber

knot le nœud
to know *(be aware of)* savoir
  (person, place) connaître
  I don't know je ne sais pas
  I don't know Paris je ne connais pas Paris
to know how to do sth savoir faire quelque chose
  to know how to swim savoir nager
kosher kascher

L

label l'étiquette *(f)*
lace la dentelle
laces *(for shoes)* les lacets *(mpl)*
ladder l'échelle *(f)*
ladies *(toilet)* les toilettes pour dames *(fpl)*
lady la dame
lager la bière
  bottled lager la bière en bouteille
  draught lager la bière pression
lake le lac
lamb l'agneau *(m)*
lamp la lampe
lamppost le réverbère
lampshade l'abat-jour *(m)*
to land atterrir
land la terre
landlady la propriétaire
landlord le propriétaire
landslide le glissement de terrain
lane la ruelle *(of motorway)* la voie
language la langue
language school l'école de langues *(f)*
laptop le portable
large grand(e)
last dernier(-ière)
  last month le mois dernier
  last night *(evening)* hier soir
  (night-time) la nuit dernière
  last time la dernière fois
  last week la semaine dernière
  last year l'année dernière
  the last bus le dernier bus
  the last train le dernier train
late tard

the train is late le train a du retard
sorry we are late excusez-nous d'arriver en retard
later plus tard
to laugh rire
launderette la laverie automatique
laundry service le service de blanchisserie
lavatory les toilettes *(fpl)*
lavender la lavande
law la loi
lawn la pelouse
lawyer l'avocat(e) *(m/f)*
laxative le laxatif
layby l'aire de stationnement *(f)*
lead *(electric)* le fil
lead *(metal)* le plomb
lead-free petrol l'essence sans plomb *(f)*
leaf la feuille
leak la fuite
to leak: *it's leaking* il y a une fuite
to learn apprendre
lease *(rental)* le bail
leather le cuir
to leave *(depart for)* partir
  (depart from) quitter
  (to leave behind) laisser
  to leave for Paris partir pour Paris
  to leave London quitter Londres
leek le poireau
left: *on/to the left* à gauche
left-handed *(person)* gaucher(-ère)
left-luggage *(office)* la consigne
left-luggage locker la consigne automatique
leg la jambe
legal légal(e)
leisure centre le centre de loisirs
lemon le citron
lemonade la limonade
to lend prêter
length la longueur
lens *(of camera, etc)* l'objectif *(m)*
  (contact lens) la lentille
lesbian la lesbienne
less moins

less than moins de
lesson la leçon
to let *(allow)* permettre
  (to hire out) louer
letter la lettre
letterbox la boîte aux lettres
lettuce la laitue
level crossing le passage à niveau
library la bibliothèque
licence le permis
lid le couvercle
to lie down s'allonger
life belt la bouée de sauvetage
lifeboat le canot de sauvetage
lifeguard le maître nageur
life insurance l'assurance-vie *(f)*
life jacket le gilet de sauvetage
life raft le radeau de sauvetage
lift *(elevator)* l'ascenseur *(m)*
lift pass *(on ski slopes)* le forfait
light *(not heavy)* léger(-ère)
light la lumière
  have you got a light? avez-vous du feu?
light bulb l'ampoule *(f)*
lighter le briquet
lighthouse le phare
lightning les éclairs *(mpl)*
like *(preposition)* comme
  like this comme ça
to like aimer
  I like coffee j'aime le café
  I don't like coffee je n'aime pas le café
  I'd like... je voudrais...
  we'd like... nous voudrions...
lilo® le matelas pneumatique
lime *(fruit)* le citron vert
line *(mark)* la ligne
  (row) la file d'attente
  (telephone) la ligne
linen le lin
lingerie la lingerie
lip la lèvre
lip-reading lire sur les lèvres
lip salve le baume pour les lèvres
lipstick le rouge à lèvres

liqueur la liqueur
list la liste
to listen to écouter
litre le litre
litter (rubbish) les ordures (fpl)
little petit(e)
 a little... un peu de...
to live (in a place) vivre ; habiter
 I live in London j'habite à Londres
 he lives in a flat il habite dans un
 appartement
liver le foie
living room le salon
loaf le pain
local local(e)
lock la serrure
 the lock is broken la serrure est
 cassée
to lock fermer à clé
locker (for luggage) le casier
locksmith le serrurier
log (for fire) la bûche
logbook (of car) la carte grise
lollipop la sucette
London Londres
 to/in London à Londres
long long(ue)
 for a long time longtemps
long-sighted hypermétrope
to look after garder
to look at regarder
to look for chercher
loose (not fastened) desserré(e)
 it's come loose
 (unscrewed) ça s'est desserré
 (detached) ça s'est détaché
lorry le camion
to lose perdre
lost (object) perdu(e)
 I've lost... j'ai perdu...
 I'm lost je suis perdu(e)
lost property office le bureau des
 objets trouvés
lot: *a lot of* beaucoup de
lotion la lotion
lottery le loto
loud fort(e)

lounge (in hotel, airport) le salon
love l'amour (m)
to love (person) aimer
 (food, activity, etc) adorer
 I love you je t'aime
 I love swimming j'adore nager
lovely beau (belle)
low bas (basse)
low-alcohol peu alcoolisé(e)
to lower baisser
low-fat allégé(e)
low tide la marée basse
luck la chance
lucky chanceux(-euse)
luggage les bagages (mpl)
luggage allowance le poids
 maximum autorisé
luggage rack le porte-bagages
luggage tag l'étiquette à bagages (f)
luggage trolley le chariot
 (à bagages)
lump (swelling) la bosse
lunch le déjeuner
lunchbreak la pause de midi
lung le poumon
luxury le luxe

M

machine la machine
mad fou (folle)
magazine la revue
maggot l'asticot (m)
magnet l'aimant (m)
magnifying glass la loupe
maid la domestique
maiden name le nom de jeune fille
mail le courrier
 by mail par la poste
main principal(e)
mains (electricity, water) le secteur
main course (of meal) le plat
 principal
main road la route principale
to make faire
make-up le maquillage
male (person) masculin

mallet le maillet
man l'homme (m)
to manage (to be in charge of) gérer
manager le/la directeur(-trice)
manual (car) manuel(le)
many beaucoup de
map la carte
   road map la carte routière
   street map le plan de la ville
March mars
margarine la margarine
marina la marina
mark (stain) la tache
market le marché
   where is the market? où est le
   marché?
   when is the market? le marché,
   c'est quel jour?
market place le marché
marmalade la marmelade d'oranges
married marié(e)
   I'm married je suis marié(e)
   are you married? vous êtes
   marié(e)?
marsh le marais
mascara le mascara
mass (in church) la messe
mast le mât
masterpiece le chef-d'œuvre
match (game) la partie
matches les allumettes (fpl)
material (cloth) le tissu
to matter: *it doesn't matter* ça ne
   fait rien
   what's the matter? qu'est-ce
   qu'il y a?
mattress le matelas
May mai
mayonnaise la mayonnaise
mayor le maire
maximum le maximum
me moi
meal le repas
to mean vouloir dire
   what does this mean? qu'est-ce
   que ça veut dire?
measles la rougeole

to measure mesurer
meat la viande
mechanic le mécanicien
medical insurance l'assurance
   maladie (f)
medical treatment les soins
   médicaux (mpl)
medicine le médicament
Mediterranean Sea la Méditerranée
medium rare (meat) à point
to meet rencontrer
meeting la réunion
meeting point le point de rencontre
melon le melon
to melt fondre
member (of club, etc) le membre
membership card la carte de
   membre
memory la mémoire
   memory card la carte de mémoire
men les hommes (mpl)
to mend réparer
meningitis la méningite
menu (choices) le menu
   (card) la carte
message le message
metal le métal
meter le compteur
metre le mètre
metro le métro
metro station la station de métro
microwave oven le four à
   micro-ondes
midday midi
   at midday à midi
middle le milieu
middle-aged d'un certain âge
midge le moucheron
midnight minuit
   at midnight à minuit
migraine la migraine
   I have a migraine j'ai la migraine
mild (weather, cheese) doux (douce)
   (curry) peu épicé(e)
   (tobacco) léger(-ère)
milk le lait
   baby milk (formula) le lait maternisé

fresh milk le lait frais
full cream milk le lait entier
hot milk le lait chaud
long-life milk le lait longue
  conservation
powdered milk le lait en poudre
semi-skimmed milk le lait demi-
  écrémé
skimmed milk le lait écrémé
soya milk le lait de soja
UHT milk le lait UHT
with/without milk avec/sans lait
milkshake le milk-shake
millimetre le millimètre
mince *(meat)* la viande hachée
to mind: *do you mind if I...?* ça vous
  gêne si je...?
  I don't mind ça m'est égal
  do you mind? vous permettez?
mineral water l'eau minérale *(f)*
minibar le minibar
minimum le minimum
minister *(church)* le pasteur
minor road la route secondaire
mint *(herb)* la menthe
  (sweet) le bonbon à la menthe
minute la minute
mirror le miroir
  (in car) le rétroviseur
miscarriage la fausse couche
to miss *(train, flight, etc)* rater
Miss Mademoiselle
missing *(disappeared)* disparu(e)
mistake l'erreur *(f)*
misty brumeux(-euse)
misunderstanding le malentendu
to mix mélanger
mobile phone le portable
modem le modem
modern moderne
moisturizer la crème hydratante
mole *(on skin)* le grain de beauté
moment: *at the moment* en ce
  moment
monastery le monastère
Monday lundi
money l'argent *(m)*

I have no money je n'ai pas d'argent
moneybelt la ceinture porte-
  monnaie
money order le mandat
month le mois
  this month ce mois-ci
  last month le mois dernier
  next month le mois prochain
monthly mensuel(-elle)
monument le monument
moon la lune
mooring *(place)* le mouillage
mop *(for floor)* le balai à franges
moped le vélomoteur
more encore
  more wine plus de vin
more than plus de
  more than three plus de trois
morning le matin
  in the morning le matin
  this morning ce matin
  tomorrow morning demain matin
morning-after pill la pilule du
  lendemain
mosque la mosquée
mosquito le moustique
mosquito bite la piqûre de
  moustique
mosquito coil la spirale antimoustiques
mosquito net la moustiquaire
mosquito repellent le produit
  antimoustiques
most (of the) la plupart (de)
moth *(clothes)* la mite
mother la mère
mother-in-law la belle-mère
motor le moteur
motorbike la moto
motorboat le bateau à moteur
motorway l'autoroute *(f)*
mountain la montagne
mountain bike le VTT (vélo tout-
  terrain)
mountain rescue le sauvetage
  en montagne
mountaineering l'alpinisme *(m)*

mouse (animal, computer) la souris
moustache la moustache
mouth la bouche
mouthwash le bain de bouche
to move bouger
  it's moving ça bouge
movie le film
Mr Monsieur
Mrs Madame
Ms Madame
much beaucoup
  too much trop
muddy boueux(-euse)
mug: *I've been mugged* je me suis
  fait agresser
mugging l'agression (f)
mumps les oreillons (mpl)
muscle le muscle
museum le musée
mushrooms les champignons (mpl)
music la musique
musical (show) la comédie musicale
Muslim musulman(e)
mussels les moules (fpl)
must devoir
  I/we must go il faut que j'y aille/
  que nous y allions
  you must be there il faut que vous y
  soyez
mustard la moutarde
my mon/ma/mes
  my passport mon passeport
  my room ma chambre
  my suitcases mes valises

N
nail (metal) le clou
  (finger) l'ongle (m)
nailbrush la brosse à ongles
nail clippers le coupe-ongles
nail file la lime à ongles
nail polish le vernis à ongles
nail polish remover le dissolvant
nail scissors les ciseaux à ongles (mpl)
name le nom
  my name is… je m'appelle…
  what is your name? comment
  vous appelez-vous?

nanny le/la baby-sitter
napkin la serviette de table
nappy la couche
narrow étroit(e)
national national(e)
nationality la nationalité
national park le parc national
natural naturel(le)
nature reserve la réserve naturelle
nature trail le sentier de grande
  randonnée
navy blue bleu marine
near près de
  near the bank près de la banque
  is it near? c'est près d'ici?
necessary nécessaire
neck le cou
necklace le collier
nectarine le brugnon
to need (to) avoir besoin de
  I need… j'ai besoin de…
  we need… nous avons besoin de…
  I need to phone j'ai besoin de
  téléphoner
needle l'aiguille (f)
  a needle and thread du fil et une
  aiguille
negative (photography) le négatif
neighbour le/la voisin(e)
nephew le neveu
net le filet
  the net le net ; l'internet (m)
never jamais
  I never drink wine je ne bois jamais
  de vin
new nouveau(-elle)
news (TV, radio) les informations (fpl)
newsagent's le magasin de journaux
newspaper le journal
news stand le kiosque
New Year le Nouvel An
  happy New Year! bonne année!
New Year's Eve la Saint-Sylvestre
New Zealand la Nouvelle-Zélande
next prochain(e)
  (after) ensuite
  the next train le prochain train

next month le mois prochain
next week la semaine prochaine
next Monday lundi prochain
next to à côté de
we're going to Paris next ensuite nous allons à Paris
nice beau (belle)
  (enjoyable) bon (bonne)
  (person) sympathique
niece la nièce
night *(night-time)* la nuit
  (evening) le soir
  at night la nuit/le soir
  last night hier soir
  tomorrow night (evening) demain soir
  tonight ce soir
nightclub la boîte de nuit
nightdress la chemise de nuit
night porter le gardien de nuit
no non *(without)* sans
  no problem pas de problème
  no thanks non merci
  no ice sans glaçons
  no sugar sans sucre
nobody personne
noise le bruit
  it's very noisy il y a beaucoup de bruit
non-alcoholic sans alcool
none aucun(e)
non-smoker: *I'm a non-smoker* je ne fume pas
non-smoking *(seat, compartment)* non-fumeurs
north le nord
Northern Ireland l'Irlande du Nord
North Sea la mer du Nord
nose le nez
not ne ... pas
  I am not... je ne suis pas...
note *(banknote)* le billet
  (letter) le mot
note pad le bloc-notes
nothing rien
  nothing else rien d'autre
notice *(warning)* l'avis *(m)*
  (sign) le panneau

notice board le panneau d'affichage
novel le roman
November novembre
now maintenant
nowhere nulle part
nuclear nucléaire
number *(quantity)* le nombre
  (of room, house) le numéro
  phone number le numéro de téléphone
numberplate *(of car)* la plaque d'immatriculation
nurse l'infirmier/l'infirmière *(m/f)*
nursery la garderie
nursery slope la piste pour débutants
nut *(to eat)* la noix
  (for bolt) l'écrou *(m)*

O

oar l'aviron *(m)* ; la rame
oats l'avoine *(f)*
to obtain obtenir
occupation *(work)* l'emploi *(m)*
ocean l'océan *(m)*
October octobre
odd *(strange)* bizarre
of de
  a glass of... un verre de...
  made of... en...
off *(light)* éteint(e)
  (rotten) mauvais(e) ; pourri(e)
office le bureau
often souvent
oil *(for car, food)* l'huile *(f)*
oil filter le filtre à huile
oil gauge la jauge de niveau d'huile
ointment la pommade
OK! *(agreed)* d'accord!
old vieux (vieille)
  how old are you? quel âge avez-vous?
  I'm... years old j'ai... ans
old-age pensioner le/la retraité(e)
olive l'olive *(f)*
olive oil l'huile d'olive *(f)*

on (light) allumé(e)
  (engine, etc) en marche
  on the table sur la table
  on time à l'heure
once une fois
  at once tout de suite
one-way (street) à sens unique
onion l'oignon (m)
only seulement
open ouvert(e)
to open ouvrir
opera l'opéra (m)
operation (surgical) l'opération (f)
operator (phone) le/la standardiste
opposite en face de
  opposite the bank en face de la
  banque
  quite the opposite bien au contraire
optician l'opticien/l'opticienne (m/f)
or ou
orange (fruit) l'orange (f)
  (colour) orange
orange juice le jus d'orange
orchestra l'orchestre (m)
order (in restaurant) la commande
  out of order en panne
to order (in restaurant) commander
organic biologique
to organize organiser
ornament le bibelot
other autre
  have you any others? vous en
  avez d'autres?
our (sing) notre
  (plural) nos
  our room notre chambre
  our passports nos passeports
  our baggage nos bagages
out (light) éteint(e)
  he's/she's out il/elle est sorti(e)
outdoor (pool, etc) en plein air
outside dehors
oven le four
ovenproof dish le plat qui va
  au four
over (on top of) au-dessus de
to overbook faire du surbooking

to overcharge faire payer trop cher
overdone (food) trop cuit(e)
overdose la surdose
to overheat surchauffer
to overload surcharger
to oversleep se réveiller en retard
to overtake (car) doubler ; dépasser
to owe devoir
  you owe me... vous me devez...
to own posséder
owner le/la propriétaire
oyster l'huître (f)

P

pace le pas
pacemaker le stimulateur
  (cardiaque)
to pack (luggage) faire les bagages
package le paquet
package tour le voyage organisé
packet le paquet
padded envelope l'enveloppe
  matelassée
paddling pool la pataugeoire
padlock le cadenas
page la page
paid payé(e)
  I've paid j'ai payé
pain la douleur
painful douloureux(-euse)
painkiller l'analgésique (m)
to paint peindre
painting (picture) le tableau
pair la paire
palace le palais
pale pâle
pan (saucepan) la casserole
  (frying pan) la poêle
pancake la crêpe
panniers (for bike) les sacoches (fpl)
panties la culotte
pants (underwear) le slip
panty liner le protège-slip
paper le papier
paper hankies les mouchoirs
  en papier (mpl)

paper napkins les serviettes en papier *(fpl)*
paragliding le parapente
paralysed paralysé(e)
parcel le colis
pardon? comment?
  I beg your pardon! pardon!
parents les parents *(mpl)*
Paris Paris
park le parc
to park garer (la voiture)
parking disk le disque de stationnement
parking meter le parcmètre
parking ticket le p.-v.
part: *spare parts* les pièces de rechange
partner *(business)* l'associé(e) *(m/f)* *(boy/girlfriend)* le compagnon/la compagne
party *(group)* le groupe *(celebration)* la fête ; la soirée *(political)* le parti
pass *(bus, train)* la carte *(mountain)* le col
passenger le passager/la passagère
passport le passeport
passport control le contrôle des passeports
password le mot de passe
pasta les pâtes *(fpl)*
pastry la pâte *(cake)* la pâtisserie
path le chemin
patient *(in hospital)* le/la patient(e)
pavement le trottoir
to pay payer
  I'd like to pay je voudrais payer
  where do I pay? où est-ce qu'il faut payer?
payment le paiement
payphone le téléphone public
peace *(after war)* la paix
peach la pêche
peak rate le plein tarif
peanut allergy l'allergie aux cacahuètes *(f)*
pear la poire

peas les petits pois *(mpl)*
pedal la pédale
pedalo le pédalo®
pedestrian le/la piéton(ne)
pedestrian crossing le passage clouté
to pee faire pipi
to peel *(fruit)* peler
peg *(for clothes)* la pince à linge *(for tent)* le piquet
pen le stylo
pencil le crayon
penfriend le/la correspondant(e)
penicillin la pénicilline
penis le pénis
penknife le canif
pensioner le/la retraité(e)
people les gens *(mpl)*
pepper *(spice)* le poivre *(vegetable)* le poivron
per par
  per day par jour
  per hour à l'heure
  per person par personne
  per week par semaine
  100 km per hour 100 km à l'heure
perfect parfait(e)
performance *(show)* le spectacle
perfume le parfum
perhaps peut-être
period *(menstruation)* les règles *(fpl)*
perm la permanente
permit le permis
person la personne
personal organizer l'agenda *(m)*
personal stereo le baladeur
pet l'animal domestique *(m)*
pet food les aliments pour animaux *(mpl)*
pet shop la boutique d'animaux
petrol l'essence *(f)*
  4-star le super
  unleaded l'essence sans plomb
petrol cap le bouchon de réservoir
petrol pump la pompe à essence
petrol station la station-service
petrol tank le réservoir

pharmacy la pharmacie
phone le téléphone
  by phone par téléphone
  mobile le portable
to phone téléphoner
phonebook l'annuaire *(m)*
phonebox la cabine (téléphonique)
phone call l'appel *(m)*
phonecard la télécarte
photocopy la photocopie
to photocopy photocopier
photograph la photo
  to take a photograph prendre une
  photo
phrase book le guide de
  conversation
piano le piano
to pick *(choose)* choisir
  (pluck) cueillir
pickpocket le pickpocket
picnic le pique-nique
  to have a picnic pique-niquer
picnic hamper le panier à
  pique-nique
picnic rug la couverture
picture *(painting)* le tableau
  (photo) la photo
pie *(savoury)* la tourte
piece le morceau
pier la jetée
pig le cochon
pill la pilule
  I'm on the pill je prends la pilule
pillow l'oreiller *(m)*
pillowcase la taie d'oreiller
pilot le pilote
pin l'épingle *(f)*
pineapple l'ananas *(m)*
pink rose
pint: *a pint of...* un demi-litre de...
pipe *(for water, gas)* le tuyau
  (smoking) la pipe
pity: *what a pity* quel dommage
pizza la pizza
place l'endroit *(m)*
place of birth le lieu de naissance
plain *(unflavoured)* ordinaire ; nature

plait la natte
to plan prévoir
plan *(map)* le plan
plane *(aircraft)* l'avion *(m)*
plant *(in garden)* la plante
plaster *(sticking plaster)* le sparadrap
  (for broken limb, on wall) le plâtre
plastic *(made of)* en plastique
plastic bag le sac en plastique
plate l'assiette *(f)*
platform *(railway)* le quai
  which platform? quel quai?
play *(at theatre)* la pièce
to play *(games)* jouer
playpark l'aire de jeux *(f)*
playroom la salle de jeux
pleasant agréable
please s'il vous plaît
pleased content(e)
  pleased to meet you! enchanté(e)!
plenty of beaucoup de
pliers la pince
plug *(electrical)* la prise
  (for sink) la bonde
to plug in brancher
plum la prune
plumber le plombier
plumbing la tuyauterie
plunger *(to clear sink)* le débouchoir
  à ventouse
p.m. de l'après-midi
poached poché(e)
pocket la poche
points *(in car)* les vis platinées
poison le poison
poisonous vénéneux
police *(force)* la police
policeman le policier
  (police woman) la femme policier
police station le commissariat ;
  la gendarmerie
polish *(for shoes)* le cirage
pollen le pollen
polluted pollué(e)
pony-trekking la randonnée à cheval
pool *(swimming)* la piscine

pool attendant le/la surveillant(e) de baignade
poor pauvre
popcorn le pop-corn
pop socks les mi-bas *(mpl)*
popular populaire
pork le porc
port *(seaport)* le port
  (wine) le porto
porter *(for luggage)* le porteur
portion la portion
Portugal le Portugal
possible possible
post *(letters)* le courrier
  by post par courrier
to post poster
postbox la boîte aux lettres
postcard la carte postale
postcode le code postal
poster l'affiche *(f)*
postman/woman le facteur/ la factrice
post office la poste
to postpone remettre à plus tard
pot *(for cooking)* la casserole
potato la pomme de terre
  baked potato la pomme de terre cuite au four
  boiled potatoes les pommes vapeur
  fried potatoes les pommes de terres sautées
  mashed potatoes la purée
  roast potatoes les pommes de terre rôties
  potato salad la salade de pommes de terre
pothole le nid de poule
pottery la poterie
pound *(money)* la livre
to pour verser
powder la poudre
powdered milk le lait en poudre
power *(electricity)* le courant
power cut la coupure de courant
pram le landau
to pray prier
to prefer préférer

pregnant enceinte
  I'm pregnant je suis enceinte
to prepare préparer
to prescribe prescrire
prescription l'ordonnance *(f)*
present *(gift)* le cadeau
preservative le conservateur
president le président
pressure la pression
  tyre pressure la pression des pneus
pretty joli(e)
price le prix
price list le tarif
priest le prêtre
print *(photo)* la photo
printer l'imprimante *(f)*
prison la prison
private privé(e)
prize le prix
probably probablement
problem le problème
professor le professeur d'université
programme *(TV, etc)* l'émission *(f)*
prohibited interdit(e)
promise la promesse
to promise promettre
to pronounce prononcer
  how's it pronounced? comment ça se prononce?
Protestant protestant(e)
to provide fournir
public public(-ique)
public holiday le jour férié
pudding le dessert
to pull tirer
  to pull a muscle se faire une élongation
to pull over *(car)* s'arrêter
pullover le pull
pump la pompe
puncture la crevaison
puncture repair kit la boîte de rustines®
puppet la marionnette
puppet show le spectacle de marionnettes

purple violet(-ette)
purpose le but
  on purpose exprès
purse le porte-monnaie
to push pousser
pushchair la poussette
to put *(place)* mettre
pyjamas le pyjama
Pyrenees les Pyrénées

Q

quality la qualité
quantity la quantité
quarantine la quarantaine
to quarrel se disputer
quarter le quart
quay le quai
queen la reine
query la question
question la question
queue la queue
to queue faire la queue
quick rapide
quickly vite
quiet *(place)* tranquille
quilt la couette
quite *(rather)* assez
  (completely) complètement
  quite good pas mal
  it's quite expensive c'est assez cher
quiz le jeu-concours

R

rabbit le lapin
rabies la rage
race *(people)* la race
  (sport) la course
race course le champ de courses
racket la raquette
radiator le radiateur
radio la radio
  digital la radio numérique
  car l'autoradio *(m)*
radish le radis
railcard la carte d'abonnement (de chemin de fer)

railway le chemin de fer
railway station la gare
rain la pluie
to rain: *it's raining* il pleut
raincoat l'imperméable *(m)*
rake le râteau
rape le viol
to rape violer
raped: *to be raped* être violé(e)
rare *(uncommon)* rare
  (steak) saignant(e)
rash *(skin)* la rougeur
raspberry la framboise
rat le rat
rate *(price)* le tarif
rate of exchange le taux de change
raw cru(e)
razor le rasoir
razor blades les lames de rasoir *(fpl)*
to read lire
ready prêt(e)
real vrai(e)
to realize (that ...) se rendre compte (que ...)
rearview mirror le rétroviseur
receipt le reçu
receiver *(of phone)* le récepteur
reception *(desk)* la réception
receptionist le/la réceptionniste
to recharge *(battery, etc)* recharger
  recharger le rechargeur
recipe la recette
to recognize reconnaître
to recommend recommander
to record enregistrer
to recover *(from illness)* se remettre
to recycle recycler
red rouge
to reduce réduire
reduction la réduction
to refer to parler de
refill la recharge
to refund rembourser
to refuse refuser
regarding concernant
region la région

register le registre
to register (at hotel) se présenter
registered (letter) recommandé(e)
registration form la fiche
to reimburse rembourser
relation (family) le/la parent(e)
relationship les rapports (mpl)
to remain rester
remember se rappeler
    I don't remember je ne m'en
    rappelle pas
remote control la télécommande
removal firm les déménageurs (mpl)
to remove enlever
rent le loyer
to rent louer
rental la location
repair la réparation
to repair réparer
to repeat répéter
to reply répondre
report (of theft, etc) la déclaration
to report (theft, etc) déclarer
request la demande
to request demander
to require avoir besoin de
to rescue sauver
reservation la réservation
to reserve réserver
reserved réservé(e)
resident l'habitant(e) (m/f)
resort (seaside) la station balnéaire
    ski resort la station de ski
rest (relaxation) le repos
    (remainder) le reste
to rest se reposer
restaurant le restaurant
restaurant car le wagon-restaurant
retired retraité(e)
to return (to a place) retourner
    (to return something) rendre
return ticket le billet aller retour
to reverse faire marche arrière
to reverse the charges appeler
    en PCV
reverse-charge call l'appel en PCV (m)

reverse gear la marche arrière
rheumatism le rhumatisme
rib la côte
ribbon le ruban
rice le riz
rich (person, food) riche
to ride (horse) faire du cheval
right (correct) exact(e)
right la droite
    on/to the right à droite
right of way la priorité
ring (on finger) la bague
to ring (bell) sonner
    it's ringing (phone) ça sonne
    to ring sb (phone) téléphoner à
    quelqu'un
ring road le périphérique
ripe mûr(e)
river la rivière
Riviera (French) la Côte d'Azur
road la route
road map la carte routière
road sign le panneau
roadworks les travaux (mpl)
roast rôti(e)
roll (bread) le petit pain
roller blades les rollers (mpl)
romantic romantique
roof le toit
roof-rack la galerie
room (in house) la pièce
    (in hotel) la chambre
    (space) la place
    double room la chambre pour deux
    personnes
    family room la chambre pour une
    famille
    single room la chambre pour une
    personne
room number le numéro de
    chambre
room service le service des
    chambres
rope la corde
rose la rose
rosé wine le rosé
rotten (fruit, etc) pourri(e)

rough: *rough sea* la mer agitée
round rond(e)
roundabout *(traffic)* le rond-point
route la route ; l'itinéraire *(m)*
row *(theatre, etc)* la rangée
rowing *(sport)* l'aviron *(m)*
rowing boat la barque
rubber *(material)* le caoutchouc
    (eraser) la gomme
rubber band l'élastique *(m)*
rubber gloves les gants en
    caoutchouc *(mpl)*
rubbish les ordures *(fpl)*
rubella la rubéole
rucksack le sac à dos
rug *(carpet)* le tapis
ruler *(for measuring)* la règle
to run courir
rush hour l'heure de pointe *(f)*
rusty rouillé(e)

S

sad triste
saddle la selle
safe *(for valuables)* le coffre-fort
safe sûr ; sans danger
    is it safe? ce n'est pas dangereux?
safety belt la ceinture de sécurité
safety pin l'épingle de sûreté *(f)*
sail la voile
sailboard la planche à voile
sailing *(sport)* la voile
sailing boat le voilier
saint le/la saint(e)
salad la salade
    green salad la salade verte
    mixed salad la salade composée
    potato salad la salade
    de pommes de terre
    tomato salad la salade
    de tomates
salad dressing la vinaigrette
salami le salami
salary le salaire
sale la vente
sales *(reductions)* les soldes *(mpl)*

salesman/woman le vendeur/
    la vendeuse
sales rep le/la représentant(e)
salt le sel
salt water l'eau salée *(f)*
salty salé(e)
same même
sample l'échantillon *(m)*
sand le sable
sandals les sandales *(fpl)*
sandwich le sandwich
    toasted sandwich
    le croque-monsieur
sanitary towel la serviette
    hygiénique
satellite dish l'antenne parabolique *(f)*
satellite TV la télévision par satellite
Saturday samedi
sauce la sauce
saucepan la casserole
saucer la soucoupe
sauna le sauna
sausage la saucisse
to save *(life)* sauver
    (money) épargner ; économiser
savoury salé(e)
saw la scie
to say dire
scales *(for weighing)* la balance
to scan scanner
    scan le scanner
    scanner le scanner
scarf *(headscarf)* le foulard
    (woollen) l'écharpe *(f)*
scenery le paysage
schedule le programme
school l'école *(f)*
    primary school l'école primaire
    secondary school (11-15) le collège
    (15-18) le lycée
scissors les ciseaux *(mpl)*
score *(of match)* le score
to score *(goal, point)* marquer
Scot l'Écossais(e) *(m/f)*
Scotland l'Écosse *(f)*
Scottish écossais(e)
scouring pad le tampon à récurer

screen l'écran (m)
screenwash le lave-glace
screw la vis
screwdriver le tournevis
  phillips screwdriver® le tournevis cruciforme
scuba diving la plongée sous-marine
sculpture la sculpture
sea la mer
seafood les fruits de mer (mpl)
seam (of dress) la couture
to search fouiller
seasickness le mal de mer
seaside le bord de la mer
  at the seaside au bord de la mer
season (of year, holiday time) la saison
  in season de saison
seasonal saisonnier
season ticket la carte d'abonnement
seat (chair) le siège
  (in train) la place
  (cinema, theatre) le fauteuil
seatbelt la ceinture de sécurité
second second(e)
second (time) la seconde
second class seconde classe
second-hand d'occasion
secretary le/la secrétaire
security guard le/la vigile
sedative le calmant
to see voir
to seize saisir
self-catering flat l'appartement indépendant (avec cuisine)
self-employed: to be self employed travailler à son compte
self-service le libre-service
to sell vendre
  do you sell...? vous vendez...?
sell-by date la date limite de vente
Sellotape® le Scotch®
to send envoyer
senior citizen le/la senior
sensible raisonnable
separated séparé(e)
separately: to pay separately payer séparément

September septembre
serious grave
to serve servir
service (church) l'office (m)
  (in restaurant, shop, etc) le service
  is service included? le service est compris?
service charge le service
service station la station-service
set menu le menu à prix fixe
settee le canapé
several plusieurs
to sew coudre
sex le sexe
shade l'ombre (f)
  in the shade à l'ombre
to shake (bottle, etc) agiter
shallow peu profond(e)
shampoo le shampooing
shampoo and set le shampooing et la mise en plis
to share partager
sharp (razor, knife) tranchant
to shave se raser
shaving cream la crème à raser
shawl le châle
she elle
sheep le mouton
sheet (for bed) le drap
shelf le rayon
shell (seashell) le coquillage
sheltered abrité(e)
to shine briller
shingles (illness) le zona
ship le navire
shirt la chemise
shock le choc
shock absorber l'amortisseur (m)
shoe la chaussure
shoelaces les lacets (mpl)
shoe polish le cirage
shoeshop le magasin de chaussures
shop le magasin
to shop faire du shopping
shop assistant le vendeur/la vendeuse

shop window la vitrine
shopping centre le centre commercial
shore le rivage
short court(e)
shortage le manque
short circuit le court-circuit
short cut le raccourci
shortly bientôt
shorts le short
short-sighted myope
shoulder l'épaule (f)
to shout crier
show le spectacle
to show montrer
shower (wash) la douche
  to take a shower prendre une douche
shower cap le bonnet de douche
shower gel le gel douche
to shrink (clothes) rétrécir
shut (closed) fermé(e)
to shut fermer
shutter (on window) le volet
shuttle service la navette
sick (ill) malade
  I feel sick j'ai envie de vomir
side le côté
side dish la garniture
sidelight le feu de position
sidewalk le trottoir
sieve la passoire
sightseeing le tourisme
  to go sightseeing faire du tourisme
sightseeing tour l'excursion touristique (f)
sign (notice) le panneau
to sign signer
signature la signature
signpost le poteau indicateur
silk la soie
silver l'argent (m)
similar (to) semblable (à)
since depuis
to sing chanter
single (unmarried) célibataire
  (bed, room) pour une personne

single ticket l'aller simple (m)
sink (washbasin) l'évier (m)
sir Monsieur
sister la sœur
sister-in-law la belle-sœur
to sit s'asseoir
  sit down! asseyez-vous!
size (clothes) la taille
  (shoe) la pointure
skates (ice) les patins à glace (mpl)
  roller les patins à roulettes (mpl)
to skate (on ice) patiner
  (roller) faire du patin à roulettes
skateboard le skate-board
  to go skateboarding faire du skate-board
ski le ski
to ski faire du ski
ski boots les chaussures de ski (fpl)
ski instructor le/la moniteur (-trice) de ski
ski jump (place) le tremplin de ski
ski lift le remonte-pente
ski pants le fuseau
ski pass le forfait
ski pole le bâton (de ski)
ski run la piste
ski suit la combinaison de ski
ski tow le remonte-pente
skilled adroit(e) ; qualifié(e)
skin la peau
skirt la jupe
sky le ciel
slate l'ardoise (f)
sledge la luge
to sleep dormir
sleeper la couchette
  (carriage) la voiture-lit
  (train) le train-couchettes
to sleep in faire la grasse matinée
sleeping bag le sac de couchage
sleeping car la voiture-lit
sleeping pill le somnifère
slice (bread, cake, etc) la tranche
sliced bread le pain de mie en tranches
slide (photograph) la diapositive

to slip glisser
slippers les pantoufles *(fpl)*
slow lent(e)
to slow down ralentir
slowly lentement
small petit(e)
  smaller than plus petit(e) que
smell l'odeur *(f)*
  a bad smell une mauvaise odeur
smile le sourire
to smile sourire
smoke la fumée
to smoke fumer
  I don't smoke je ne fume pas
  can I smoke? on peut fumer?
smoke alarm le détecteur de fumée
smoked fumé(e)
smokers *(sign)* fumeurs
smooth lisse
snack le casse-croûte
  to have a snack casser la croûte
snack bar le snack-bar
snail l'escargot *(m)*
snake le serpent
snake bite la morsure de serpent
to sneeze éternuer
snorkel le tuba
snow la neige
to snow: *it's snowing* il neige
snowboard le snowboard
snowboarding le surf des neiges
  to go snowboarding faire du
  snowboard
snow chains les chaînes *(fpl)*
snowed up enneigé(e)
snow tyres les pneus cloutés *(mpl)*
soap le savon
soap powder *(detergent)* la lessive
sober: *to be sober* ne pas avoir bu
socket *(for plug)* la prise de courant
socks les chaussettes *(fpl)*
soda water l'eau de Seltz *(f)*
sofa le canapé
sofa bed le canapé-lit
soft doux (douce)
soft drink le soda

software le logiciel
soldier le soldat
sole *(shoe)* la semelle
soluble soluble
some de (du/de la/des)
someone quelqu'un
something quelque chose
sometimes quelquefois
son le fils
son-in-law le gendre
song la chanson
soon bientôt
  as soon as possible dès que
  possible
sore douloureux(-euse)
sore throat: *to have a sore throat*
  avoir mal à la gorge
sorry: *I'm sorry!* excusez-moi!
sort la sorte
  what sort de quelle sorte?
soup le potage ; la soupe
sour aigre
soured cream la crème fermentée
south le sud
souvenir le souvenir
spa la station thermale
space la place
spade la pelle
Spain l'Espagne *(f)*
Spanish espagnol(e)
spanner la clé plate
spare parts les pièces de
  rechange *(fpl)*
spare room la chambre d'amis
spare tyre le pneu de rechange
spare wheel la roue de secours
sparkling *(wine)* mousseux(-euse)
  (water) gazeux(-euse)
spark plug la bougie
to speak parler
  do you speak English? vous parlez
  anglais?
special spécial(e)
specialist *(medical)* le/la spécialiste
speciality la spécialité
speeding l'excès de vitesse *(m)*

a speeding ticket un p.-v. pour excès de vitesse
speed limit la limitation de vitesse
  to exceed the speed limit dépasser la vitesse permise
speedboat le hors-bord
speedometer le compteur
to spell: *how is it spelt?* comment ça s'écrit?
to spend *(money)* dépenser
  (time) passer
spice l'épice *(f)*
spicy épicé(e)
spider l'araignée *(f)*
to spill renverser
spinach les épinards *(mpl)*
spine la colonne vertébrale
spin dryer le sèche-linge
spirits *(alcohol)* les spiritueux *(mpl)*
splinter *(in finger)* l'écharde *(f)*
spoke *(of wheel)* le rayon
sponge l'éponge *(f)*
spoon la cuiller
sport le sport
sports centre le centre sportif
sports shop le magasin de sports
spot *(pimple)* le bouton
sprain l'entorse *(f)*
spring *(season)* le printemps
  (metal) le ressort
spring onion la ciboule
square *(in town)* la place
squeeze presser
squid le calmar
stadium le stade
stage la scène
staff le personnel
stain la tache
stained glass window le vitrail
stairs l'escalier *(m)*
stale *(bread)* rassis(e)
stalls *(in theatre)* l'orchestre *(m)*
stamp le timbre
to stand *(get up)* se lever
  (be standing) être debout
star l'étoile *(f)* *(celebrity)* la vedette

to start commencer
starter *(in meal)* le hors d'œuvre
  (in car) le démarreur
station la gare
stationer's la papeterie
statue la statue
stay le séjour
  enjoy your stay! bon séjour!
to stay *(remain)* rester
  (reside for while) loger
  I'm staying at... je loge à...
steak le bifteck
to steal voler
steam la vapeur
steamed cuit(e) à la vapeur
steel l'acier *(m)*
steep raide
steeple le clocher
steering wheel le volant
step le pas
stepdaughter la belle-fille
stepfather le beau-père
stepmother la belle-mère
stepson le beau-fils
stereo la chaîne (stéréo)
sterling la livre sterling
steward le steward
stewardess l'hôtesse *(f)*
sticking-plaster le sparadrap
still: *still water* l'eau plate *(f)*
still *(yet)* encore
sting la piqûre
to sting piquer
stitches *(surgical)* les points de suture *(mpl)*
stockings les bas *(mpl)*
stolen volé(e)
stomach l'estomac *(m)*
stomach ache: *to have a stomach ache* avoir mal au ventre
stomach upset l'estomac dérangé
stone la pierre
to stop arrêter
store *(shop)* le magasin
storey l'étage *(m)*
storm l'orage *(m)*

story l'histoire *(f)*
straightaway tout de suite
straight on tout droit
strange bizarre
straw *(for drinking)* la paille
strawberries les fraises *(fpl)*
stream le ruisseau
street la rue
street map le plan des rues
strength la force
stress le stress
strike *(of workers)* la grève
string la ficelle
striped rayé(e)
stroke *(haemorrhage)* l'attaque
(d'apoplexie)
to have a stroke avoir une attaque
strong fort(e)
stuck bloqué(e)
student *(male)* l'étudiant
(female) l'étudiante
student discount le tarif étudiant
stuffed farci(e)
stung piqué(e)
stupid stupide
subscription l'abonnement *(m)*
subtitles les sous-titres *(mpl)*
subway le passage souterrain
suddenly soudain
suede le daim
sugar le sucre
sugar-free sans sucre
to suggest suggérer
suit *(man's)* le costume
(woman's) le tailleur
suitcase la valise
sum la somme
summer l'été *(m)*
summer holidays les vacances
d'été *(fpl)*
summit le sommet
sun le soleil
to sunbathe prendre un bain
de soleil
sunblock l'écran total *(m)*
sunburn le coup de soleil

Sunday le dimanche
sunflower le tournesol
sunglasses les lunettes de soleil *(fpl)*
sunny: *it's sunny* il fait beau
sunrise le lever du soleil
sunroof le toit ouvrant
sunscreen *(lotion)* l'écran solaire *(m)*
sunset le coucher de soleil
sunshade le parasol
sunstroke l'insolation *(f)*
suntan le bronzage
suntan lotion le lait solaire
supermarket le supermarché
supper *(dinner)* le souper
supplement le supplément
to supply fournir
to surf faire du surf
to surf the net surfer sur Internet
surfboard la planche de surf
surfing le surf
surgery *(operation)* l'opération
chirurgicale *(f)*
surname le nom de famille
surprise la surprise
to survive survivre
to swallow avaler
to sweat transpirer
sweater le pull
sweatshirt le sweat-shirt
sweet sucré(e)
sweetener l'édulcorant *(m)*
sweets les bonbons *(mpl)*
to swell enfler
to swim nager
swimming pool la piscine
swimsuit le maillot de bain
swing *(for children)* la balançoire
Swiss suisse
switch le bouton
to switch off éteindre
to switch on allumer
Switzerland la Suisse
swollen enflé(e)
synagogue la synagogue
syringe la seringue

T

table la table
tablecloth la nappe
table tennis le tennis de table
table wine le vin de table
tablet le comprimé
to take *(something)* prendre
to take away *(something)* emporter
to take off *(clothes)* enlever
  (plane) décoller
talc le talc
to talk (to) parler (à)
tall grand(e)
tampons les tampons
  hygiéniques *(mpl)*
tangerine la mandarine
tank *(petrol)* le réservoir
  (fish) l'aquarium *(m)*
tap le robinet
tap water l'eau du robinet *(f)*
tape le ruban *(cassette)* la cassette
  adhesive tape le Scotch®
  video tape la cassette vidéo
tape measure le mètre à ruban
tape recorder le magnétophone
tart la tarte
taste le goût
to taste goûter
  can I taste some? je peux goûter?
tax l'impôt *(m)*
taxi le taxi
taxi driver le chauffeur de taxi
taxi rank la station de taxis
tea le thé
  herbal tea la tisane
  lemon tea le thé au citron
  tea with milk le thé au lait
teabag le sachet de thé
teapot la théière
teaspoon la cuiller à café
tea towel le torchon
to teach enseigner
teacher le professeur
team l'équipe *(f)*
tear *(in material)* la déchirure
teat *(on bottle)* la tétine

teenager l'adolescent(e) *(m/f)*
teeth les dents *(fpl)*
telegram le télégramme
telephone le téléphone
to telephone téléphoner
telephone box la cabine
  téléphonique
telephone call le coup de téléphone
telephone card la télécarte
telephone directory l'annuaire *(m)*
telephone number le numéro de
  téléphone
television la télévision
to tell dire
temperature la température
  to have a temperature avoir de la
  fièvre
temporary temporaire
tenant le/la locataire
tendon le tendon
tennis le tennis
tennis ball la balle de tennis
tennis court le court de tennis
tennis racket la raquette de tennis
tent la tente
tent peg le piquet de tente
terminal *(airport)* l'aérogare *(f)*
terrace la terrasse
terracotta la terre cuite
to test *(try out)* tester
testicles les testicules *(fpl)*
tetanus injection la piqûre
  antitétanique
to text envoyer un message SMS
text message le message SMS
than que
to thank remercier
thank you merci
  thank you very much merci
  beaucoup
that cela
  that one celui-là/celle-là
the le/la/l'/les
theatre le théâtre
theft le vol
their *(sing)* leur
  (plural) leurs

140

them eux
there là
there is/are... il y a...
thermometer le thermomètre
these ces
  these ones ceux-ci/celles-ci
they ils/elles
thick *(not thin)* épais(se)
thief le voleur/la voleuse
thigh la cuisse
thin *(person)* mince
thing la chose
  my things mes affaires
to think penser
thirsty: *I'm thirsty* j'ai soif
this ceci
  this one celui-ci/celle-ci
thorn l'épine *(f)*
those ces
  those ones ceux-là/celles-là
thread le fil
throat la gorge
throat lozenges les pastilles pour
  la gorge *(fpl)*
through à travers
thumb le pouce
thunder le tonnerre
thunderstorm l'orage *(m)*
Thursday jeudi
thyme le thym
ticket le billet ; le ticket
  a single ticket un aller simple
  a return ticket un aller-retour
  book of tickets le carnet de tickets
ticket inspector le contrôleur/la
  contrôleuse
ticket office le guichet
tide la marée
  low tide la marée basse
  high tide la marée haute
tidy bien rangé(e)
to tidy up tout ranger
tie la cravate
tight *(fitting)* serré(e)
tights le collant
tile *(on roof)* la tuile
  (on wall, floor) le carreau

till *(cash desk)* la caisse
till *(until)* jusqu'à
  till 2 o'clock jusqu'à deux heures
time le temps *(of day)* l'heure *(f)*
  this time cette fois
  what time is it? quelle heure est-il?
timer le minuteur
timetable l'horaire *(m)*
tin *(can)* la boîte
tinfoil le papier alu(minium)
tin-opener l'ouvre-boîtes *(m)*
tip *(to waiter, etc)* le pourboire
to tip *(waiter, etc)* donner un
  pourboire à
tipped *(cigarette)* à bout filtre
tired fatigué(e)
tissue *(hanky)* le kleenex®
to à *(with name of country)* en/au
  to London à Londres
  to the airport à l'aéroport
  to France en France
  to Canada au Canada
toadstool le champignon vénéneux
toast *(to eat)* le pain grillé ; le toast
tobacco le tabac
tobacconist's le bureau de tabac
today aujourd'hui
toddler l'enfant en bas âge *(m)*
toe le doigt de pied
together ensemble
toilet les toilettes *(fpl)*
  toilet for disabled les toilettes pour
  handicapés
toilet brush la brosse pour les WC
toilet paper le papier hygiénique
toiletries les articles de toilette *(mpl)*
token le jeton
toll *(motorway)* le péage
tomato la tomate
  tomato sauce le ketchup®
  tomato soup la soupe
  de tomates
  tinned tomatoes les tomates en
  boîte
tomorrow demain
  tomorrow morning demain matin
  tomorrow afternoon demain après-
  midi

tomorrow evening demain soir
tongue la langue
tonic water le tonic
tonight ce soir
tonsillitis l'angine (f)
too (also) aussi
  it's too big c'est trop grand
  it's too hot il fait trop chaud
  it's too noisy il y a trop de bruit
toolkit la trousse à outils
tools les outils (mpl)
tooth la dent
toothache le mal de dents
  I have toothache j'ai mal aux dents
toothbrush la brosse à dents
toothpaste le dentifrice
toothpick le cure-dent
top: *the top floor* le dernier étage
top (of bottle) le bouchon
  (of pen) le capuchon
  (of pyjamas, bikini) le haut
  (of hill, mountain) le sommet
  on top of sur
topless: *to go topless* enlever
  le haut
torch la lampe de poche
torn déchiré(e)
total (amount) le total
to touch toucher
tough (meat) dur(e)
tour l'excursion (f)
  guided tour la visite guidée
tour guide le/la guide
tour operator le tour-opérateur ;
  le voyagiste
tourist le/la touriste
tourist (information) office
  le syndicat d'initiative
tourist route l'itinéraire
  touristique (m)
tourist ticket le billet touristique
to tow remorquer
towbar (on car) le crochet d'attelage
tow rope le câble de remorquage
towel la serviette
tower la tour
town la ville

town centre le centre-ville
town hall la mairie
town plan le plan de la ville
toxic toxique
toy le jouet
toyshop le magasin de jouets
tracksuit le survêtement
traditional traditionnel(-elle)
traffic la circulation
traffic jam l'embouteillage (m)
traffic lights les feux (mpl)
traffic warden le/la contractuel(le)
trailer la remorque
train le train
  by train par le train
  the next train le prochain train
  the first train le premier train
  the last train le dernier train
trainers les baskets (fpl)
tram le tramway
tranquillizer le tranquillisant
to translate traduire
translation la traduction
to travel voyager
travel agent's l'agence de voyages (f)
travel guide le guide
travel insurance l'assurance
  voyage (f)
travel pass la carte de transport
travel sickness le mal des transports
traveller's cheques les chèques
  de voyage
tray le plateau
tree l'arbre (m)
trip l'excursion (f)
trolley le chariot
trouble les ennuis (mpl)
  to be in trouble avoir des ennuis
trousers le pantalon
truck le camion
true vrai(e)
trunk (luggage) la malle
trunks (swimming) le maillot (de bain)
to try essayer
to try on (clothes, etc) essayer
t-shirt le tee-shirt

Tuesday mardi
tumble dryer le sèche-linge
tunnel le tunnel
to turn tourner
  to turn round faire demi-tour
to turn off *(light, etc)* éteindre
  (engine) couper le moteur
to turn on *(light, etc)* allumer
  (engine) mettre en marche
turnip le navet
turquoise *(colour)* turquoise
tweezers la pince à épiler
twice deux fois
twin-bedded room la chambre
  à deux lits
twins *(male)* les jumeaux
  (female) les jumelles
to type taper à la machine
typical typique
tyre le pneu
tyre pressure la pression des pneus

U

ugly laid(e)
ulcer l'ulcère *(m)*
  mouth ulcer l'aphte *(m)*
umbrella le parapluie
  (sunshade) le parasol
uncle l'oncle *(m)*
uncomfortable inconfortable
unconscious sans connaissance
under sous
undercooked pas assez cuit(e)
underground le métro
underpants *(man's)* le caleçon
underpass le passage souterrain
to understand comprendre
  I don't understand je ne
  comprends pas
  do you understand? vous
  comprenez?
underwear les sous-vêtements *(mpl)*
to undress se déshabiller
unemployed au chômage
to unfasten *(seatbelt)* détacher
United Kingdom le Royaume-Uni

United States les États-Unis *(mpl)*
university l'université *(f)*
unkind pas gentil(-ille)
unleaded petrol l'essence sans
  plomb *(f)*
unlikely peu probable
to unlock ouvrir
to unpack *(suitcase)* défaire
unpleasant désagréable
to unplug débrancher
to unscrew dévisser
up: *to get up* *(out of bed)* se lever
upside down à l'envers
upstairs en haut
urgent urgent(e)
urine l'urine *(f)*
us nous
to use utiliser
useful utile
usual habituel(-elle)
usually d'habitude
U-turn le demi-tour

V

vacancy *(in hotel)* la chambre
vacant libre
vacation les vacances *(fpl)*
vaccination le vaccin
vacuum cleaner l'aspirateur *(m)*
vagina le vagin
valid *(ticket, driving licence, etc)* valable
valley la vallée
valuable d'une grande valeur
valuables les objets de valeur *(mpl)*
value la valeur
valve la soupape
van la camionnette
vase le vase
VAT la TVA
vegan végétalien(ne)
  I'm a vegan je suis végétalien(ne)
vegetables les légumes *(mpl)*
vegetarian végétarien(ne)
  I'm vegetarian je suis
  végétarien(ne)
vehicle le véhicule

vein la veine
velvet le velours
vending machine le distributeur automatique
venereal disease la maladie vénérienne
ventilator le ventilateur
very très
vest le maillot de corps
vet le/la vétérinaire
via par
to video (from TV) enregistrer
video (machine) le magnétoscope (cassette) la (cassette) vidéo
video camera la caméra vidéo
video cassette la cassette vidéo
video game le jeu vidéo
video recorder le magnétoscope
video tape la cassette vidéo
view la vue
villa la maison de campagne
village le village
vinegar le vinaigre
vineyard le vignoble
viper la vipère
virus le virus
visa le visa
visit le séjour
to visit visiter
visiting hours les heures de visite
visitor le/la visiteur(-euse)
vitamin la vitamine
voice la voix
volcano le volcan
volleyball le volley-ball
voltage le voltage
to vomit vomir
voucher le bon

W

wage le salaire
waist la taille
waistcoat le gilet
to wait for attendre
waiter le/la serveur(-euse)
waiting room la salle d'attente

waitress la serveuse
to wake up se réveiller
Wales le pays de Galles
walk la promenade
  to go for a walk faire une promenade
to walk aller à pied ; marcher
walking boots les chaussures de marche *(fpl)*
walking stick la canne
wall le mur
wallet le portefeuille
to want vouloir
  I want... je veux...
  we want... nous voulons...
war la guerre
ward (hospital) la salle
wardrobe l'armoire *(f)*
warehouse l'entrepôt *(m)*
warm chaud(e)
  it's warm (weather) il fait bon
  it's too warm il fait trop chaud
to warm up (milk, etc) faire chauffer
warning triangle le triangle de présignalisation
to wash laver
  to wash oneself se laver
washbasin le lavabo
washing machine la machine à laver
washing powder la lessive
washing-up bowl la cuvette
washing-up liquid le produit pour la vaisselle
wasp la guêpe
wasp sting la piqûre de guêpe
waste bin la poubelle
watch la montre
to watch (look at) regarder
watchstrap le bracelet de montre
water l'eau *(f)*
  bottled water l'eau en bouteille
  cold water l'eau froide
  drinking water (fit to drink) l'eau potable
  hot water l'eau chaude
  sparkling mineral water l'eau minérale gazeuse
  still mineral water l'eau minérale plate

waterfall la cascade
water heater le chauffe-eau
watermelon la pastèque
waterproof imperméable
water-skiing le ski nautique
water sports les sports nautiques (mpl)
waterwings les bracelets gonflables (mpl)
waves (on sea) les vagues (fpl)
waxing (hair removal) l'épilation à la cire (f)
way (manner) la manière (route) le chemin
way in (entrance) l'entrée (f)
way out (exit) la sortie
we nous
weak faible (coffee, etc) léger(-ère)
to wear porter
weather le temps
weather forecast la météo
web (internet) le Web
website le site web
wedding le mariage
wedding anniversary l'anniversaire de mariage (m)
wedding present le cadeau de mariage
Wednesday mercredi
week la semaine
last week la semaine dernière
next week la semaine prochaine
per week par semaine
this week cette semaine
weekday le jour de semaine
weekend le week-end
next weekend le week-end prochain
this weekend ce week-end
weekly par semaine ; hebdomadaire (pass, ticket) valable pendant une semaine
to weigh peser
weight le poids
welcome! bienvenu(e)!
well (for water) le puits
well (healthy) en bonne santé

I'm very well je vais très bien
he's not well il ne va pas bien
well done (steak) bien cuit(e)
wellingtons les bottes en caoutchouc (fpl)
Welsh gallois(e)
west l'ouest (m)
wet mouillé(e)
wetsuit la combinaison de plongée
what que ; quel/quelle ; quoi
what is it? qu'est-ce que c'est?
wheel la roue
wheelchair le fauteuil roulant
wheel clamp le sabot
when quand
(at what time?) à quelle heure?
when is it? c'est quand? ; à quelle heure?
where où
where is it? c'est où?
where is the hotel? où est l'hôtel?
which quel/quelle
which (one)? lequel/laquelle?
which (ones)? lesquels/lesquelles?
while pendant que
in a while bientôt ; tout à l'heure
white blanc (blanche)
who qui
who is it? qui c'est?
whole entier(-ière)
wholemeal bread le pain complet
whose: *whose is it?* c'est à qui?
why pourquoi
wide large
widow la veuve
widower le veuf
width la largeur
wife la femme
wig la perruque
to win gagner
wind le vent
windbreak (camping, etc) le pare-vent
windmill le moulin à vent
window la fenêtre (shop) la vitrine
windscreen le pare-brise
windscreen wipers les essuie-glaces (mpl)

windsurfing la planche à voile
  to go windsurfing faire de la planche à voile
windy: *it's windy* il y a du vent
wine le vin
  dry wine le vin sec
  house wine le vin en pichet
  red wine le vin rouge
  rosé wine le rosé
  sparkling wine le vin mousseux
  sweet wine le vin doux
  white wine le vin blanc
wine list la carte des vins
wing *(bird, aircraft)* l'aile *(f)*
wing mirror le rétroviseur latéral
winter l'hiver *(m)*
wire le fil
with avec
  with ice avec des glaçons
  with milk/sugar avec du lait/sucre
without sans
  without ice sans glaçons
  without milk/sugar sans lait/sucre
witness le témoin
woman la femme
wonderful merveilleux(-euse)
wood le bois
wooden en bois
wool la laine
word le mot
work le travail
to work *(person)* travailler
  (machine, car) fonctionner ; marcher
  it doesn't work ça ne marche pas
work permit le permis de travail
world le monde
worried inquiet(-iète)
worse pire
worth: *it's worth...* ça vaut...
to wrap (up) emballer
wrapping paper le papier d'emballage
wrinkles les rides *(fpl)*
wrist le poignet
to write écrire
  please write it down vous me l'écrivez, s'il vous plaît?

writing paper le papier à lettres
wrong faux (fausse)
wrought iron le fer forgé

X

X-ray la radiographie
to x-ray radiographier

Y

yacht le yacht
year l'an *(m)* ; l'année *(f)*
  this year cette année
  next year l'année prochaine
  last year l'année dernière
yearly annuel(le)
yellow jaune
Yellow Pages les pages jaunes
yes oui
  yes please oui, merci
yesterday hier
yet: *not yet* pas encore
yoghurt le yaourt
  plain yoghurt le yaourt nature
yolk le jaune d'œuf
you *(familiar)* tu
  (polite) vous
young jeune
your *(familiar sing)* ton/ta
  (familiar plural) tes
  (polite singular) votre
  (polite plural) vos
youth hostel l'auberge de jeunesse *(f)*

Z

zebra crossing le passage pour piétons
zero le zéro
zip la fermeture éclair
zone la zone
zoo le zoo
zoom lens le zoom
zucchini les courgettes *(fpl)*

A

à to ; at
abbaye f abbey
abcès m abscess
abeille f bee
abîmer to damage
abonné(e) m/f subscriber ; season ticket holder
abonnement m subscription ; season ticket
abri m shelter
abricot m apricot
abrité(e) sheltered
accélérateur m accelerator
accepter to accept
accès m access
  accès aux trains to the trains
  accès interdit no entry
  accès réservé authorized entry only
accident m accident
accompagner to accompany
accord m agreement
accotement m verge
accueil m reception ; information
accueillir to greet ; to welcome
ACF m Automobile Club de France
achat m purchase
acheter to buy
acier m steel
acte de naissance m birth certificate
activité f activity
adaptateur m adaptor (electrical)
addition f bill
adhérent(e) m/f member
adolescent(e) m/f teenager
adresse f address
  adresse électronique e-mail address
adresser to address
  adressez-vous à enquire at (office)
adroit(e) skilful
adulte m/f adult
aérogare f terminal
aéroglisseur m hovercraft
aéroport m airport

affaires fpl business ; belongings
  bonne affaire bargain
affiche f poster ; notice
affluence f crowd
affreux(-euse) awful
âge m age
  d'un certain âge middle-aged
  du troisième âge senior citizen
âgé(e) elderly
  âgé de ... ans aged ... years
agence f agency ; branch
  agence de voyages travel agency
  agence immobilière estate agent's
agenda m diary
  agenda électronique personal organizer
agent m agent
  agent de police police officer
agiter to shake
  agiter avant emploi shake before use
agneau m lamb
agrandissement m enlargement
agréable pleasant ; nice
agréé(e) registered ; authorized
agression f attack (mugging)
aider to help
aigre sour
aiguille f needle
ail m garlic
aimer to enjoy ; to love (person)
air: en plein air in the open air
aire: aire de jeux play area
  aire de repos rest area
  aire de service service area
  aire de stationnement layby
airelles fpl bilberries ; cranberries
alarme f alarm
alcool m alcohol ; fruit brandy
alcoolisé(e) alcoholic
alentours mpl surroundings
algues fpl seaweed
alimentation f food
allée f driveway ; path
allégé(e) low-fat
Allemagne f Germany
allemand(e) German
aller to go

aller (simple) m single ticket
aller retour m return ticket
allergie f allergy
allô? hello? (on telephone)
allumage m ignition
allumé(e) on (light)
allume-feu m fire lighter
allumer to turn on ; to light
   allumez vos phares switch
   on headlights
allumette f match
alpinisme m mountaineering
alsacien(ne) Alsatian
ambassade f embassy
ambulance f ambulance
améliorer to improve
amende f fine
amer(-ère) bitter
américain(e) American
Amérique f America
ameublement m furniture
ami(e) m/f friend
   petit(e) ami(e) boyfriend/
   girlfriend
amortisseur m shock absorber
amour m love
   faire l'amour to make love
ampoule f blister ; light bulb
amusant(e) funny (amusing)
amuser to entertain
   (bien) s'amuser to enjoy oneself
an m year
   Nouvel An New Year
analgésique m painkiller
ananas m pineapple
ancien(ne) old ; former
ancre f anchor
anesthésique m anaesthetic
ange m angel
angine f tonsillitis
   angine de poitrine angina
Anglais m Englishman
anglais m English (language)
anglais(e) English
Angleterre f England
animal m animal
   animal domestique pet

animations fpl entertainment ;
   activities
anis m aniseed
anisette f aniseed liqueur
année f year ; vintage
   bonne année! happy New Year!
anniversaire m anniversary ;
   birthday
annonce f advertisement
annuaire m directory
annulation f cancellation
annuler to cancel
antenne f aerial
   antenne parabolique satellite dish
anti-insecte m insect repellent
antibiotique m antibiotic
antigel m antifreeze
antihistaminique m antihistamine
antimoustique m mosquito repellent
antiquaire m/f antique dealer
antiquités fpl antiques
antiseptique m antiseptic
antivol m bike lock
août August
apéritif m apéritif
aphte m mouth ulcer
appareil m appliance ; camera
   appareil acoustique hearing aid
   appareil photo camera
   appareil photo numérique
   digital camera
appartement m apartment
appât m bait (for fishing)
appel m phone call
appeler to call (speak, phone)
   appeler en PCV to reverse
   the charges
appendicite f appendicitis
apporter to bring
apprendre to learn
appuyer to press
après after
après-midi m afternoon
après-rasage m after-shave
après-shampooing m conditioner
aquarium m fish tank
arachide f groundnut

araignée f **spider**

arbre m **tree**

arête f **fishbone**

argent m **money ; silver**
  argent de poche **pocket money**
  argent liquide **cash**

argot m **slang**

armoire f **wardrobe**

arranger **to arrange**

arrêt m **stop**
  arrêt d'autobus **bus stop**
  arrêt facultatif **request stop**

arrêter **to arrest ; to stop**
  arrêter le moteur **to turn off the engine**

arrêtez! **stop! stop it!**

arrhes fpl **deposit** (part payment)

arrière m **rear ; back**

arrivées fpl **arrivals**

arriver **to arrive ; to happen**

arrobase @

arrondissement m **district**

art m **art**

arthrite f **arthritis**

artichaut m **artichoke**

article m **item ; article**
  articles de toilette **toiletries**

articulation f **joint** (body)

artisan(e) m/f **craftsman/woman**

artisanat m **arts and crafts**

artiste m/f **artist**

ascenseur m **lift**

asperge f **asparagus**

aspirateur m **vacuum cleaner**

aspirine f **aspirin**

assaisonnement m **seasoning ; dressing**

asseoir **to sit (someone) down**
  s'asseoir **to sit down**

assez **enough ; quite** (rather)

assiette f **plate**

associé(e) m/f **partner** (business)

assorti(e) **assorted ; matching**

assurance f **insurance**

assuré(e) **insured**

assurer **to assure ; to insure**

asthme m **asthma**

atelier m **workshop ; artist's studio**

attacher **to fasten** (seatbelt)

attaque f **fit** (medical)
  attaque (d'apoplexie) **stroke**

attendre **to wait (for)**

attention! **look out!**
  attention au feu **danger of fire**
  faire attention **to be careful**

attestation f **certificate**
  l'attestation d'assurance **green card**

attrayant(e) **attractive**

au-delà de **beyond**

au-dessus de **above ; on top of**

au lieu de **instead of**

au revoir **goodbye**

au secours! **help!**

aube f **dawn**

auberge f **inn**
  auberge de jeunesse **youth hostel**

aubergine f **aubergine**

aucun(e) **none ; no ; not any**

audiophone m **hearing aid**

augmenter **to increase**

aujourd'hui **today**

aussi **also**

aussitôt **immediately**
  aussitôt que possible **as soon as possible**

Australie f **Australia**

australien(ne) **Australian**

autel m **altar**

auteur m **author**

auto-école f **driving school**

auto-stop m **hitch-hiking**

autobus m **bus**

autocar m **coach**

automatique **automatic**

automne m **autumn**

automobiliste m/f **motorist**

autoradio m **car radio**

autorisé(e) **permitted ; authorized**

autoroute f **motorway**

autre **other**
  autres directions **other routes**

avalanche f **avalanche**

avaler **to swallow**

ne pas avaler not to be taken internally
avance *f* advance
  à l'avance in advance
avant before ; front
  à l'avant at the front
  en avant forward
avec with
avenir *m* future
avenue *f* avenue
avertir to inform ; to warn
avion *m* aeroplane
aviron *m* oar ; rowing (sport)
avis *m* notice ; warning
aviser to advise
avocat *m* avocado ; lawyer
avoine *f* oats
avoir to have
avortement *m* abortion
avril April

B

bacon *m* bacon
bagages *mpl* luggage
  bagages à main hand luggage
  faire les bagages to pack
bague *f* ring (on finger)
baguette *f* stick of French bread
baie *f* bay (along coast)
baignade *f* bathing
  baignade interdite no bathing
baignoire *f* bath (tub)
bain *m* bath
  bain de bouche mouthwash
  bain moussant bubble bath
baiser *m* kiss
baisser to lower
bal *m* ball ; dance
balade *f* walk ; drive ; trek
balai *m* broom (brush)
  balai à franges mop
balance *f* weighing scales
balançoire *f* swing
balcon *m* circle (theatre) ; balcony
ball-trap *m* clay pigeon shooting
balle *f* ball (small: golf, tennis)
ballet *m* ballet

ballon *m* balloon ; ball (large) ; brandy glass
banane *f* banana ; bumbag
banc *m* seat ; bench
banlieue *f* suburbs
banque *f* bank
bar *m* bar
barbe *f* beard
  barbe à papa candy floss
barque *f* rowing boat
barrage *m* dam
  barrage routier road block
barré: *route barrée* road closed
barrer to cross out
barrière *f* barrier
bas *m* bottom (of page, etc) ; stocking
  en bas below ; downstairs
bas(se) low
baskets *fpl* trainers
bassin *m* pond ; washing-up bowl
bateau *m* boat ; ship
  bateau à rames row boat
  bateau-mouche river boat
bâtiment *m* building
bâton (de ski) *m* ski pole
batte *f* bat (baseball, cricket)
batterie *f* battery (for car)
  batterie à plat flat battery
baume pour les lèvres *m* lip salve
bavoir *m* bib (baby's)
beau (belle) lovely ; handsome ; beautiful ; nice (enjoyable)
beau-frère *m* brother-in-law
beau-père *m* father-in-law ; stepfather
beaucoup (de) much/many ; a lot of
bébé *m* baby
beignet *m* fritter ; doughnut
belge Belgian
Belgique *f* Belgium
belle-fille *f* daughter-in-law
belle-mère *f* mother-in-law ; step-mother
béquilles *fpl* crutches
berger *m* shepherd
berlingots *mpl* boiled sweets
besoin: *avoir besoin de* to need

beurre m butter
  beurre doux unsalted butter
biberon m baby's bottle
bibliothèque f library
bicyclette f bicycle
bien well ; right ; good
  bien cuit(e) well done (steak)
bientôt soon ; shortly
bienvenu(e) welcome!
bière f beer
  bière (à la) pression draught beer
  bière blonde lager
  bière bouteille bottled lager
  bière brune bitter
bifteck m steak
bijouterie f jeweller's ; jewellery
bijoux mpl jewellery
bikini m bikini
billet m note ; ticket
  billet aller-retour return ticket
  billet d'avion plane ticket
  billet de banque banknote
  billet simple one-way ticket
bio(logique) organic
biscotte f breakfast biscuit ; rusk
biscuit m biscuit
bisque f thick seafood soup
blanc (blanche) white ; blank
  en blanc blank (on form)
blanc d'œuf m egg white
blanchisserie f laundry
blé m wheat
blessé(e) injured
blesser to injure
bleu m bruise
bleu(e) blue ; very rare (steak)
  bleu marine navy blue
bloc-notes m note pad
blond(e) fair (hair)
bloqué(e) stuck
body m body (clothing)
bœuf m beef
boire to drink
bois m wood
boisson f drink
  boisson non alcoolisée soft drink
boîte f can ; box ; tin
  boîte à fusibles fuse box

boîte à lettres post box
boîte de conserve tin (of food)
boîte de nuit night club
boîte de rustines® bicycle repair kit
boîte de vitesses gearbox
bol m bowl (for soup, etc)
bombe f aerosol ; bomb
bon m token ; voucher
bon (bonne) good ; right ; nice
  bon anniversaire happy birthday
  bon marché inexpensive
bonbon m sweet
bondé(e) crowded
bonhomme m chap
  bonhomme de neige snowman
bonjour hello ; good
  morning/afternoon
bonnet m hat
  bonnet de bain bathing cap
bonneterie f hosiery
bonsoir good evening
bord m border ; edge ; verge
  à bord on board
  au bord de la mer at the seaside
bosse f lump (swelling)
botte f boot ; bunch
bouche f mouth
  bouche d'incendie fire hydrant
bouché(e) blocked
bouchée f mouthful ; chocolate
  bouchée à la reine vol-au-vent
boucherie f butcher's shop
bouchon m cork ; plug (for sink) ;
  top (of bottle)
boucle d'oreille f earring
bouée de sauvetage f life belt
bougie f candle ; spark plug
bouillabaisse f rich fish soup/stew
bouilli(e) boiled
bouillir to boil
bouilloire f kettle
bouillon m stock
bouillotte f hot-water bottle
boulangerie f bakery
boule f ball
boules fpl game similar to bowls
bouquet m bunch (of flowers)
Bourgogne Burgundy

boussole f compass
bout m end
  à bout filtre filter-tipped
bouteille f bottle
boutique f shop
bouton m button ; switch ; spot
  bouton de fièvre cold sore
  boutons de manchette cufflinks
boxe f boxing
bracelet m bracelet
  bracelet de montre watchstrap
braisé(e) braised
bras m arm
brasserie f café ; brewery
Bretagne f Brittany
breton(ne) from Brittany
bricolage m do-it-yourself
briquet m cigarette lighter
briser to break ; to smash
britannique British
brocante f second-hand goods ; flea
  market
broche f brooch ; spit
brochette f skewer ; kebab
brocoli m broccoli
brodé main hand-embroidered
bronzage m suntan
bronze m bronze
brosse f brush
  brosse à cheveux hairbrush
  brosse à dents toothbrush
brouillard m fog
bru f daughter-in-law
bruit m noise
brûlé(e) burnt
brûler to burn
brûlures d'estomac fpl heartburn
brun(e) brown ; dark
brushing m blow-dry
brut(e) gross ; raw
Bruxelles Brussels
bûche f log *(for fire)*
buisson m bush
bulletin de consigne m left-luggage
  ticket
bureau m desk ; office
  bureau de change foreign

  exchange office
  bureau de location booking office
  bureau de poste post office
  bureau de renseignements
  information office
  bureau des objets trouvés
  lost-property
bus m bus
butane m camping gas

C

ça va it's OK ; I'm OK
  ça va? are you OK?
cabaret m cabaret
cabine f beach hut ; cubicle
  cabine d'essayage changing room
cabinet m office
câble de remorquage m tow rope
cacahuète f peanut
cacao m cocoa
cacher to hide
cadeau m gift
cadenas m padlock
cadre m picture frame
cafard m cockroach
café m coffee ; café
  café au lait white coffee
  café crème white coffee
  café décaféiné decaff coffee
  café instantané instant coffee
  café noir black coffee
cafetière f coffee pot
cahier m exercise book
caisse f cash desk ; case
  caisse d'épargne savings bank
caissier(-ière) m/f cashier ; teller
calculatrice f calculator
caleçon m boxer shorts
calendrier m calendar ; timetable
calmant m sedative
cambriolage m break-in
cambrioleur(-euse) m/f burglar
caméra vidéo f video camera
caméscope m camcorder
camion m lorry ; truck
camionnette f van
camomille f camomile

campagne f countryside ; campaign
camper to camp
camping m camping ; camp-site
  camping sauvage camping on
  unofficial sites
  camping-gaz® camping stove
Canada m Canada
canadien(ne) Canadian
canal m canal
canapé m sofa ; open sandwich
  canapé-lit sofa bed
canard m duck
canif m penknife
canne f walking stick
  canne à pêche fishing rod
cannelle f cinnamon
canoë m canoe
canot m boat
  canot de sauvetage lifeboat
canotage m boating
caoutchouc m rubber
capable efficient
capitale f capital (city)
capot m bonnet ; hood (of car)
câpres fpl capers
capuchon m hood ; top (of pen)
car m coach
carabine de chasse f hunting rifle
carafe f carafe ; decanter
caravane f caravan
carburateur m carburettor
Carême m Lent
carnet m notebook ; book
  carnet de billets book of tickets
  carnet de chèques cheque book
carotte f carrot
carré m square
carreau m tile (on wall, floor)
carrefour m crossroads
carte f map ; card ; menu ;
  pass (bus, train)
  carte bleue credit card
  carte d'abonnement season ticket
  carte d'embarquement boarding
  card/pass
  carte d'identité identity card
  carte de crédit credit card
  carte des vins wine list

carte grise log book (car)
carte de mémoire memory card
carte orange monthly or yearly
  season ticket (for Paris transport
  system)
carte postale postcard
carte routière road map
carte vermeille senior citizen's
  rail pass
cartes (à jouer) fpl playing cards
carton m cardboard
cartouche f carton (of cigarettes)
cas m case
cascade f waterfall
caserne f barracks
casier m rack ; locker
casino m casino
casque m helmet
  casque (à écouteurs) headphones
casquette f cap (hat)
cassé(e) broken
casse-croûte m snacks
casser to break
  casser la croûte to have a snack
casserole f saucepan
cassette f cassette
catch m wrestling
cathédrale f cathedral
catholique Catholic
cause f cause
  pour cause de on account of
caution f security (for loan) ; deposit
  caution à verser deposit required
cave f cellar
caveau m cellar
caviar m caviar(e)
CD m CD
  CD vierge blank CD
ceci this
cédez le passage give way
CE f EC (European Community)
ceinture f belt
  ceinture de sécurité seatbelt
  ceinture porte-monnaie moneybelt
cela that
célèbre famous
céleri m celery
célibataire single (unmarried)

cendrier m ashtray
cent m hundred
centimètre m centimetre
central(e) central
centre m centre
  centre commercial shopping centre
  centre de loisirs leisure centre
  centre équestre riding school
  centre-ville city centre
céramique f ceramics
cercle m circle ; ring
céréales fpl cereal (for breakfast)
cerise f cherry
certain(e) certain (sure)
certificat m certificate
cerveau m brain
cervelle f brains (as food)
cesser to stop
cette this ; that
ceux-ci/celles-ci these ones
ceux-là/celles-là those ones
CFF mpl Swiss Railways
chacun/chacune each
chaîne f chain ; channel ; mountain range
  chaîne (stéréo) stereo
  chaînes obligatoires snow chains compulsory
chair f flesh
chaise f chair
  chaise de bébé high chair
  chaise longue deckchair
châle m shawl
chalet m chalet
chambre f bedroom ; room
  chambre à air inner tube
  chambre à coucher bedroom
  chambre à deux lits twin-bedded room
  chambre d'hôte bed and breakfast
  chambre individuelle single room
  chambre pour deux personnes double room
  chambres rooms to let
champ m field
  champ de courses racecourse
champagne m champagne

champignon m mushroom
  champignon vénéneux toadstool
chance f luck
change m exchange
changement m change
changer to change
  changer de l'argent to change money
  changer de train to change train
  se changer to change clothes
chanson f song
chanter to sing
chanterelle f chanterelle
chantier m building site ; roadworks
chapeau m hat
chapelle f chapel
chaque each ; every
charbon m coal
  charbon de bois charcoal
charcuterie f pork butcher's ; delicatessen ; cooked meat
chariot m trolley
charter m charter flight
chasse f hunting ; shooting
  chasse gardée private hunting
chasse-neige m snowplough
chasser to hunt
chasseur m hunter
chat m cat
châtaigne f chestnut
château m castle ; mansion
chaud(e) hot
chauffage m heating
chauffer to heat up (milk, water)
chauffeur m driver
chaussée f carriageway
  chaussée déformée uneven road surface
  chaussée rétrécie road narrows
  chaussée verglacée icy road
chaussette f sock
chaussure f shoe ; boot
chauve bald (person)
chauve-souris f bat (creature)
chef m chef ; chief ; head ; leader
  chef de train train guard
chef-d'œuvre m masterpiece

chef-lieu m **county town**

chemin m **path** ; **lane** ; **track** ; **way**
  chemin de fer **railway**

cheminée f **chimney** ; **fireplace**

chemise f **shirt**
  chemise de nuit **nightdress**

chemisier m **blouse**

chèque m **cheque**
  chèque de voyage **traveller's cheque**

cher (chère) **dear** ; **expensive**

chercher **to look for**
  aller chercher **to fetch** ; **to collect**

cheval m **horse**
  faire du cheval **to ride**

cheveux mpl **hair**

cheville f **ankle**

chèvre f **goat**

chevreau m **kid** (goat, leather)

chevreuil m **venison**

chez **at the house of**
  chez moi **at my home**

chien m **dog**

chiffon m **duster** ; **rag**

chips fpl **crisps**

chirurgien m **surgeon**

chocolat m **chocolate**
  chocolat à croquer **plain chocolate**
  chocolat au lait **milk chocolate**
  chocolat noir **plain chocolate**

choisir **to choose**

choix m **range** ; **choice** ; **selection**

chômage: au chômage **unemployed**

chope f **tankard**

chorale f **choir**

chose f **thing**

chou m **cabbage**

chou-fleur m **cauliflower**

chute f **fall**

ciboule f **spring onion**

cidre m **cider**

ciel m **sky**

cigare m **cigar**

cigarette f **cigarette**

cil m **eyelash**

cimetière m **cemetery** ; **graveyard**

cinéma m **cinema**

cintre m **coat hanger**

cirage m **shoe polish**

circuit m **round trip** ; **circuit**

circulation f **traffic**

circuler **to operate** (train, bus, etc)

cire f **wax** ; **polish**

cirque m **circus**

ciseaux mpl **scissors**

cité f **city** ; **housing estate**

citron m **lemon**
  citron vert **lime**

citronnade f **still lemonade**

clair(e) **clear** ; **light**

classe f **grade** ; **class**

clavicule f **collar bone**

clavier m **keyboard**

clé f **key** ; **spanner**
  clé de contact **ignition key**
  clé minute **keys cut while you wait**

clef f **key**

client(e) m/f **client** ; **customer**

clignotant m **indicator** (on car)

climatisation f **air-conditioning**

climatisé(e) **air-conditioned**

clinique f **clinic** (private)

cloche f **bell** (church, school)

clocher m **steeple**

clou m **nail** (metal)
  clou de girofle **clove**

cocher **to tick** (on form)

cochon m **pig**

cocktail m **cocktail**

cocotte f **casserole dish**

cocotte-minute f **pressure cooker**

code m **code**
  code barres **barcode**
  code postal **postcode**
  code secret **pin number**

cœur m **heart**

coffre-fort m **safe**

cognac m **brandy**

coiffeur m **hairdresser** ; **barber**

coiffeuse f **hairdresser**

coin m **corner**

coincé(e) **jammed** ; **stuck**

col m **collar** ; **mountain pass**

colis m **parcel**

collant m **pair of tights**
colle f **glue**
collège m **secondary school**
collègue m/f **colleague**
coller **to stick ; to glue**
collier m **necklace ; dog collar**
colline f **hill**
collision f **crash** (car)
colonne f **column**
  colonne vertébrale **spine**
combien **how much/many**
combinaison de plongée f **wetsuit**
combinaison de ski f **ski suit**
combustible m **fuel**
comédie f **comedy**
  comédie musicale **musical**
commande f **order** (in restaurant)
commander **to order**
comme **like**
  comme ça **like this ; like that**
commencer **to begin**
comment? **pardon? ; how?**
commerçant(e) m/f **trader**
commerce m **commerce ; business ; trade**
commissariat (de police) m **police station**
commode f **chest of drawers**
commotion f **shock**
  commotion (cérébrale) **concussion**
communication f **communication ; call** (on telephone)
communion f **communion**
compagne f **girlfriend**
compagnie f **firm ; company**
compagnon m **boyfriend**
compartiment m **compartment** (train)
complet(-ète) **full (up)**
complètement **completely**
comporter **to consist of**
  se comporter **to behave**
composer **to dial** (a number)
composter **to date-stamp/ punch** (ticket)
  compostez votre billet **validate your ticket**
comprenant **including**

comprendre **to understand**
comprimé m **tablet**
compris(e) **included**
  non compris **not included**
comptant m **cash**
compte m **number ; account**
  compte en banque **bank account**
compter **to count** (add up)
compteur m **speedometer ; meter**
comptoir m **counter** (in shop, bar, etc)
comte m **count ; earl**
concert m **concert**
concierge m/f **caretaker ; janitor**
concombre m **cucumber**
concours m **contest ; aid**
concurrent(e) m/f **competitor**
conducteur(-trice) m/f **driver**
conduire **to drive**
conduite f **driving ; behaviour**
confection f **ready-to-wear clothes**
conférence f **conference**
confession f **confession**
confirmer **to confirm**
confiserie f **sweetshop**
confiture f **jam ; preserve**
congélateur m **freezer**
congelé(e) **frozen**
connaître **to know**
conseil m **advice ; council**
conseiller **to advise**
conserver **to keep ; to retain** (ticket, etc)
consigne f **deposit ; left luggage**
consommation f **drink**
consommé m **clear soup**
constat m **report**
constipé(e) **constipated**
construire **to build**
consulat m **consulate**
contacter **to contact**
contenir **to contain**
content(e) **pleased**
contenu m **contents**
continuer **to continue**
contraceptif m **contraceptive**
contrat m **contract**

contrat de location lease
contravention f fine *(penalty)*
contre against ; versus
contre-filet m sirloin
contrôle m check
  contrôle des passeports
  passport control
  contrôle radar speed trap
contrôler to check
contrôleur(-euse) m/f ticket inspector
convenu(e) agreed
convoi exceptionnel m large load
copie f copy *(duplicate)*
copier to copy
coque f shell ; cockle
coquelicot m poppy
coquet(te) pretty *(place, etc)*
coquillages mpl shellfish
coquille f shell
  coquille Saint-Jacques scallop
corail m coral ; type of train
corde f rope
  corde à linge clothes line
cordonnerie f shoe repairer's
cornet m cone
corniche f coast road
cornichon m gherkin
corps m body
correspondance f connection
  (transport)
correspondant(e) m/f penfriend
corrida f bull-fight
Corse f Corsica
costume m suit *(man's)*
côte f coast ; hill ; rib
  Côte d'Azur French Riviera
côté m side
  à côté de beside ; next to
côtelette f cutlet
coton m cotton
  coton hydrophile cotton wool
  coton-tige® cotton bud
cou m neck
couche (de bébé) f nappy
coucher de soleil m sunset
couchette f bunk ; berth
coude m elbow

coudre to sew
couette f continental quilt ; duvet
couler to run *(water)*
couleur f colour
coulis m purée
couloir m corridor ; aisle
coup m stroke ; shot ; blow
  coup de pied kick
  coup de soleil sunburn
  coup de téléphone phone call
coupe f goblet *(ice cream)*
  coupe (de cheveux) haircut
coupe-ongles m nail clippers
couper to cut
couple m couple *(two people)*
coupure f cut
  coupure de courant power cut
cour f court ; courtyard
courant m power ; current
courant(e) common ; current
courgette f courgette
courir to run
couronne f crown
courrier m mail ; post
  courrier électronique e-mail
courroie de ventilateur f fan belt
cours m lesson ; course ; rate
course f race *(sport)* ; errand
  course hippique horse race
  faire des courses to go shopping
court de tennis m tennis court
court(e) short
cousin(e) m/f cousin
coussin m cushion
coût m cost
couteau m knife
coûter to cost
coûteux(-euse) expensive
couture f sewing ; seam
couvent m convent ; monastery
couvercle m lid
couvert m cover charge ; place
  setting
  couverts cutlery
couvert(e) covered
couverture f blanket ; cover
crabe m crab

crapaud m toad
cravate f tie
crayon m pencil
crème f cream (food, lotion)
  crème à raser shaving cream
  crème anglaise custard
  crème Chantilly whipped cream
  crème fermentée soured cream
  crème hydratante moisturizer
  crème pâtissière confectioner's
  custard
crémerie f dairy
crêpe f pancake
crêperie f pancake shop/restaurant
cresson m watercress
crevaison f puncture
crevette f shrimp ; prawn
cric m jack (for car)
crier to shout
crime m crime ; offence ; murder
crise f crisis ; attack (medical)
  crise cardiaque heart attack
cristal m crystal
crochet d'attelage m towbar
croire to believe
croisement m junction (road)
croisière f cruise
croix f cross
croquant(e) crisp ; crunchy
croque-madame m toasted cheese
  sandwich with ham and fried egg
croque-monsieur m toasted ham and
  cheese sandwich
croûte f crust
cru(e) raw
crudités fpl raw vegetables
crue subite f flash flood
crustacés mpl shellfish
cube de bouillon m stock cube
cuiller f spoon
  cuiller à café teaspoon
cuir m leather
cuisiné(e) cooked
cuisine f cooking ; cuisine ; kitchen
  cuisine familiale home cooking
  faire la cuisine to cook
cuisiner to cook

cuisinier m cook
cuisinière f cook ; cooker
cuisse f thigh
  cuisses de grenouille frogs' legs
cuit(e) cooked
  bien cuit well done (steak)
cuivre m copper
  cuivre jaune brass
culotte f panties
curieux(-euse) strange
curseur m cursor (computer)
cuvée f vintage
cuvette f washing up bowl
cyclisme m cycling
cystite f cystitis

D

daltonien(ne) colour-blind
dame f lady
  dames ladies
danger m danger
dangereux(-euse) dangerous
dans into ; in ; on
danser to dance
date f date (day)
  date de naissance date of birth
  date limite de vente sell-by date
daube f stew
de from ; of ; some
dé m dice
début m beginning
débutant(e) m/f beginner
décaféiné(e) decaffeinated
décembre December
décès m death
décharge f electric shock
  décharge publique rubbish dump
déchargement m unloading
déchirer to rip
déclaration f statement ; report
  déclaration de douane
  customs declaration
décollage m takeoff
décoller to take off (plane)
décolleté m low neck
décongeler to defrost
découvrir to discover

décrire to describe
décrocher to lift the receiver
dedans inside
défaire to unfasten ; to unpack
défaut m fault ; defect
défectueux(-euse) faulty
défense de... no.../... forbidden
    défense de fumer no smoking
    défense de stationner no parking
dégâts mpl damage
dégeler to thaw
dégivrer to de-ice
dégustation f tasting
    dégustation de vins wine tasting
dehors outside ; outdoors
déjeuner m lunch
délicieux(-euse) delicious
délit m offence
deltaplane m hang-glider
demain tomorrow
demande f application ; request
    demandes d'emploi situations
    wanted
demander to ask (for)
demandeur d'emploi m job seeker
démaquillant m make-up remover
démarqué(e) reduced (goods)
démarreur m starter (in car)
demi(e) half
demi-pension f half board
demi-sec medium-dry
demi-tarif m half fare
demi-tour m U-turn
dent f tooth
dentelle f lace
dentier m dentures
dentifrice m toothpaste
dentiste m/f dentist
déodorant m deodorant
dépannage m breakdown service
dépanneuse f breakdown van
départ m departure
département m county
dépasser to exceed ; to overtake
dépenses fpl expenditure
dépliant m brochure
dépôt m deposit ; depot

dépôt d'ordures rubbish dump
dépression f depression ; nervous
    breakdown
depuis since
déranger to disturb
dernier(-ère) last ; latest
derrière at the back ; behind
derrière m bottom (buttocks)
dès from ; since
    dès votre arrivée as soon as you
    arrive
désagréable unpleasant
descendre to go down ; to get off
description f description
déshabiller to undress
    se déshabiller to get undressed
désirer to want
désodorisant m air freshener
désolé(e) sorry
dessein m design ; plan
desserré(e) loose (not fastened)
dessert m pudding
dessous (de) underneath
dessus (de) on top (of)
destinataire m/f addressee
destination f destination
    à destination de bound for
détail m detail
    au détail retail
détergent m detergent
détourner to divert
deux two
    deux fois twice
    les deux both
deuxième second
devant in front (of)
développer to develop
devenir to become
déviation f diversion
devis m quotation (price)
devises fpl currency
dévisser to unscrew
devoir to have to; to owe
diabète m diabetes
diabétique diabetic
diamant m diamond
diaphragme m cap (contraceptive)

diapositive f slide *(photograph)*
diarrhée f diarrhoea
dictionnaire m dictionary
diététique f dietary ; health foods
différent(e) different
difficile difficult
digue f dyke ; jetty
dimanche m Sunday
dinde f turkey
dîner to have dinner
dîner m dinner
  dîner spectacle cabaret dinner
dire to say ; to tell
direct: *train direct* through train
directeur m manager ; headmaster
direction f management ; direction
directrice f manageress ;
  headmistress
discothèque f disco ; nightclub
discussion f argument
disjoncteur m circuit breaker
disloquer to dislocate
disparaître to disappear
disparu(e) missing *(disappeared)*
disponible available
disque m record ; disk
  disque de stationnement parking
  disk
  disque dur hard disk
disquette f floppy disk
dissolvant m nail polish remover
distractions fpl entertainment
distributeur m dispenser
  distributeur automatique vending
  machine ; cash machine
divers(e) various
divertissements mpl entertainment
divorcé(e) divorced
docteur m doctor
doigt m finger
  doigt de pied toe
domestique m/f servant ; maid
domicile m home ; address
donner to give ; to give away
doré(e) golden
dormir to sleep
dos m back *(of body)*

dossier m file
douane f customs
double double
doubler to overtake
douche f shower
douleur f pain
douloureux(-euse) painful
doux (douce) mild ; gentle ; soft ;
  sweet
douzaine f dozen
dragée f sugared almond
drap m sheet
drapeau m flag
drogue f drug
droguerie f hardware shop
droit m right *(entitlement)*
droit(e) right *(not left)* ; straight
droite f right-hand side
  à droite on/to the right
  tenez votre droite keep to right
dur(e) hard ; hard-boiled ; tough
durée f duration

E

eau f water
  eau de Javel bleach
  eau douce fresh water *(not salt)*
  eau du robinet tap-water
  eau minérale mineral water
  eau potable drinking water
  eau salée salt water
  eau-de-vie brandy
ébène f ebony
échanger to exchange
échantillon m sample
échapper to escape
écharpe f scarf *(woollen)*
échelle f ladder
  échelle de secours fire escape
éclairage m lighting
éclairs mpl lightning
écluse f lock *(in canal)*
école f school
  école maternelle nursery school
écorce f peel *(of fruit)*
écossais(e) Scottish
Écosse f Scotland

écouter to listen to
écran m screen
  écran solaire sunscreen lotion
  écran total sunblock
écrire to write
écrivain m author
écrou m nut (for bolt)
écurie f stable
édulcorant m sweetener
église f church
élastique m elastic band
électricien m electrician
électricité f electricity
électrique electric
élément m unit ; element
emballer to wrap (up)
embarcadère m jetty
embarquement m boarding
embouteillage m traffic jam
embrayage m clutch (in car)
émission f programme ; broadcast
emplacement m parking space ;
  pitch for tent
emploi m use ; job
emporter to take away
  à emporter take-away
emprunter to borrow
en some ; any ; in ; to ; made of
  en cas de in case of
  en face de opposite
  en gros in bulk ; wholesale
  en panne out of order
  en retard late
  en train by train
encaisser to cash (cheque)
enceinte pregnant
enchanté(e)! pleased to meet you!
encore still ; yet ; again
encre f ink
endommager to damage
endroit m place ; spot
enfant m/f child
  enfant en bas âge toddler
enfler to swell
enlever to take away ; to take
  off (clothes)
  enlever le haut to go topless

enneigé(e) snowed up
ennui m boredom ; nuisance ;
  trouble
ennuyeux boring
enregistrement m check-in desk
enregistrer to record ; to check in ;
  to video
enseignement m education
enseigner to teach
ensemble together
ensuite next ; after that
entendre to hear
entier(-ière) whole
entorse f sprain
entracte m interval
entre between
entrecôte f rib steak
entrée f entrance ; admission ;
  starter (food)
  entrée gratuite admission free
  entrée interdite no entry
entreprise f firm ; company
entrer to come in ; to go in
entretien m maintenance ; interview
enveloppe f envelope
  enveloppe matelassée padded
  envelope
envers: l'envers wrong side
  à l'envers upside down ; back
  to front
environ around ; about
environs mpl surroundings
envoyer to send
  envoyer un message SMS to text
épais(se) thick
épargner to save (money)
épaule f shoulder
épi m ear (of corn)
  épi de maïs corn-on-the-cob
épice f spice
épicerie f grocer's shop
  épicerie fine delicatessen
épilation f hair removal
  épilation à la cire f waxing
épileptique epileptic
épinards mpl spinach

épine f thorn
épingle f pin
  épingle de sûreté safety pin
éponge f sponge
époque f age
  d'époque period (furniture)
épuisé(e) sold out ; used up
épuiser to use up ; to run out of
équipage m crew
équipe f team ; shift
équipement m equipment
équitation f horse-riding
erreur f mistake
escalade f climbing
escalator m escalator
escalier m stairs
  escalier de secours fire escape
  escalier mécanique escalator
escargot m snail
escarpement m cliff
Espagne f Spain
espagnol(e) Spanish
espèce f sort
espérer to hope
esquimau m ice lolly
essai m trial ; test
essayer to try ; to try on
essence f petrol
  essence sans plomb unleaded
  petrol
essorer to spin(-dry) ; to wring
essoreuse f spin dryer
essuie-glace m windscreen wipers
essuie-tout m kitchen paper
esthéticienne f beautician
estivants mpl summer holiday-
  makers
estomac m stomach
estragon m tarragon
et and
étage m storey
  dernier étage top floor
étain m tin ; pewter
étang m pond
étape f stage
état m state
  États-Unis United States

été m summer
éteindre to turn off
éteint(e) out (light)
étiquette f label
  étiquette à bagages luggage tag
étoile f star
étranger(-ère) m/f foreigner
  à l'étranger overseas ; abroad
être to be
étroit(e) narrow ; tight
étudiant(e) m/f student
étudier to study
étui m case (camera, glasses)
étuvée: à l'étuvée braised
eurochèque m eurocheque
Europe f Europe
européen(ne) European
eux them
évanoui(e) fainted
événement m occasion ; event
éventail m fan (handheld)
éventé(e) flat (beer)
évêque m bishop
évier m sink (washbasin)
éviter to avoid
exact(e) right (correct)
examen m examination
excédent de bagages m excess
  baggage
excellent(e) excellent
excès de vitesse m speeding
exclu(e) excluded
exclure to expel
exclusif (-ive) exclusive
excursion f trip ; outing ; excursion
excuses fpl apologies
excusez-moi! excuse me!
exemplaire m copy
exercice m exercise
expéditeur m sender
expert(e) m/f expert
expirer to expire
expliquer to explain
exporter to export
exposition f exhibition
exprès on purpose ; deliberately

en exprès **express** *(parcel, etc)*
extérieur **outside**
extincteur m **fire extinguisher**
extra **top-quality ; first-rate**

F

fabrication f **manufacturing**
fabriquer **to manufacture**
  fabriqué en... **made in...**
face: *en face (de)* **opposite**
fâché(e) **angry**
facile **easy**
façon f **way ; manner**
facteur(-trice) m/f **postman/woman**
facture f **invoice**
  facture détaillée **itemized bill**
faible **weak**
faïence f **earthenware**
faim f **hunger**
  avoir faim **to be hungry**
faire **to make ; to do**
  faire du stop **to hitchhike**
faisan m **pheasant**
fait main **handmade**
falaise f **cliff**
famille f **family**
farci(e) **stuffed**
farine f **flour**
fatigue f **tiredness**
fatigué(e) **tired**
fausse couche f **miscarriage**
faute f **mistake ; foul** *(football)*
fauteuil m **armchair ; seat**
  fauteuil roulant **wheelchair**
faux (fausse) **fake ; false ; wrong**
fax m **fax**
faxer **to fax**
félicitations fpl **congratulations**
femme f **woman ; wife**
  femme au foyer **housewife**
  femme d'affaires **businesswoman**
  femme de chambre **chambermaid**
  femme de ménage **cleaner**
  femme policier **policewoman**
fenêtre f **window**
fenouil m **fennel**
fente f **crack ; slot**

fer m **iron** *(material, golf club)*
  fer à repasser **iron** *(for clothes)*
férié(e): *jour férié* **public holiday**
ferme f **farmhouse ; farm**
fermé(e) **closed**
fermer **to close/shut ; to turn off**
  fermer à clé **to lock**
fermeture f **closing**
  fermeture Éclair® **zip**
ferroviaire **railway ; rail**
ferry m **car ferry**
fête f **holiday ; fête ; party**
  fête des rois **Epiphany**
  fête foraine **funfair**
feu m **fire ; traffic lights**
  feu (de joie) **bonfire** *(celebration)*
  feu d'artifice **fireworks**
  feu de position **sidelight**
  feu rouge **red light**
feuille f **leaf ; sheet** *(of paper)*
feuilleton m **soap opera**
feutre m **felt ; felt-tip pen**
février **February**
fiancé(e) **engaged** *(to marry)*
ficelle f **string ; thin French stick**
fiche f **token ; form ; slip** *(of paper)*
fichier m **file** *(computer)*
fièvre f **fever**
  avoir de la fièvre **to have**
  a temperature
figue f **fig**
fil m **thread ; lead** *(electrical)*
  fil dentaire **dental floss**
file f **lane ; row**
filet m **net ; fillet** *(of meat, fish)*
  filet à bagages **luggage rack**
fille f **daughter ; girl**
film m **film**
  film alimentaire **Clingfilm®**
film m **film**
fils m **son**
filtre m **filter** *(on cigarette)*
  filtre à huile **oil filter**
fin f **end**
fin(e) **thin** *(material)* **; fine** *(delicate)*
fini(e) **finished**
finir **to end ; to finish**
fixer **to fix**

flacon m **bottle** (small)
flamand(e) **Flemish**
flan m **custard tart**
flash m **flash** (for camera)
fleur f **flower**
fleuriste m/f **florist**
fleuve m **river**
flipper m **pinball**
flûte f **long, thin loaf**
foie m **liver**
  foie gras **goose liver**
foire f **fair**
  foire à/aux... **special offer on...**
fois f **time**
  cette fois **this time**
  une fois **once**
folle **mad**
foncé(e) **dark** (colour)
fonctionner **to work** (machine)
fond m **back** (of hall, room) ; **bottom**
fondre **to melt**
force f **strength**
forêt f **forest**
forfait m **fixed price** ; **ski pass**
forme f **shape** ; **style**
formidable **great** (wonderful)
formulaire m **form** (document)
fort(e) **loud; strong**
forteresse f **fort**
fosse f **pit** ; **grave**
  fosse septique **septic tank**
fou (folle) **mad**
fouetté(e) **whipped** (cream, eggs)
foulard m **scarf** (headscarf)
foule f **crowd**
four m **oven**
  four à micro-ondes **microwave**
fourchette f **fork**
fournir **to supply**
fourré(e) **filled** ; **fur-lined**
fourrure f **fur**
fraîche **fresh** ; **cool** ; **wet** (paint)
frais **fresh** ; **cool**
frais mpl **costs** ; **expenses**
fraise f **strawberry**
framboise f **raspberry**
français(e) **French**

Français(e) **Frenchman/woman**
frapper **to hit** ; **to knock** (on door)
frein m **brake**
freiner **to brake**
fréquent(e) **frequent**
frère m **brother**
fret m **freight** (goods)
frigo m **fridge**
frit(e) **fried**
friterie f **chip shop**
frites fpl **French fries** ; **chips**
friture f **small fried fish**
froid(e) **cold**
fromage m **cheese**
froment m **wheat**
front m **forehead**
frontière f **border** ; **boundary**
frotter **to rub**
fruit m **fruit**
  fruits de mer **seafood**
  fruits secs **dried fruit**
fuite f **leak**
fumé(e) **smoked**
fumée f **smoke**
fumer **to smoke**
fumeurs mpl **smokers**
fumier m **manure**
funiculaire m **funicular railway**
fuseau m **ski pants**
fusible m **fuse**
fusil m **gun**

G

gagner **to earn** ; **to win**
galerie f **art gallery** ; **arcade** ;
  roof-rack
gallois(e) **Welsh**
gambas fpl **large prawns**
gant m **glove**
  gant de toilette **face cloth**
  gants de ménage **rubber gloves**
garage m **garage**
garantie f **guarantee**
garçon m **boy** ; **waiter**
garde f **custody** ; **guard**
  garde-côte **coastguard**

garder to keep ; to look after
gardien(ne) m/f caretaker ; warden
gare f railway station
  gare routière bus terminal
garer to park
garni(e) served with vegetables
  or chips
gas-oil m diesel fuel
gâteau m cake ; gateau
gauche left
  à gauche to/on the left
gâteau m cake
gaufre f waffle
gaz m gas
  gaz d'échappement exhaust fumes
gazole m diesel fuel
gazeux(-euse) fizzy
gel m frost
  gel pour cheveux hair gel
gelé(e) frozen
gelée f jelly ; aspic
gênant inconvenient
gendarme m policeman (in rural areas)
gendarmerie f police station
gendre m son-in-law
généreux(-euse) generous
genou m knee
gentil(-ille) kind (person)
gérant(e) m/f manager/manageress
gérer to manage (be in charge of)
gibier m game (hunting)
gilet m waistcoat
  gilet de sauvetage life jacket
gingembre m ginger
gîte m self-catering house/flat
glace f ice ; ice cream ; mirror
glacé(e) chilled ; iced
glacier m glacier ; ice-cream maker
glacière f cool-box (for picnic)
glaçon m ice cube
glissant(e) slippery
glisser to slip
gomme f rubber (eraser)
gorge f throat ; gorge
gosse m/f kid (child)
gothique Gothic
goût m flavour ; taste

goûter to taste
graine f seed
gramme m gram
grand(e) great ; high (speed, number) ;
  big ; tall
grand-mère f grandmother
grand-père f grandfather
Grande-Bretagne f Great Britain
grands-parents mpl grandparents
grange f barn
granité m flavoured crushed ice
grappe f bunch (of grapes)
gras(se) fat ; greasy
gratis for free
gratuit(e) free of charge
grave serious
graver to burn (CD)
gravure f print (picture)
grêle f hail
grenier m attic
grenouille f frog
grève f strike
grillé(e) grilled
grille-pain m toaster
Grèce f Greece
grippe f flu
gris(e) grey
gros(se) big ; large ; fat
gros lot m jackpot
grotte f cave
groupe m group ; party ; band
  groupe sanguin blood group
guêpe f wasp
guerre f war
gueule de bois f hangover
guichet m ticket office ; counter
guide m guide ; guidebook
  guide de conversation
  phrase book
guidon m handlebars
guitare f guitar

H

habillé(e) dressed
habiller to dress
  s'habiller to get dressed

habitant(e) m/f inhabitant
habiter to live (in)
habituel(le) usual ; regular
haché(e) minced
  steak haché m hamburger
hachis m minced meat
halles fpl central food market
hamburger m burger
hameçon m hook (fishing)
hanche f hip
handicapé(e) disabled (person)
haricot m bean
  haricots verts French beans
haut m top (of ladder, bikini)
  en haut upstairs
haut(e) high ; tall
hauteur f height
hebdomadaire weekly
hébergement m lodging
hépatite f hepatitis
herbe f grass
  fines herbes herbs
hernie f hernia
heure f hour ; time of day
  à l'heure on time
  heure de pointe rush hour
heureux(-euse) happy
hibou m owl
hier yesterday
hippisme m horse riding
hippodrome m racecourse
historique historic
hiver m winter
hollandais(e) Dutch
homard m lobster
homéopathie f homeopathy
homme m man
  homme au foyer house-husband
  homme d'affaires businessman
  hommes gents
homo m gay (person)
honnête honest
honoraires mpl fee
hôpital m hospital
horaire m timetable ; schedule
horloge f clock
hors: hors de out of

  hors service out of order
  hors-taxe duty-free
  hors-saison off-season
hôte m host ; guest
hôtel m hotel
  hôtel de ville town hall
hôtesse f stewardess
huile f oil
  huile d'olive olive oil
  huile d'arachide groundnut oil
  huile de tournesol sunflower oil
huître f oyster
hypermarché m hypermarket
hypermétrope long-sighted
hypertension f high blood pressure

I

ici here
idée f idea
il y a... there is/are...
  il y a un défaut there's a fault
  il y a une semaine a week ago
île f island
illimité(e) unlimited
immédiatement immediately
immeuble m building (offices, flats)
immunisation f immunisation
impair(e) odd (number)
impasse f dead end
imperméable waterproof
important(e) important
importer to import
impossible impossible
impôt m tax
imprimer to print
incendie m fire
inclus(e) included ; inclusive
inconfortable uncomfortable
incorrect(e) wrong
indicateur m guide ; timetable
indicatif m dialling code
indications fpl instructions ;
  directions
indigestion f indigestion
indispensable essential
infectieux(-euse) infectious
infection f infection

inférieur(e) inferior ; lower
infirmerie f infirmary
infirmier(-ière) m/f nurse
informations fpl news ; information
infusion f herbal tea
ingénieur m/f engineer
ingrédient m ingredient
inhalateur m inhaler
inondation f flood
inquiet(-iète) worried
inscrire to write (down) ; to enrol
insecte m insect
insolation f sunstroke
installations fpl facilities
instant m moment
  un instant! just a minute!
institut m institute
  institut de beauté beauty salon
insuline f insulin
intelligent(e) intelligent
interdit forbidden
intéressant(e) interesting
intérieur: à l'intérieur indoors
international(e) international
interprète m/f interpreter
intervention f operation (surgical)
intoxication alimentaire f food
  poisoning
introduire to introduce ; to insert
inutile useless ; unnecessary
invalide m/f disabled person
invité(e) m/f guest
inviter to invite
irlandais(e) Irish
Irlande f Ireland
Irlande du Nord f Northern Ireland
issue de secours f emergency exit
Italie f Italy
italien(ne) Italian
itinéraire m route
  itinéraire touristique scenic route
ivoire m ivory
ivre drunk

J

jaloux(-ouse) jealous
jamais never

jambe f leg
jambon m ham
janvier January
Japon m Japan
jardin m garden
jauge (de niveau d'huile) f dipstick
jaune yellow
jaune d'œuf m egg yolk
jaunisse f jaundice
jetable disposable
jetée f pier
jeter to throw
jeton m token
jeu m game ; set (of tools, etc) ;
  gambling
  jeu électronique computer game
  jeu vidéo video game
  jeu-concours quiz
jeudi m Thursday
jeune young
jeunesse f youth
joindre to join ; to enclose
joli(e) pretty
jonquille f daffodil
joue f cheek
jouer to play (games)
jouet m toy
jour m day
  jour férié public holiday
journal m newspaper
journaliste m/f journalist
journée f day (length of time)
juge m/f judge
juif (juive) Jewish
juillet July
juin June
jumeaux mpl twins
jumelles fpl twins ; binoculars
jupe f skirt
jus m juice
  jus d'orange orange juice
  jus de fruit fruit juice
  jus de viande gravy
jusqu'à (au) until ; till
juste fair ; reasonable

K

kart m go-cart
kas(c)her kosher
kayak m canoe
Ketchup® m tomato sauce
kilo m kilo
kilométrage m mileage
  kilométrage illimité unlimited
  mileage
kilomètre m kilometre
kiosque m kiosk ; newsstand
klaxonner to sound one's horn
kyste m cyst

L

là there
lac m lake
lacets mpl shoelaces
laid(e) ugly
laine f wool
  laine polaire fleece *(top/jacket)*
laisse f leash
laisser to leave
  laissez en blanc leave blank
lait m milk
  lait cru unpasteurised milk
  lait démaquillant cleansing milk
  lait demi-écrémé semi-skimmed
  milk
  lait écrémé skim(med) milk
  lait entier full-cream milk
  lait longue conservation long-life
  milk
  lait maternisé baby milk *(formula)*
  lait solaire suntan lotion
laiterie f dairy
laitue f lettuce
lame f blade
  lames de rasoir razor blades
lampe f light ; lamp
  lampe de poche torch
landau m pram ; baby carriage
langue f tongue ; language
lapin m rabbit
laque f hair spray
lard m fat ; *(streaky)* bacon
lardons mpl diced bacon

large wide ; broad
largeur f width
laurier m sweet bay ; bay leaves
lavable washable
lavabo m washbasin
  lavabos toilets
lavage m washing
lavande f lavender
lave-auto m car wash
lave-glace m screen wash
lave-linge m washing machine
laver to wash
  se laver to wash oneself
laverie automatique f launderette
lave-vaisselle m dishwasher
laxatif m laxative
layette f baby clothes
leçon f lesson
  leçons particulières private lessons
lecture f reading
légal(e) legal
léger(-ère) light ; weak *(tea, etc)*
légume m vegetable
lendemain m next day
lent(e) slow
lentement slowly
lentille f lentil ; lens *(of glasses)*
  lentille de contact contact lens
lesbienne f lesbian
lessive f soap powder ; washing
lettre f letter
  lettre recommandée registered
  letter
leur(s) their
levée f collection *(of mail)*
lever to lift
  se lever to get up *(out of bed)*
lever de soleil m sunrise
lèvre f lip
levure f yeast
libellule f dragonfly
librairie f bookshop
libre free ; vacant
libre-service self-service
lieu m place *(location)*
lièvre m hare
ligne f line ; service ; route

lime à ongles f nail file
limitation de vitesse f speed limit
limonade f lemonade
lin m linen (cloth)
linge m linen (bed, table); laundry
lingerie f lingerie
lingettes fpl baby wipes
lion m lion
liquide f liquid
  liquide de freins brake fluid
lire to read
liste f list
lit m bed
  lit d'enfant cot
  lit simple single bed
  lits jumeaux twin beds
  grand lit double bed
litre m litre
livraison f delivery (of goods)
  livraison des bagages baggage
  reclaim
livre f pound
livre m book
local(e) local
locataire m/f tenant; lodger
location f hiring (out); letting
logement m accommodation
loger to stay (reside for while)
logiciel m computer software
loi f law
loin far
lointain(e) distant
loisir m leisure
Londres London
long(ue) long
  le long de along
longe f loin (of meat)
longtemps for a long time
longueur f length
lot m prize; lot (at auction)
loterie f lottery
lotion f lotion
loto m numerical lottery
lotte f monkfish; angler fish
louer to let; to hire; to rent
  à louer for hire/to rent
loup m wolf; sea perch

loupe f magnifying glass
lourd(e) heavy
loyer m rent
luge f sledge; toboggan
lumière f light
lundi m Monday
lune f moon
  lune de miel honeymoon
lunettes fpl glasses
  lunettes de soleil sunglasses
  lunettes protectrices goggles
luxe m luxury
lycée m secondary school

M

M sign for the Paris metro
machine f machine
  machine à laver washing machine
mâchoire f jaw
Madame f Mrs; Ms; Madam
madeleine f small sponge cake
Mademoiselle f Miss
madère m Madeira (wine)
magasin m shop
  grand magasin department store
magnétophone m tape recorder
magnétoscope m video-cassette
  recorder
magret de canard m breast fillet
  of duck
mai May
maigre lean (meat)
maigrir to slim
maillet m mallet
maillot m vest
  maillot de bain swimsuit
main f hand
maintenant now
maire m mayor
mairie f town hall
mais but
maison f house; home
  maison de campagne villa
maître d'hôtel m head waiter
majuscule f capital letter
mal badly
mal m harm; pain

mal de dents toothache
mal de mer seasickness
mal de tête headache
faire du mal à quelqu'un to harm someone
malade sick *(ill)*
malade *m/f* sick person ; patient
maladie *f* disease
malentendu *m* misunderstanding
malle *f* trunk *(luggage)*
maman *f* mummy
manche *f* sleeve
Manche *f* the Channel
mandat *m* money order
manger to eat
manière *f* way *(manner)*
manifestation *f* demonstration
manque *m* shortage ; lack
manteau *m* coat
maquereau *m* mackerel
maquillage *m* make-up
marais *m* marsh
marbre *m* marble *(material)*
marc *m* white grape spirit
marchand *m* dealer ; merchant
  marchand de poisson fishmonger
  marchand de vin wine merchant
marche *f* step ; march; walking
  marche arrière reverse gear
marché *m* market
  marché aux puces flea market
marcher to walk ; to work *(machine, car)*
  en marche on *(machine)*
mardi *m* Tuesday
  mardi gras Shrove Tuesday
marée *f* tide
  marée basse low tide
  marée haute high tide
margarine *f* margarine
mari *m* husband
mariage *m* wedding
marié *m* bridegroom
marié(e) married
mariée *f* bride
marier to marry
  se marier to get married

mariné(e) marinated
marionnette *f* puppet
marque *f* make ; brand
marquer to score *(goal, point)*
marron brown
marron *m* chestnut
mars March
marteau *m* hammer
masculin male *(person, on forms)*
mât *m* mast
match de football *m* football match
  match en nocturne floodlit fixture
matelas *m* mattress
  matelas pneumatique lilo®
matériel *m* equipment ; kit
matin *m* morning
mauvais(e) bad ; wrong ; off *(food)*
maximum *m* maximum
mazout *m* oil *(for heating)*
mécanicien *m* mechanic
méchant(e) naughty ; wicked
médecin *m* doctor
médicament *m* medicine ; drug ; medication
médiéval(e) medieval
Méditerranée *f* Mediterranean Sea
méduse *f* jellyfish
meilleur(e) best ; better
  meilleurs vœux best wishes
mél *m* e-mail address
melon *m* melon
membre *m* member *(of club, etc)*
même same
mémoire *f* memory
ménage *m* housework
méningite *f* meningitis
mensuel(le) monthly
menthe *f* mint ; mint tea
menu *m* menu *(set)*
  menu à prix fixe set price menu
  menu du jour today's menu
mer *f* sea
  mer du Nord North Sea
mercerie *f* haberdasher's
merci thank you
mercredi *m* Wednesday
mère *f* mother

merlan *m* whiting
merlu *m* hake
mérou *m* grouper
merveilleux(-euse) wonderful
message *m* message
  message SMS text message
messe *f* mass *(church)*
messieurs *mpl* men
  Messieurs gentlemen
messieurs gents
mesure *f* measurement
mesurer to measure
métal *m* metal
météo *f* weather forecast
métier *m* trade ; occupation
mètre *m* metre
  mètre à ruban tape measure
métro *m* underground
mettre to put ; to put on
  mettre au point to focus *(camera)*
  mettre en marche to turn on
meublé(e) furnished
meubles *mpl* furniture
  meubles de style period furniture
mi-bas *mpl* pop-socks ; knee-highs
midi *m* midday ; noon
Midi *m* the south of France
miel *m* honey
mieux better ; best
migraine *f* headache ; migraine
milieu *m* middle
mille *m* thousand
millimètre *m* millimetre
million *m* million
mince slim ; thin
mine *f* expression ; mine *(coal, etc)*
mineur *m* miner
mineur(e) under age ; minor
minimum *m* minimum
minuit *m* midnight
minuscule tiny
minute *f* minute
minuteur *m* timer
mirabelle *f* plum ; plum brandy
miroir *m* mirror
mise en plis *f* set *(for hair)*
mistral *m* strong cold dry wind

mite *f* moth *(clothes)*
mixte mixed
mobilier *m* furniture
mode *f* fashion
  à la mode fashionable
  mode d'emploi instructions for use
modem *m* modem
moderne modern
moelle *f* marrow *(beef, etc)*
moi me
moineau *m* sparrow
moins less ; minus
  moins (de) less (than)
  moins cher cheaper
moins *m* the least
mois *m* month
moisissure *f* mould *(fungus)*
moitié *f* half
  à moitié prix half-price
moka *m* coffee cream cake ;
  mocha coffee
molle soft
moment *m* moment
  en ce moment at the moment
mon/ma/mes my
monastère *m* monastery
monde *m* world
  il y a du monde there's a lot
  of people
moniteur *m* instructor ; coach
monitrice *f* instructress ; coach
monnaie *f* currency ; change
monnayeur *m* automatic change
  machine
monsieur *m* gentleman
Monsieur *m* Mr ; Sir
montagne *f* mountain
montant *m* amount *(total)*
monter to take up ; to go up ;
  to rise ; to get in *(car)*
  monter à cheval to horse-ride
montre *f* watch
montrer to show
monument *m* monument
moquette *f* fitted carpet
morceau *m* piece ; bit ; cut *(of meat)*
mordu(e) bitten

morsure f bite
  morsure de serpent snake bite
mort(e) dead
mosquée f mosque
mot m word ; note (letter)
  mot de passe password
  mots croisés crossword puzzle
motel m motel
moteur m engine ; motor
  moteur de recherche search
  engine
motif m pattern
moto f motorbike
mou (molle) soft
mouche f fly
moucheron m midge
mouchoir m handkerchief
mouette f seagull
mouillé(e) wet
moule f mussel
moulin m mill
  moulin à vent windmill
moulinet m reel (fishing)
mourir to die
mousse f foam ; mousse
  mousse à raser shaving foam
  mousse coiffante hair mousse
mousseux(-euse) sparkling (wine)
moustache f moustache
moustique m mosquito
moutarde f mustard
mouton m sheep ; lamb ; mutton
moyen(ne) average
moyenne f average
muguet m lily of the valley ; thrush
  (candida)
muni(e) de supplied with ;
  in possession of
mur m wall
mûr(e) mature ; ripe
mûre f blackberry
muscade f nutmeg
musée m museum
  musée d'art art gallery
musique f music
Musulman(e) Muslim
myope short-sighted

N

nager to swim
naissance f birth
nappe f tablecloth
nappé(e) coated (with chocolate, etc)
natation f swimming
national(e) national
nationalité f nationality
natte f plait
nature f wildlife
naturel(le) natural
nautique nautical ; water
navet m turnip
navette f shuttle (bus service)
navigation f sailing
navire m ship
né(e) born
nectarine f nectarine
négatif m negative (photography)
neige f snow
neiger to snow
nettoyage m cleaning
  nettoyage à sec dry-cleaning
nettoyer to clean
neuf (neuve) new
neveu m nephew
névralgie f headache
nez m nose
niche f kennel
nid m nest
  nid de poule pothole
nièce f niece
niveau m level ; standard
noce f wedding
nocturne m late opening
Noël m Christmas
  joyeux Noël! merry Christmas!
noir(e) black
noisette f hazelnut
noix f nut ; walnut
nom m name ; noun
  nom de famille family name
  nom de jeune fille maiden name
nombre m number
nombreux(-euse) numerous

non no ; not
non alcoolisé(e) non-alcoholic
non-fumeur non-smoking
nord m north
normal(e) normal ; standard (size)
nos our
notaire m solicitor
note f note ; bill ; memo
notre our
nœud m knot
nourrir to feed
nourriture f food
nouveau (nouvelle) new
  de nouveau again
nouvelles fpl news
novembre November
nu(e) naked ; bare
nuage m cloud
nuageux(-euse) cloudy
nucléaire nuclear
nuit f night
  bonne nuit good night
numéro m number ; act ; issue

O

objectif m objective ; lens (of camera)
objet m object
  objets de valeur valuable items
  objets trouvés lost property
obligatoire compulsory
oblitérer to stamp (ticket, stamp)
obsèques fpl funeral
obtenir to get ; to obtain
occasion f occasion ; bargain
occupé(e) busy ; hired (taxi) ;
  engaged (toilet)
océan m ocean
octobre October
odeur f smell
œuf m egg
  œuf de Pâques Easter egg
office m service (church) ; office
  office du tourisme tourist office
offre f offer
oie f goose
oignon m onion
œil m eye

œillet m carnation
oiseau m bird
olive f olive
ombre f shade/shadow
  à l'ombre in the shade
oncle m uncle
onde f wave
ongle m nail (finger)
opéra m opera
or m gold
orage m storm
orange orange ; amber (traffic light)
orange f orange
orangeade f orange squash
orchestre m orchestra ; stalls
  (in theatre)
ordinaire ordinary
ordinateur m computer
ordonnance f prescription
ordre m order
  à l'ordre de payable to
ordures fpl litter (rubbish)
oreille f ear
oreiller m pillow
oreillons mpl mumps
organiser to organize
orge f barley
origan m oregano
os m bone
oseille f sorrel
osier m wicker
ou or
où where
oublier to forget
ouest m west
oui yes
ours(e) m/f bear (animal)
oursin m sea urchin
outils mpl tools
ouvert(e) open ; on (tap, gas, etc)
ouverture f overture ; opening
ouvrable working (day)
ouvre-boîtes m tin-opener
ouvre-bouteilles m bottle-opener
ouvrir to open

P

page f page
  pages jaunes Yellow Pages
paiement m payment
paille f straw
pain m bread ; loaf of bread
  pain bis brown bread
  pain complet wholemeal bread
  pain grillé toast
pair(e) even
paire f pair
paix f peace
palais m palace
pâle pale
palmes fpl flippers
palourde f clam
pamplemousse m grapefruit
panaché m shandy
pané(e) in breadcrumbs
panier m basket
  panier repas packed lunch
panne f breakdown
panneau m sign
pansement m bandage
pantalon m trousers
pantoufles fpl slippers
pape m pope
papeterie f stationer's shop
papier m paper
  papier à lettres writing paper
  papier alu(minium) foil
  papier cadeau gift-wrap
  papier hygiénique toilet paper
  papiers identity papers ; driving
  licence
papillon m butterfly
pâquerette f daisy
Pâques m or fpl Easter
paquet m package ; packet
par by ; through ; per
  par example for example
  par jour per day
  par téléphone by phone
  par voie orale take by mouth
  (medicine)
paradis m heaven
paralysé(e) paralysed

parapluie m umbrella
parasol m sunshade
parc m park
  parc d'attractions funfair
parce que because
parcmètre m parking meter
parcours m route
pardon! sorry! ; excuse me!
parer to ward off
pare-brise m windscreen
pare-chocs m bumper
parent(e) m/f relative
parents mpl parents
paresseux(-euse) lazy
parfait(e) perfect
parfum m perfume ; flavour
parfumerie f perfume shop
pari m bet
parier sur to bet on
parking m car park
  parking assuré parking facilities
  parking souterrain underground
  car park
  parking surveillé attended car park
parler (à) to speak (to) ; to talk (to)
paroisse f parish
partager to share
parterre m flowerbed
parti m political party
partie f part ; match (game)
partir to leave ; to go
  à partir de from
partout everywhere
pas not
  pas encore not yet
pas m step ; pace
passage m passage
  passage à niveau level crossing
  passage clouté pedestrian crossing
  passage interdit no through way
  passage souterrain underpass
passager(-ère) m/f passenger
passé(e) past
passe-temps m hobby
passeport m passport
passer to pass ; to spend (time)
  se passer to happen

passerelle f **gangway** *(bridge)*
passionnant(e) **exciting**
passoire f **sieve** ; **colander**
pastèque f **watermelon**
pasteur m **minister** *(of religion)*
pastille f **lozenge**
pastis m **aniseed-flavoured apéritif**
pataugeoire f **paddling pool**
pâte f **pastry** ; **dough** ; **paste**
pâté m **pâté**
pâtes fpl **pasta**
patient(e) m/f **patient** *(in hospital)*
patin m **skate**
  patins à glace **ice skates**
  patins à roulettes **roller skates**
patinoire f **skating rink**
pâtisserie f **cake shop** ; **little cake**
patron m **boss** ; **pattern** *(knitting, dress, etc)*
patronne f **boss**
pauvre **poor**
payer **to pay (for)**
  payé(e) **paid**
  payé(e) d'avance **prepaid**
pays m **land** ; **country**
  du pays **local**
Pays-Bas mpl **Netherlands**
paysage m **countryside** ; **scenery**
péage m **toll** *(motorway, etc)*
peau f **hide** *(leather)* ; **skin**
pêche f **peach** ; **fishing**
pêcher **to fish**
pêcheur m **angler**
pédale f **pedal**
pédalo m **pedal boat/pedalo**
pédicure m/f **chiropodist**
peigne m **comb**
peignoir m **dressing gown** ; **bath-robe**
peindre **to paint** ; **to decorate**
peinture f **painting** ; **paintwork**
peler **to peel** *(fruit)*
pèlerinage m **pilgrimage**
pelle f **spade**
  pelle à poussière **dustpan**
pellicule f **film** *(for camera)*
  pellicule couleur **colour film**

pellicule noir et blanc **black and white film**
pelote f **ball** *(of string, wool)*
  pelote basque **pelota** *(ball game for 2 players)*
pelouse f **lawn**
pencher **to lean**
pendant **during**
pendant que **while**
pénicilline f **penicillin**
péninsule f **peninsula**
pénis m **penis**
penser **to think**
pension f **guesthouse**
  pension complète **full board**
pente f **slope**
Pentecôte f **Whitsun**
pépin m **pip**
perceuse électrique f **electric drill**
perdre **to lose**
perdu(e) **lost** *(object)*
père m **father**
périmé(e) **out of date**
périphérique m **ring road**
perle f **bead** ; **pearl**
permanente f **perm**
permettre **to permit**
permis m **permit** ; **licence**
  permis de chasse **hunting permit**
  permis de conduire **driving licence**
  permis de pêche **fishing permit**
perruque f **wig**
persil m **parsley**
personne f **person**
peser **to weigh**
pétanque f **type of bowls**
pétillant(e) **fizzy**
petit(e) **small** ; **slight**
  petit déjeuner **breakfast**
  petit pain **roll**
petit-fils m **grandson**
petite-fille f **granddaughter**
pétrole m **oil** *(petroleum)* ; **paraffin**
peu **little** ; **few**
  à peu près **approximately**
  un peu (de) **a bit (of)**
peur f **fear**

avoir peur (de) to be afraid (of)

peut-être perhaps

phare m headlight ; lighthouse

pharmacie f chemist's ; pharmacy

phoque m seal (animal)

photo f photograph

photocopie f photocopy

photocopier to photocopy

piano m piano

pichet m jug ; carafe

pie f magpie

pièce f room (in house) ; play (theatre) ; coin
  pièce d'identité means of identification
  pièce de rechange spare part
  pièce jointe attachment (e-mail)

pied m foot
  à pied on foot

pierre f stone

piéton m pedestrian

pignon m pine kernel

pile f pile ; battery

pilon m drumstick (of chicken)

pilote m/f pilot

pilule f pill

pin m pine

pince f pliers
  pince à cheveux hairgrip
  pince à épiler tweezers
  pince à linge clothes peg

pipe f pipe (smoking)

piquant(e) spicy ; hot

pique-nique m picnic

piquer to sting

piquet m peg (for tent)

piqûre f insect bite ; injection ; sting

pire worse

piscine f swimming pool

pissenlit m dandelion

pistache f pistachio (nut)

piste f ski-run ; runway
  piste cyclable cycle track
  piste de luge toboggan run
  piste pour débutants nursery slope
  pistes tous niveaux slopes for all levels of skiers

pistolet m pistol ; gun

placard m cupboard

place f square (in town) ; seat ; space (room)
  places debout standing room

plafond m ceiling

plage f beach

plainte f complaint

plaisanterie f joke

plaisir m enjoyment ; pleasure

plaît: s'il vous/te plaît please

plan m map (of town)
  plan de la ville street map

planche f plank
  planche à découper chopping board
  planche à repasser ironing board
  planche à voile sailboard ; windsurfing
  planche de surf surfboard

plancher m floor (of room)

plante f plant ; sole

plaque f sheet ; plate
  plaque d'immatriculation numberplate

plat m dish ; course (of meal)
  plat de résistance main course
  plat principal main course
  plat à emporter take-away meal

plat(e) level (surface) ; flat
  à plat flat (battery)

platane m plane tree

plateau m tray

plâtre m plaster

plein(e) (de) full (of)
  le plein! fill it up! (car)
  plein sud facing south
  plein tarif peak rate

pleurer to cry (weep)

pleuvoir to rain
  il pleut it's raining

plier to fold

plomb m lead ; fuse

plombage m filling (in tooth)

plombier m plumber

plonger to dive

pluie f rain

plume f feather

plus more ; most

plus grand(e) (que) bigger (than)
plus tard later
plusieurs **several**
pneu *m* **tyre**
 pneu de rechange **spare tyre**
 pneu dégonflé **flat tyre**
 pneus cloutés **snow tyres**
poche *f* **pocket**
poché(e) **poached**
poêle *f* **frying-pan**
poème *m* **poem**
poids *m* **weight**
 poids lourd **heavy goods vehicle**
poignée *f* **handle**
poignet *m* **wrist**
poil *m* **hair ; coat** *(of animal)*
poinçonner **to punch** *(ticket, etc)*
point *m* **place ; point ; stitch ; dot**
 à point **medium rare** *(meat)*
pointure *f* **size** *(of shoes)*
poire *f* **pear ; pear brandy**
poireau *m* **leek**
pois *m* **pea ; spot** *(dot)*
 petits pois **peas**
poison *m* **poison**
poisson *m* **fish**
poissonnerie *f* **fishmonger's shop**
poitrine *f* **breast ; chest**
poivre *m* **pepper**
poivron *m* **pepper** *(capsicum)*
police *f* **policy** *(insurance)* **; police**
policier *m* **policeman ; detective film/novel**
pollué(e) **polluted**
pommade *f* **ointment**
pomme *f* **apple ; potato**
pomme de terre *f* **potato**
pompe *f* **pump**
pompes funèbres *fpl* **undertaker's**
pompier *m* **fireman**
 pompiers **fire brigade**
poney *m* **pony**
pont *m* **bridge ; deck** *(of ship)*
 faire le pont **to have a long weekend**
populaire **popular**
porc *m* **pork ; pig**

port *m* **harbour ; port**
portable *m* **mobile phone ; laptop**
portatif **portable**
porte *f* **door ; gate**
portefeuille *m* **wallet**
porter **to wear; to carry**
porte-bagages *m* **luggage rack**
porte-clefs *m* **keyring**
porte-monnaie *m* **purse**
porteur *m* **porter**
portier *m* **doorman**
portion *f* **helping ; portion**
porto *m* **port** *(wine)*
poser **to put ; to lay down**
posologie *f* **dosage**
posséder **to own**
poste *f* **post ; post office**
 poste de contrôle **checkpoint**
 poste de secours **first-aid post**
poste *m* **radio/television set ; extension** *(phone)*
poster *m* **poster** *(decorative)*
poster **to post**
pot *m* **pot ; carton**
 pot d'échappement **exhaust pipe**
potable **ok to drink**
potage *m* **soup**
poteau *m* **post** *(pole)*
 poteau indicateur **signpost**
poterie *f* **pottery**
poubelle *f* **dustbin**
pouce *m* **thumb**
poudre *f* **powder**
poule *f* **hen**
poulet *m* **chicken**
poumon *m* **lung**
poupée *f* **doll**
pour **for**
pourboire *m* **tip**
pourquoi **why**
pourri(e) **rotten** *(fruit, etc)*
pousser **to push**
poussette *f* **push chair**
pousser **to push**
poussière *f* **dust**
pouvoir **to be able to**
pré *m* **meadow**

préfecture de police f police headquarters
préféré(e) favourite
préférer to prefer
premier(-ière) first
  premier cru first-class wine
  premiers secours first aid
prendre to take ; to get ; to catch
prénom m first name
préparer to prepare ; to cook
près de near (to)
présenter to present ; to introduce
préservatif m condom
pressé(e) squeezed ; pressed
pressing m dry cleaner's
pression f pressure
  pression des pneus tyre pressure
prêt(e) ready
  prêt à cuire ready to cook
prêt-à-porter m ready-to-wear
prêter to lend
prêtre m priest
prévision f forecast
prier to pray
prière de... please...
prince m prince
princesse f princess
principal(e) main
printemps m spring
priorité f right of way
  priorité à droite give way to traffic from right
prise f plug ; socket
privé(e) private
prix m price ; prize
  à prix réduit cut-price
  prix d'entrée admission fee
  prix de détail retail price
probablement probably
problème m problem
prochain(e) next
proche close (near)
produits mpl produce ; product
professeur m teacher
profiter de to take advantage of
profond(e) deep
programme m schedule ;

programme (list of performers, etc)
  programme informatique computer program
promenade f walk ; promenade ; ride (in vehicle)
  faire une promenade to go for a walk
promettre to promise
promotionnel(le) special low-price
prononcer to pronounce
propre clean ; own
propriétaire m/f owner
propriété f property
protège-slip m panty-liner
protestant(e) Protestant
provenance f origin ; source
provisions fpl groceries
province f province
provisoire temporary
provisoirement for the time being
proximité: à proximité nearby
prune f plum ; plum brandy
pruneau m prune
public m audience
public(-ique) public
publicité f advert (on TV)
puce f flea
puissance f power
puits m well (for water)
pull m sweater
pullover m sweater
purée f purée ; mashed
PV m parking ticket
pyjama m pyjamas

Q

quai m platform
qualifié(e) skilled
qualité f quality
quand when
quantité f quantity
quarantaine f quarantine
quart m quarter
quartier m neighbourhood ; district
que that ; than ; whom ; what
  qu'est-ce que c'est? what is it?

quel(le) which ; what
quelqu'un someone
quelque some
quelque chose something
quelquefois sometimes
question f question
queue f queue ; tail
  faire la queue to queue (up)
qui who ; which
quincaillerie f hardware ; hardware shop
quinzaine f fortnight
quitter to leave a place
quoi what
quotidien(ne) daily

R

rabais m reduction
raccourci m short cut
raccrocher to hang up *(phone)*
race f race *(people)*
racine f root
radiateur m radiator
radio f radio
  radio numérique digital radio
radiographie f X-ray
radis m radish
rafraîchissements *mpl* refreshments
rage f rabies
ragoût m stew ; casserole
raide steep
raie f skate *(fish)*
raifort m horseradish
raisin m grapes
  raisins secs sultanas ; raisins ; currants
  raisin blanc green grapes
  raisin noir black grapes
raison f reason
ralentir to slow down
ralentissement m tailback
rallonge f extension *(electrical)*
randonnée f hike
  randonnée à cheval pony-trekking
râpe f grater
râpé(e) grated
rappel m reminder *(on signs)*

rappeler to remind
  se rappeler to remember
rapide quick ; fast
rapide m express train
raquette f racket ; bat ; snowshoe
rare rare ; unusual
raser to shave off
  se raser to shave
rasoir m razor
rater to miss *(train, flight etc)*
RATP f Paris transport authority
rayé(e) striped
rayon m shelf ; department *(in store)* ; spoke *(of wheel)*
  rayon hommes menswear
RC ground floor
reboucher to recork
récemment recently
récepteur m receiver *(of phone)*
réception f reception ; check-in
réceptionniste *m/f* receptionist
recette f recipe
recharge f refill
rechargeable refillable *(lighter, pen)*
recharger to recharge *(battery, etc)*
  le rechargeur recharger
réchaud de camping m camping stove
réclamation f complaint
réclame f advertisement
recommandé(e) registered *(mail)*
recommander to recommend
récompense f reward
reconnaître to recognize
reçu m receipt
réduction f reduction ; discount; concession
réduire to reduce
refuge m mountain hut
refuser to reject ; to refuse
regarder to look at
régime m diet *(slimming)*
région f region
règle f rule ; ruler *(for measuring)*
règles *fpl* period *(menstruation)*
  règles douloureuses cramps

règlement *m* regulation ; payment
régler to pay ; to settle
réglisse *f* liquorice
reine *f* queen
relais routier *m* roadside restaurant
rembourser to refund
remède *m* remedy
remercier to thank
remettre to put back
  remettre à plus tard to postpone
  se remettre to recover *(from illness)*
remonte-pente *m* ski tow
remorque *f* trailer
remorquer to tow
remplir to fill ; to fill in/out/up
renard *m* fox
rencontrer to meet
rendez-vous *m* date ; appointment
rendre to give back
renouveler to renew
renseignements *mpl* information
rentrée *f* return to work after break
  rentrée (des classes) start of the
  new school year
renverser to knock down *(in car)*
réparations *fpl* repairs
réparer to fix *(repair)*
repas *m* meal
repasser to iron
répondeur automatique *m* answerphone
répondre (à) to reply ; to answer
réponse *f* answer ; reply
repos *m* rest
  se reposer to rest
représentation *f* performance
requis(e) required
RER *m* Paris high-speed commuter
  train
réseau *m* network
réservation *f* reservation ; booking
réserve naturelle *f* nature reserve
réservé(e) reserved
réserver to book *(reserve)*
réservoir *m* tank
  réservoir d'essence fuel tank
respirer to breathe

ressort *m* spring *(metal)*
restaurant *m* restaurant
reste *m* rest *(remainder)*
rester to remain ; to stay
restoroute *m* roadside or motorway
  restaurant
retard *m* delay
retirer to withdraw ; to collect
  (tickets)
retour *m* return
retourner to go back
retrait *m* withdrawal ; collection
  retrait d'espèces cash withdrawal
retraité(e) retired
retraité(e) *m/f* old-age pensioner
rétrécir to shrink *(clothes)*
rétroviseur *m* rearview mirror
  rétroviseur latéral wing mirror
réunion *f* meeting
réussir (à) to succeed
réussite *f* success ; patience *(game)*
réveil *m* alarm clock
réveiller to wake *(someone)*
  se réveiller to wake up
réveillon *m* Christmas/
  New Year's Eve
revenir to come back
réverbère *m* lamppost
revue *f* review ; magazine
rez-de-chaussée *m* ground floor
rhum *m* rum
rhumatisme *m* rheumatism
rhume *m* cold *(illness)*
  rhume des foins hay fever
riche rich
rideau *m* curtain
rides *fpl* wrinkles
rien nothing ; anything
  rien à déclarer nothing to declare
rire to laugh
rivage *m* shore
rive *f* river bank
rivière *f* river
riz *m* rice
RN trunk road
robe *f* gown ; dress
robinet *m* tap

rocade f ringroad
rocher m rock (boulder)
rognon m kidney (to eat)
roi m king
roman m novel
roman(e) Romanesque
romantique romantic
romarin m rosemary
rond(e) round
rond-point m roundabout
rose pink
rose f rose
rossignol m nightingale
rôti(e) roast
rôtisserie f steakhouse ; roast meat
counter
roue f wheel
roue de secours spare wheel
rouge red
rouge à lèvres m lipstick
rouge-gorge m robin
rougeole f measles
rougeur f rash (skin)
rouillé(e) rusty
rouleau à pâtisserie m rolling pin
rouler to roll ; to go (by car)
route f road ; route
route barrée road closed
route nationale trunk road
route principale major road
route secondaire minor road
routier m lorry driver
Royaume-Uni m United Kingdom
ruban m ribbon ; tape
rubéole f rubella
rue f street
rue sans issue no through road
ruelle f lane ; alley
ruisseau m stream
russe Russian

S

SA Ltd ; plc
sable m sand
sables mouvants quicksand
sabot m wheel clamp

sac m sack ; bag
sac à dos backpack
sac à main handbag
sac de couchage sleeping bag
sac poubelle bin liner
sachet de thé m tea bag
sacoche f panniers (for bike)
safran m saffron
sage good (well-behaved) ; wise
saignant(e) rare (steak)
saigner to bleed
saint(e) m/f saint
Saint-Sylvestre f New Year's Eve
saisir to seize
saison f season
basse saison low season
de saison in season
haute saison high season
saisonnier seasonal
salade f lettuce ; salad
salade de fruits fruit salad
salaire m salary ; wage
sale dirty
salé(e) salty ; savoury
salle f lounge (airport) ; hall ; ward
(hospital)
salle à manger dining room
salle d'attente waiting room
salle de bains bathroom
salon m sitting room ; lounge
salon de beauté beauty salon
salut! hi!
samedi m Saturday
SAMU m emergency services
sandales fpl sandals
sandwich m sandwich
sang m blood
sanglier m wild boar
sans without
sans alcool alcohol-free
sans connaissance unconscious
sans issue no through road
santé f health
santé! cheers!
en bonne santé well
sapeurs-pompiers mpl fire brigade
SARL f Ltd ; plc
sauce f sauce

sauf except (for)
saumon m salmon
sauter to jump
sauvegarder to back up (computer)
sauver to rescue
savoir to know (be aware of)
  savoir faire quelque chose
  to know how to do sth
savon m soap
scanner to scan
  le scanner scan
  le scanner scanner
scène f stage
scie f saw
score m score (of match)
Scotch® m Sellotape®
séance f meeting ; performance
seau m bucket
sec (sèche) dried (fruit, beans)
sèche-cheveux m hairdryer
sèche-linge m tumble dryer
sécher to dry
seconde f second (in time)
  en seconde second class
secouer to shake
secours m help
secrétaire m/f secretary
secrétariat m office
secteur m sector ; mains
sécurité f security ; safety
séjour m stay ; visit
sel m salt
self m self-service restaurant
selle f saddle
semaine f week
sens m meaning ; direction
  sens interdit no entry
  sens unique one-way street
sentier m footpath
  sentier écologique nature trail
sentir to feel
septembre September
séparément separately
série f series ; set
seringue f syringe
serré(e) tight (fitting)
serrer to grip ; to squeeze

serrez à droite keep to the right
serrure f lock
serrurerie f locksmith's
serveur m waiter
serveuse f waitress
servez-vous help yourself
service m service ; service charge ;
  favour
  service compris service included
  service d'urgences A & E
serviette f towel ; briefcase
  serviette hygiénique sanitary
  towel
servir to dish up ; to serve
seul(e) alone ; lonely
seulement only
sexe m sex
shampooing m shampoo
  shampooing antipelliculaire anti-
  dandruff shampoo
short m shorts
si if ; yes (to negative question)
SIDA m AIDS
siècle m century
siège m seat ; head office
  siège pour bébés/enfants car seat
  (for children)
signaler to report
signer to sign
simple simple ; single ; plain
site m site
  site web web site
situé(e) located
ski m ski ; skiing
  ski de piste downhill skiing
  ski de randonnée/fond
  cross-country skiing
  ski nautique water-skiing
slip m underpants ; panties
  slip (de bain) swimming trunks
snack m snack bar
SNCB f Belgian Railways
SNCF f French Railways
société f company ; society
sœur f sister
soie f silk
soif f thirst
  avoir soif to be thirsty
soin m care

soins du visage facial
soir *m* evening
soirée *f* evening ; party
soja *m* soya ; soya bean
sol *m* ground ; soil
soldat *m* soldier
solde *m* balance *(remainder owed)*
soldes *mpl* sales
  soldes permanents sale prices
  all year round
sole *f* sole *(fish)*
soleil *m* sun ; sunshine
somme *f* sum
sommelier *m* wine waiter
sommet *m* top *(of hill, mountain)*
somnifère *m* sleeping pill
sonner to ring ; to strike
sonnette *f* doorbell
sonner to ring bell
sorbet *m* water ice
sorte *f* kind *(sort, type)*
sortie *f* exit
  sortie de secours emergency exit
  sortie interdite no exit
sortir to go out *(leave)*
soucoupe *f* saucer
soudain suddenly
souhaiter to wish
soûl(e) drunk
soulever to lift
soupape *f* valve
soupe *f* soup
souper *m* supper
sourcils *mpl* eyebrows
sourd(e) deaf
sourire to smile
souris *f* mouse *(also for computer)*
sous underneath ; under
sous-sol *m* basement
sous-titres *mpl* subtitles
sous-vêtements *mpl* underwear
souterrain(e) underground
soutien-gorge *m* bra
souvenir *m* memory ; souvenir
souvent often
sparadrap *m* sticking plaster

spécial(e) special
spécialité *f* speciality
spectacle *m* show *(in theatre)* ;
  entertainment
spectateurs *mpl* audience
spiritueux *mpl* spirits
sport *m* sport
  sports nautiques water sports
sportif(-ive) sports ; athletic
stade *m* stadium
stage *m* course
standard *m* switchboard
station *f* station *(metro)* ; resort
  station balnéaire seaside resort
  station de taxis taxi rank
  station thermale spa
  station-service service station
stationnement *m* parking
stérilet *m* coil *(IUD)*
stimulateur (cardiaque) *m*
  pacemaker
store *m* blind ; awning
stylo *m* pen
sucette *f* lollipop ; dummy
sucre *m* sugar
sucré(e) sweet
sud *m* south
suisse Swiss
Suisse *f* Switzerland
suite *f* series ; continuation ; sequel
suivant(e) following
suivre to follow
  faire suivre please forward
super *m* four-star petrol
supermarché *m* supermarket
supplément *m* extra charge
supplémentaire extra
sur on ; onto ; on top of ; upon
  sur place on the spot
sûr safe ; sure
surcharger to overload
surchauffer to overheat
surf *m* surfing
  faire du surf to surf
  surf des neiges snowboard
  surf sur neige snowboarding
surgelés *mpl* frozen foods

surveillé(e) **supervised**
survêtement m **tracksuit**
sympa(thique) **nice ; pleasant**
synagogue f **synagogue**
syndicat d'initiative m **tourist office**

T

tabac m **tobacco ; tobacconist's**
table f **table**
tableau m **painting ; picture ; board**
  tableau de bord **dashboard**
tablier m **apron**
tache f **stain**
taie d'oreiller f **pillowcase**
taille f **size** *(of clothes)* **; waist**
  taille unique **one size**
  grande taille **outsize (clothes)**
tailleur m **tailor ; suit**
talc m **talc**
talon m **heel ; stub** *(counterfoil)*
  talon minute **shoes reheeled while**
  you wait
tampon m **tampon**
  tampon Jex® **scouring pad**
tante f **aunt**
taper **to strike ; to type**
tapis m **carpet**
  tapis de sol **groundsheet**
tard **late**
  au plus tard **at the latest**
tarif m **price-list ; rate ; tarif**
tarte f **flan ; tart**
tartine f **slice of bread and butter**
  (or jam)
tartiner: *à tartiner* **for spreading**
tasse f **cup ; mug**
taureau m **bull**
tauromachie f **bull-fighting**
taux m **rate**
  taux de change **exchange rate**
  taux fixe **flat rate**
taxe f **duty ; tax** *(on goods)*
taxi m **cab** *(taxi)*
TCF m **Touring Club de France** *(AA)*
teinture f **dye**
teinturerie f **dry cleaner's**
télé f **TV**

télébenne f **gondola lift**
télécabine f **gondola lift**
télécarte f **phonecard**
télécharger **to download**
télécommande f **remote control**
téléphérique m **cable-car**
téléphone m **telephone**
  téléphone portable **mobile phone**
téléphoner (à) **to phone**
téléphoniste m/f **operator**
télésiège m **chair-lift**
téléviseur m **television (set)**
télévision f **television**
température f **temperature**
tempête f **storm**
temple m **temple ; synagogue ;**
  protestant church
temps m **weather ; time**
tendon m **tendon**
tenir **to hold ; to keep**
tennis m **tennis**
tension f **voltage ; blood pressure**
tente f **tent**
tenue f **clothes ; dress**
  tenue de soirée **evening dress**
terrain m **ground ; land ; pitch ;**
  course
terrasse f **terrace**
terre f **land ; earth ; ground**
  terre cuite **terracotta**
tête f **head**
tétine f **dummy** *(for baby)* **; teat**
  (for bottle)
TGV m **high-speed train**
thé m **tea**
  thé au lait **tea with milk**
  thé nature **black tea**
théâtre m **theatre**
théière f **teapot**
thermomètre m **thermometer**
ticket m **ticket** *(bus, cinema, museum)*
  ticket de caisse **receipt**
tiède **lukewarm**
tiers m **third ; third party**
timbre m **stamp**
tirage m **printing ; print** *(photo)*

tirage le mercredi lottery draw on Wednesdays
tire-bouchon m **corkscrew**
tire-fesses m **ski tow**
tirer to **pull**
 tirez pull
tiroir m **drawer**
tisane f **herbal tea**
tissu m **material ; fabric**
titre m **title**
 à titre indicatif for info only
 à titre provisoire provisionally
titulaire m/f **holder of**
toile f **canvas ; web** (spider)
 Toile World Wide Web
toilettes fpl **toilet ; powder room**
toit m **roof**
 toit ouvrant sunroof
tomate f **tomato**
tomber to **fall**
tonalité f **dialling tone**
tongs fpl **flip flops**
tonneau m **barrel (wine/beer)**
tonnerre m **thunder**
torchon m **tea towel**
tordre to **twist**
tôt **early**
total m **total** (amount)
toucher to **touch**
toujours **always ; still ; forever**
tour f **tower**
tour m **trip ; walk ; ride**
tourisme m **sightseeing**
touriste m/f **tourist**
touristique **tourist** (route, resort, etc)
tourner to **turn**
tournesol m **sunflower**
tournevis m **screwdriver**
 tournevis cruciforme phillips screwdriver®
tourte f **pie**
tous **all (plural)**
 tous les jours daily
Toussaint f **All Saints' Day**
tousser to **cough**
tout(e) **all ; everything**
 tout à l'heure in a while

tout compris all inclusive
tout de suite straight away
tout droit straight ahead
tout le monde **everyone**
toutes **all** (plural)
 toutes directions all routes
toux f **cough**
tradition f **custom** (tradition)
traditionnel(-elle) **traditional**
traduction f **translation**
traduire to **translate**
train m **train**
trajet m **journey**
tramway m **tram**
tranchant **sharp** (razor, knife)
tranche f **slice**
tranquille **quiet** (place)
transférer to **transfer**
transpirer to **sweat**
travail m **work**
travailler to **work** (person)
 travailler à son compte to be self employed
travaux mpl **road works ; alterations**
travers: *à travers* **through**
traversée f **crossing** (voyage)
traverser to **cross** (road, sea)
tremplin m **diving-board**
 tremplin de ski ski jump
très **very ; much**
triangle de présignalisation m **warning triangle**
tricot m **knitting ; sweater**
tricoter to **knit**
trimestre m **term**
triste **sad**
trop **too ; too much**
trottoir m **pavement ; sidewalk**
trou m **hole**
trousse f **pencil case**
 trousse de premiers secours first aid kit
trouver to **find**
 se trouver to be (situated)
tuer to **kill**
tunnel m **tunnel**
tuyau m **pipe** (for water, gas)

tuyau d'arrosage hosepipe
TVA *f* VAT
typique typical

U

UE *f* EU
ulcère *m* ulcer
ultérieur(e) later *(date, etc)*
un(e) one ; a ; an
　l'un ou l'autre either one
uni(e) plain *(not patterned)*
Union européenne *f* European Union
université *f* university
urgence *f* urgency ; emergency
　Urgences A & E
urine *f* urine
usage *m* use
usine *f* factory
utile useful
utiliser to use

V

vacances *fpl* holiday(s)
　en vacances on holiday
　grandes vacances summer holiday
vaccin *m* vaccination
vache *f* cow
vagin *m* vagina
vague *f* wave *(on sea)*
vaisselle *f* crockery
valable valid *(ticket, licence, etc)*
valeur *f* value
valider to validate
valise *f* suitcase
vallée *f* valley
valoir to be worth
　ça vaut... it's worth...
vanille *f* vanilla
vapeur *f* steam
varicelle *f* chickenpox
varié(e) varied ; various
vase *m* vase
veau *m* calf ; veal
vedette *f* speedboat ; star *(film)*
végétal(e) vegetable
végétarien(ne) vegetarian
véhicule *m* vehicle

véhicules lents slow-moving
vehicles
veille *f* the day before ; eve
　veille de Noël Christmas Eve
veine *f* vein
vélo *m* bike
　vélo tout terrain (VTT)
mountain bike
velours *m* velvet
venaison *f* venison
vendange(s) *fpl* harvest *(of grapes)*
vendeur(-euse) *m/f* sales assistant
vendre to sell
　à vendre for sale
vendredi *m* Friday
　vendredi saint Good Friday
vénéneux poisonous
venir to come
vent *m* wind
vente *f* sale
　vente aux enchères auction
ventilateur *m* ventilator ; fan
verglas *m* black ice
vérifier to check ; to audit
vernis *m* varnish
　vernis à ongles nail varnish
verre *m* glass
　verres de contact contact lenses
verrouillage central *m* central
locking
vers toward(s) ; about
versement *m* payment ; instalment
verser to pour ; to pay
vert(e) green
veste *f* jacket
vestiaire *m* cloakroom
vêtements *mpl* clothes
vétérinaire *m/f* vet
veuf *m* widower
veuillez... please...
veuve *f* widow
via by *(via)*
viande *f* meat
　viande hachée mince *(meat)*
vidange *f* oil change *(car)*
vide empty
videoclub *m* video shop

vie f life
vieux (vieille) old
vigile m security guard
vigne f vine ; vineyard
vignoble m vineyard
VIH m HIV
village m village
ville f town ; city
vin m wine
  vin en pichet house wine
  vin pétillant sparkling wine
vinaigre m vinegar
violer to rape
violet(-ette) purple
vipère f adder ; viper
virage m bend ; curve ; corner
vis f screw
  vis platinées points (in car)
visage m face
visite f visit ; consultation (of doctor)
  visite guidée guided tour
visiter to visit (a place)
visiteur(-euse) m/f visitor
visser to screw on
vite quickly ; fast
vitesse f gear (of car) ; speed
  vitesse limitée à... speed limit...
vitrail m stained-glass window
vitrine f shop window
vivre to live
VO: en VO with subtitles (film)
vœu m wish
voici here is/are
voie f lane (of road) ; line ; track
voilà there is/are
voile f sail ; sailing
voilier m sailing boat
voir to see
voisin(e) m/f neighbour
voiture f car ; coach (of train)
vol m flight ; theft
  vol intérieur domestic flight
volaille f poultry
volant m steering wheel
voler to fly (bird) ; to steal
volet m shutter (on window)
voleur(-euse) m/f thief

volonté f will
  à volonté as much as you like
vomir to vomit
V.O.S.T. original version with
  subtitles (film)
vouloir to want
voyage m journey
  voyage d'affaires business trip
  voyage organisé package holiday
voyager to travel
voyageur(-euse) m/f traveller
vrai(e) real ; true
VTT m mountain bike
vue f view ; sight

W

w-c mpl toilet
wagon m carriage ; waggon
wagon-couchettes m sleeping car
wagon-restaurant m dining car
web m internet

X

xérès m sherry

Y

yacht m yacht
yaourt m yoghurt
  yaourt nature plain yoghurt
yeux mpl eyes
youyou m dinghy

Z

zéro m zero
zona m shingles (illness)
zone f zone
  zone piétonne pedestrian area
zoo m zoo

Grammar

NOUNS

Unlike English, French nouns have a gender: they are either masculine
(**le**) or feminine (**la**). Therefore words for **the** and **a(n)** must agree with the
noun they accompany – whether *masculine*, *feminine* or *plural*:

	masc.	*fem.*	*plural*
the	le chat	la rue	les chats, les rues
a, an	un chat	une rue	des chats, des rues

If the noun begins with a vowel (**a**, **e**, **i**, **o** or **u**) or an unsounded **h**, le and
la shorten to l', i.e. l'**avion** *(m)*, l'**école** *(f)*, l'**hôtel** *(m)*.

NOTE: le and les used after the prepositions à (**to**, **at**)
and de (**any**, **some**, **of**) contract as follows:

à + **le** = au (au cinéma but à <u>la</u> gare)
à + **les** = aux (aux magasins – applies to both *(m)* and *(f)*)
de + **le** = du (du pain but de <u>la</u> confiture)
de + **les** = des (<u>des</u> pommes – applies to both *(m)* and *(f)*)

There are some broad rules as to noun endings which indicate whether
they are *masculine* or *feminine*:

Generally *masculine* endings: -er, -ier, -eau, -t, -c, -ail, -oir, -é, -on, -acle,
-ège, -ème, -o, -ou.

Generally *feminine* endings: -euse, -trice, -ère, -ière, -elle, -te, -tte, -de,
-che, -age, -aille, -oire, -ée, -té, -tié, -onne, -aison, -ion, -esse, -ie, -ine,
-une, -ure, -ance, -anse, -ence, -ense.

PLURALS

The general rule is to add an **s** to the singular:

> le chat ➜ les chats

Exceptions occur with the following noun endings: -eau, -eu, -al

> le bat<u>eau</u> ➜ les bat<u>eaux</u>
> le nev<u>eu</u> ➜ les nev<u>eux</u>
> le chev<u>al</u> ➜ les chev<u>aux</u>

Nouns ending in **s**, **x**, or **z** do not change in the plural.

> le dos ➜ les dos
> le prix ➜ les prix
> le nez ➜ les nez

ADJECTIVES

Adjectives normally follow the noun they describe in French,

e.g. **la pomme verte** (the green apple)

Some common exceptions which go in front of the noun are:

beau beautiful, **bon** good, **grand** big, **haut** high, **jeune** young, **long** long, **joli** pretty, **mauvais** bad, **nouveau** new, **petit** small, **vieux** old

e.g. **un bon livre** (a good book)

French adjectives have to reflect the gender of the noun they describe. To make an adjective feminine, an **e** is added to the *masculine* form (where this does not already end in an **e**, e.g. **jeune**). A final consonant, which is usually silent in the *masculine* form, is pronounced in the *feminine*:

masc. **le livre vert**   *fem.* **la pomme verte**
luh leevr vehr   *la pom vehrt*
(the green book)   **(the green apple)**

To make an adjective plural, an **s** is added to the singular form:

masculine plural – **verts** (remember – the ending is still silent: *vehr*) or *feminine plural* – **vertes** (because of the **e**, the **t** ending is sounded: *vehrt*).

MY, YOUR, HIS, HER

These words also depend on the gender and number of the noun they accompany and not on the sex of the 'owner'.

	with masc. sing. noun	*with fem. sing. noun*	*with plural nouns*
my	mon	ma	mes
your *(familiar, singular)*	ton	ta	tes
his/her	son	sa	ses
our	notre	notre	nos
your *(polite, plural)*	votre	votre	vos
their	leur	leur	leurs

e.g. **la clé (key)**   **sa clé (his/her key)**

le passeport (passport)   **son passeport (his/her passport)**

les billets (tickets)   **ses billets (his/her tickets)**

PRONOUNS

subject		object	
I	je, j'	**me**	me
you *(familiar)*	tu	**you**	te
you *(polite, plural)*	vous	**you**	vous
he/it	il	**him/it**	le, l'
she/it	elle	**her/it**	la, l'
we	nous	**us**	nous
they *(masc.)*	ils	**them**	les
they *(fem.)*	elles	**them**	les

In French there are two forms of **you** – tu and vous. Tu is the familiar form which is used with people you know well (friends and family). **Vous**, as well as being the plural form for **you**, is also the polite form of addressing someone. You should take care to use this form until the other person invites you to use the more familiar tu.

Object pronouns are placed before the verb,

e.g.   **il vous aime (he loves you)**
          nous la connaissons (we know her)

However, in commands or requests, object pronouns follow the verb,

e.g.   **écoutez-le (listen to him)**
          aidez-moi (help me)

NOTE: this does not apply to negative commands or requests,

e.g.   **ne le faites pas (don't do it)**

The object pronouns shown above are also used to mean **to me, to us**, etc. except:

          le and la become **lui (to him, to her)**
          les becomes **leur (to them)**,

e.g.   **il le lui donne (he gives it to him)**

VERBS

There are three main patterns of endings for verbs in French – those ending -er, -ir and -re in the dictionary.

DONNER	TO GIVE
je donne	I give
tu donnes	you give
il/elle donne	he/she gives
nous donnons	we give
vous donnez	you give
ils/elles donnent	they give

FIN**IR**	**TO FINISH**
je finis	I finish
tu finis	you finish
il/elle finit	he/she finishes
nous finissons	we finish
vous finissez	you finish
ils/elles finissent	they finish

RÉPON**DRE**	**TO REPLY**
je réponds	I reply
tu réponds	you reply
il/elle répond	he/she replies
nous répondons	we reply
vous répondez	you reply
ils/elles répondent	they reply

IRREGULAR VERBS

Among the most important irregular verbs are the following:

ÊTRE	**TO BE**
je suis	I am
tu es	you are
il/elle est	he/she is
nous sommes	we are
vous êtes	you are
ils/elles sont	they are

AVOIR	**TO HAVE**
j'ai	I have
tu as	you have
il/elle a	he/she has
nous avons	we have
vous avez	you have
ils/elles ont	they have

ALLER	**TO GO**
je vais	I go
tu vas	you go
il/elle va	he/she goes
nous allons	we go
vous allez	you go
ils/elles vont	they go

POUVOIR	TO BE ABLE
je peux	I can
tu peux	you can
il/elle peut	he/she can
nous pouvons	we can
vous pouvez	you can
ils/elles peuvent	they can

PAST TENSE

To form the simple past tense, **I gave/I have given, I finished/I have finished**, combine the present tense of the verb avoir – **to have** with the past participle of the verb (donné, fini, répondu),

e.g.

j'ai donné	**I gave/I have given**
j'ai fini	**I finished/I have finished**
j'ai répondu	**I replied/I have replied**

Not all verbs take avoir (j'ai..., il a...) as their auxiliary verb; some verbs take être (je suis..., il est...). These are intransitive verbs (which have no object),

e.g.

je suis allé	**I went**
je suis né	**I was born**

When the auxiliary verb être is used, the past participle (allé, né, etc.) becomes adjectival and agrees with the subject of the verb,

e.g.

nous sommes allés	**we went** *(plural)*
je suis née	**I was born** *(female)*